EPISODE ONE: THE DOCTOR IS IN

STORY
BRIAN FINKELSTEIN
BILL JEMAS
MICHAEL COAST

SCRIPT
BRIAN FINKELSTEIN

LAYOUTS
JULIAN ROWE

PENCILS
JOSEPH COOPER

COLORS
LIEZL BUENAVENTURA
THE HORIES

HANG

LETTERS
RICHARD BROOKS

EDITOR
RICHARD BROOKS

EPISODE TWO: FRESH FLESH

STORY
BILL JEMAS
MICHAEL COAST

SCRIPT
BILL JEMAS
MATTHEW DICKS
MICHAEL COAST

LAYOUTS
JULIAN ROWE

PENCILS
JOSEPH COOPER

COLORS
TAMRA BONVILLAIN
LIEZL BUENAVENTURA

COVER
CARLOS RENO

LETTERS
CAROLINE FLANAGAN

EDITOR
CAROLINE FLANAGAN

EPISODE THREE: BARE BONES

STORY
BILL JEMAS
MICHAEL COAST

SCRIPT
MICHAEL COAST
BRIAN FINKELSTEIN
MATTHEW DICKS
BILL JEMAS

**LAYOUTS &
PENCILS**
JULIAN ROWE
JOSEPH COOPER
YOUNG HELLER
STAN CHOU

COLORS
JAY RAMOS
LEO PACIAROTTI
STELLAR STUDIOS

COVER
CARLOS RENO

LETTERS
CAROLINE FLANAGAN
RICHARD BROOKS

EDITOR
CAROLINE FLANAGAN

EPISODE FOUR: DOCTOR'S ORDERS

STORY
BILL JEMAS
MICHAEL COAST

SCRIPT
MICHAEL COAST
BRIAN FINKELSTEIN

LAYOUTS
STAN CHOU

PENCILS
MARCO COSENTINO

COLORS
LEO PACIAROTTI
ANDREA CELESTINI

COVER
RUIZ BURGOS

LETTERS
CAROLINE FLANAGAN

EDITOR
CAROLINE FLANAGAN

EPISODE FIVE: RIGOR

STORY
BILL JEMAS
MICHAEL COAST

SCRIPT
MICHAEL COAST
BRIAN FINKELSTEIN
CAROLINE FLANAGAN

PENCILS
JOEL CARPENTER
RICARDO SANCHEZ
MARCO COSENTINO

COLORS
LEO PACIAROTTI
JUANMAR STUDIOS
FALK HANSEL
MARCO PELANDRA
MARTA MARTINEZ

LAYOUTS
DEAN KOTZ
STAN CHOU
ALLEN WATSON

COVER
ALESSANDRA De BERNARDIS

LETTERS
CAROLINE FLANAGAN

EDITOR
CAROLINE FLANAGAN

PRIME TIME GUIDE

APRIL 24TH–30TH, 1966

	Time	ABC	CBS	NBC	WJAC-TV DuBois
SUNDAY	6:30	Local	Local	Bell Telephone Hour/NBC News	Walter Kronkite
	7:00	Voyage to the Bottom of the	Lassie	Specials	Rifleman
	7:30	Sea	It's About Time	Walt Disney's Wonderful World	To Tell the Truth
	8:00	The FBI	Ed Sullivan Show	of Color	I've Got a Secret
	8:30			Hey Landlord!	Lucy Show
	9:00	The Sunday Night Movie	Garry Moore Show	Bonanza	Andy Griffith Show
	9:30				Hazel
	10:00		Candid Camera	Andy Williams Show	Strollin' 20's
	10:30		What's My Line?		
MONDAY	7:30	Iron Horse	Gilligan's Island	The Monkees	Gunsmoke
	8:00		Run, Buddy, Run	I Dream of Jeannie	Pirate Fever 66
	8:30	The Rat Patrol	The Lucy Show	Roger Miller Show	Lucy Show
	9:00	The Felony Squad	Andy Griffith Show	The Road West	Andy Griffith Show
	9:30	Peyton Place	Family Affair		Family Affair
	10:00	The Big Valley	Jess Arthur Show	Run for Your Life	Run for Your Life
	10:30		I've Got a Secret		
TUESDAY	7:30	Combat!	Daktari	The Girl from U.N.C.L.E.	12 O'Clock High
	8:00				
	8:30	The Rounders	Red Skelton Hour	Occasional Wife	Legend of Jesse James
	9:00	The Pruitts of Southampton			Shenandoah
	9:30	Love on a Rooftop	Petticoat Junction	Tuesday Night at the Movies	Peyton Place
	10:00	The Fugitive	CBS News Special		Ben Casey
	10:30				
WEDNESDAY	7:30	Batman	Lost In Space	The Virginian	Hullabaloo
	8:00	The Monroes			John Forsythe Show
	8:30		The Beverly Hillbillies		Dr. Kildare
	9:00	The Man Who Never Was	Green Acres	Bob Hope Show and Specials	Andy Williams Show
	9:30	Peyton Place	Gomer Pyle, USMC		
	10:00	ABC Stage 67	Danny Kaye Show	I Spy	Run for Your Life
	10:30				
THURSDAY	7:30	Batman	Jericho	Daniel Boone	Batman
	8:00	F Troop			Hullabaloo
	8:30	Tammy Grimes Show	My Three Sons	Star Trek	Lucy Show
	9:00	Bewitched			Family Affair
	9:30	That Girl	The CBS Thursday Night	The Hero	My Three Sons
	10:00	Hawk	Movies	Dean Martin Show	Big Valley
	10:30				
FRIDAY	7:30	The Green Hornet	The Wild, Wild West	Tarzan	World Today
	8:00	The Time Tunnel			12 O'Clock High
	8:30		Hogan's Heroes	The Man from U.N.C.L.E.	Hazel
	9:00	Milton Barie Show	The CBS Friday Night Movies		Peyton Place
	9:30			T.H.E. Cat	Lucy Show
	10:00	12 O'Clock High		Laredo	Merv Griffin Show
	10:30				
SATURDAY	7:30	Shane	Jackie Gleeson Show	Flipper	Pitt at Johnstown Quiz
	8:00			Please Don't Eat the Daisies	John Forsythe Show
	8:30	The Lawrence Welk Show	Pistols 'N' Petticoats	Get Smart	Dr. Kildare
	9:00		Mission: Impossible	Saturday Night at the Movies	Andy Williams Show
	9:30	The Hollywood Palace			
	10:00		Gunsmoke		Run for Your Life
	10:30	ABC Scope			

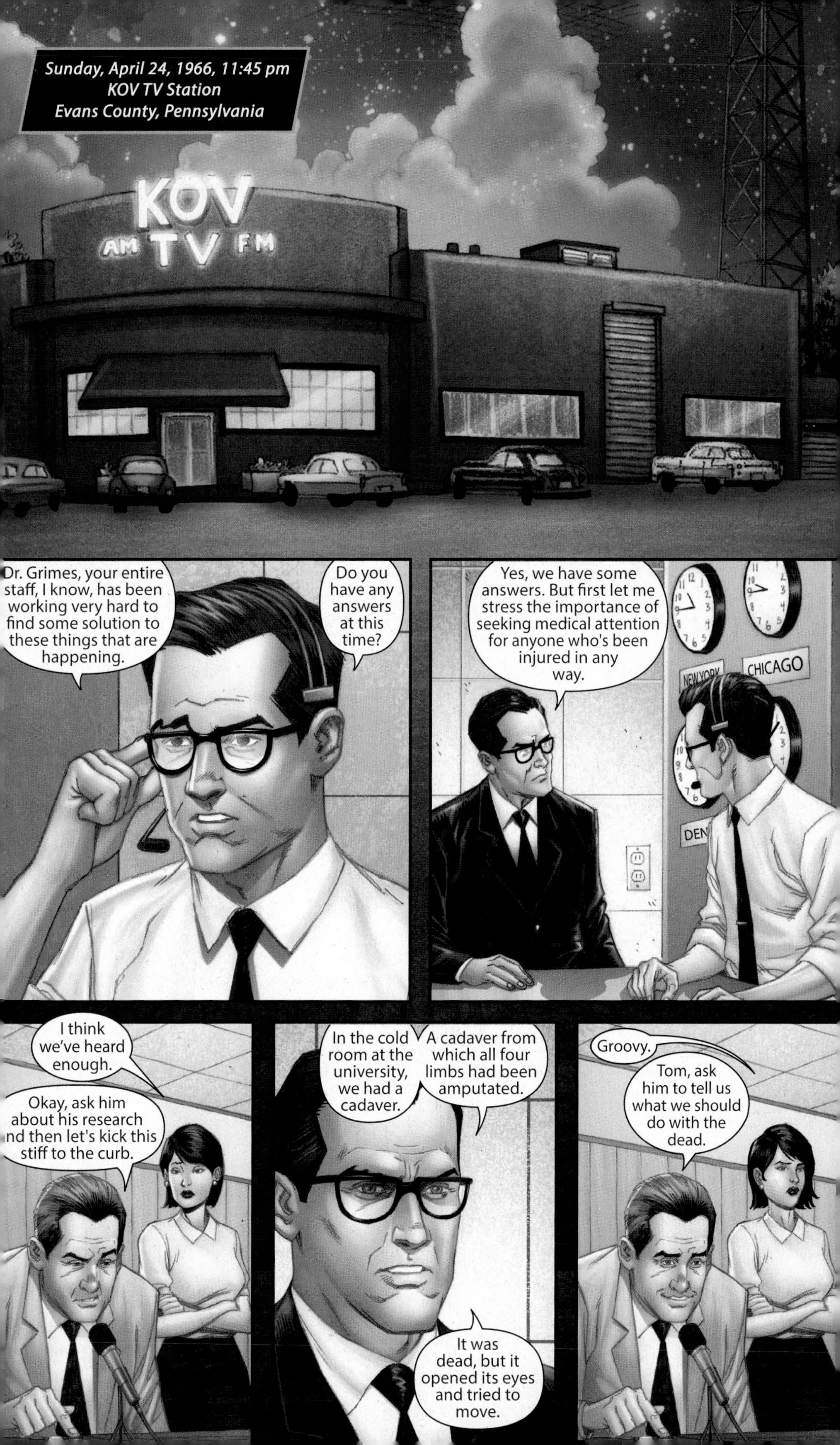
Sunday, April 24, 1966, 11:45 pm
KOV TV Station
Evans County, Pennsylvania
KOV
AM TV FM
Dr. Grimes, your entire staff, I know, has been working very hard to find some solution to these things that are happening.
Do you have any answers at this time?
Yes, we have some answers. But first let me stress the importance of seeking medical attention for anyone who's been injured in any way.
NEW YORK
CHICAGO
DEN
I think we've heard enough.
Okay, ask him about his research nd then let's kick this stiff to the curb.
In the cold room at the university, we had a cadaver.
A cadaver from which all four limbs had been amputated.
It was dead, but it opened its eyes and tried to move.
Groovy.
Tom, ask him to tell us what we should do with the dead.

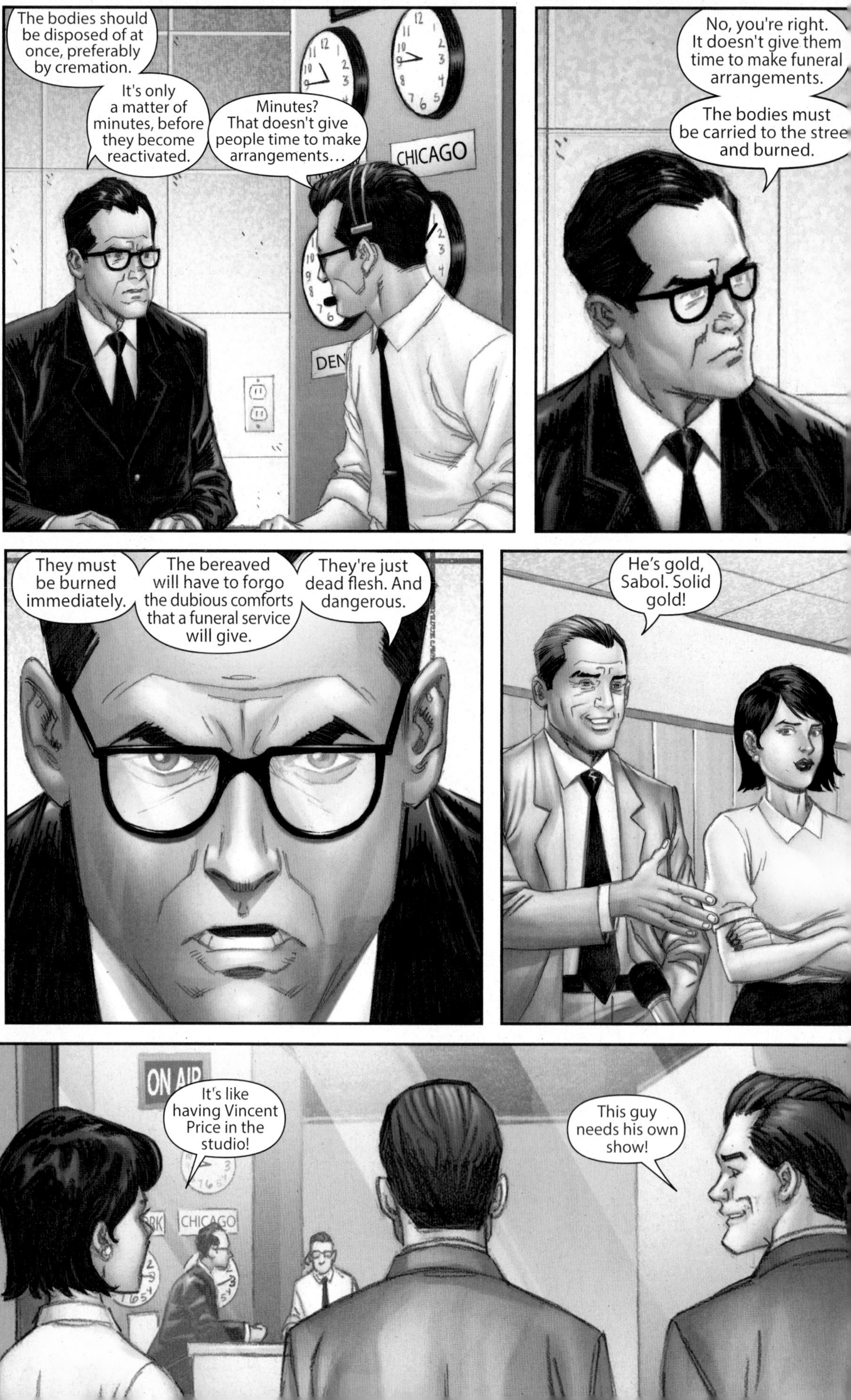
The bodies should be disposed of at once, preferably by cremation.
It's only a matter of minutes, before they become reactivated.
Minutes? That doesn't give people time to make arrangements…
CHICAGO
DEN
No, you're right. It doesn't give them time to make funeral arrangements.
The bodies must be carried to the stree and burned.
They must be burned immediately.
The bereaved will have to forgo the dubious comforts that a funeral service will give.
They're just dead flesh. And dangerous.
He's gold, Sabol. Solid gold!
ON AIR
It's like having Vincent Price in the studio!
This guy needs his own show!
CHICAGO

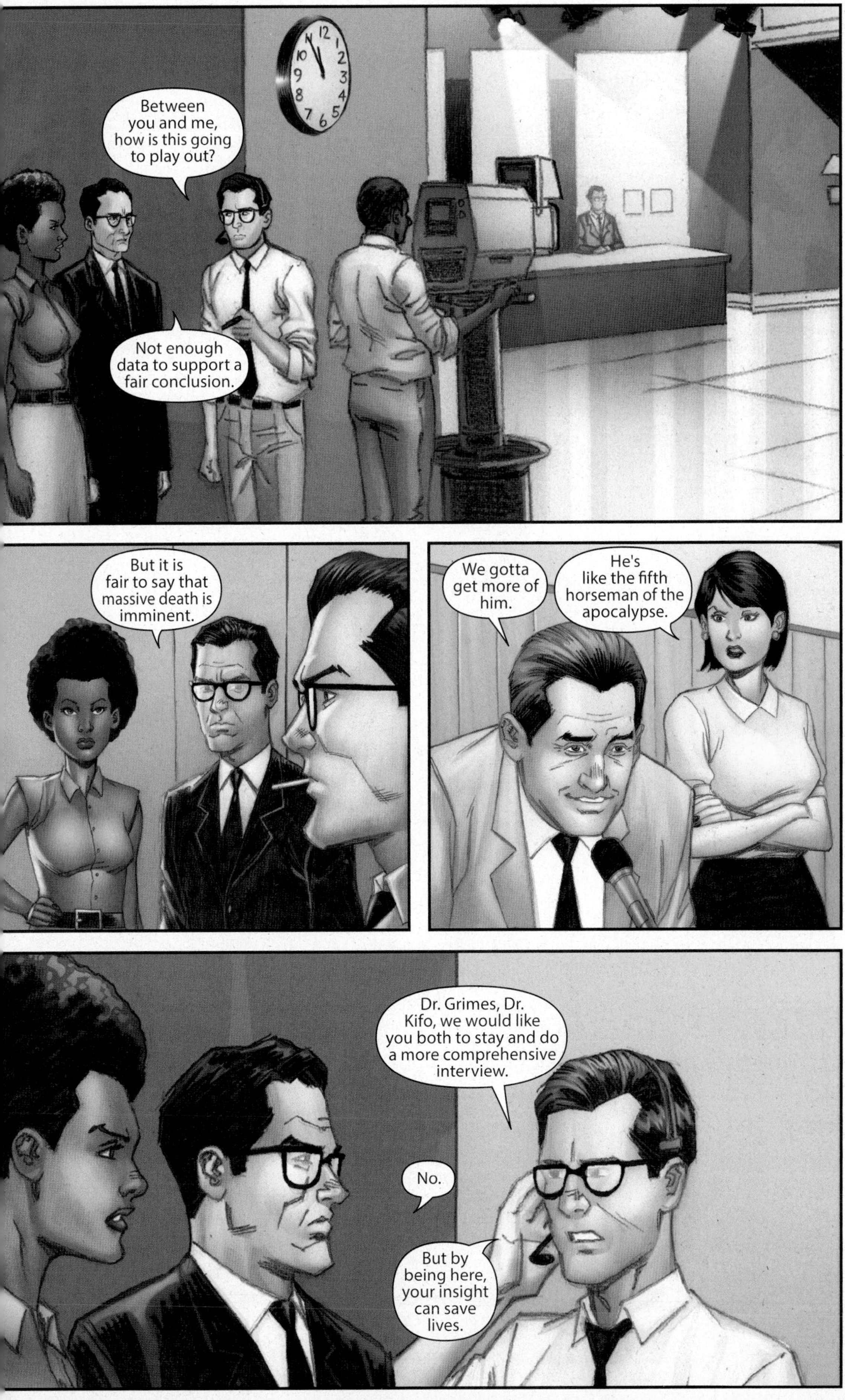
Between you and me, how is this going to play out?
Not enough data to support a fair conclusion.
But it is fair to say that massive death is imminent.
We gotta get more of him.
He's like the fifth horseman of the apocalypse.
Dr. Grimes, Dr. Kifo, we would like you both to stay and do a more comprehensive interview.
No.
But by being here, your insight can save lives.

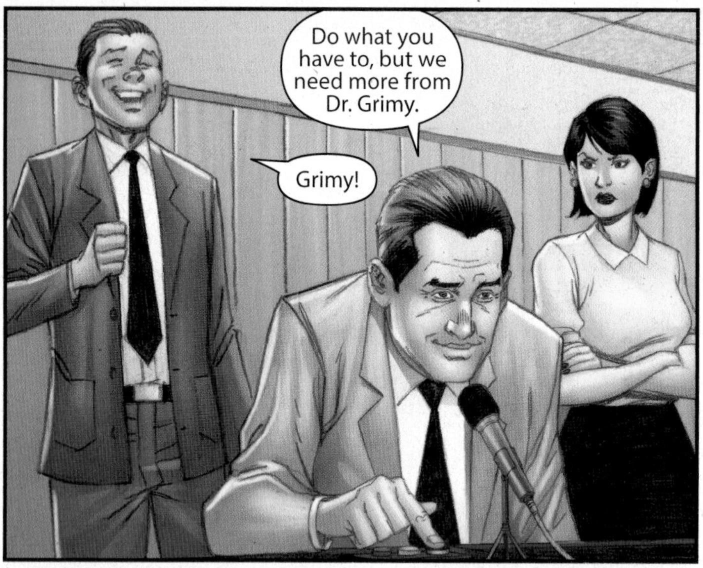
Do what you have to, but we need more from Dr. Grimy.
Grimy!

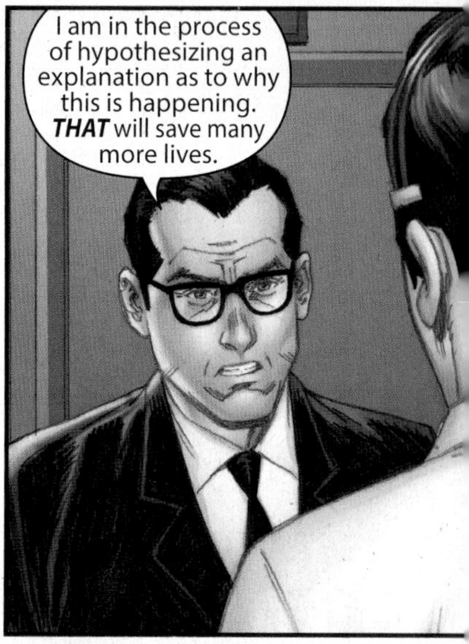
I am in the process of hypothesizing an explanation as to why this is happening. ***THAT*** will save many more lives.

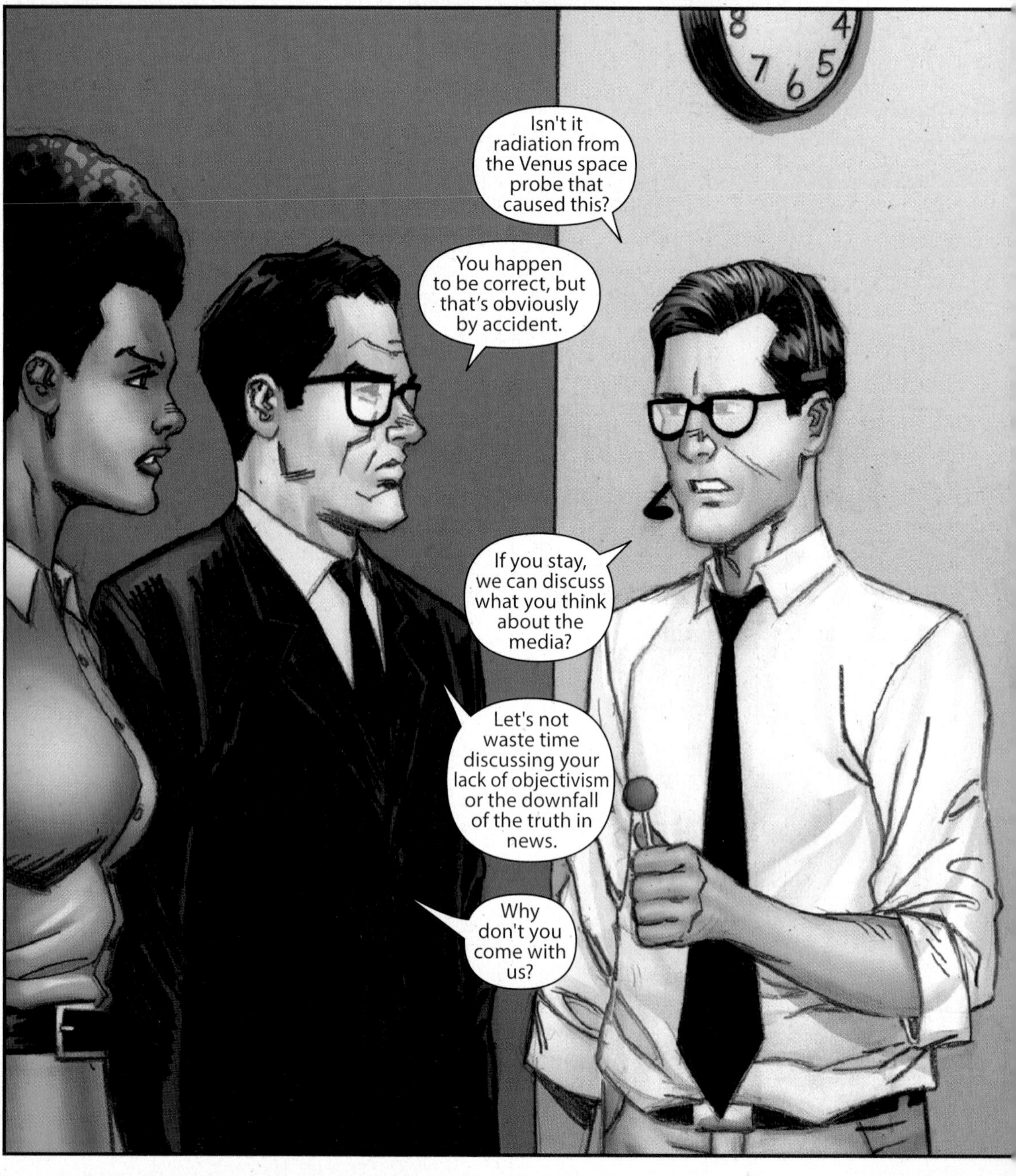
Isn't it radiation from the Venus space probe that caused this?
You happen to be correct, but that's obviously by accident.
If you stay, we can discuss what you think about the media?
Let's not waste time discussing your lack of objectivism or the downfall of the truth in news.
Why don't you come with us?

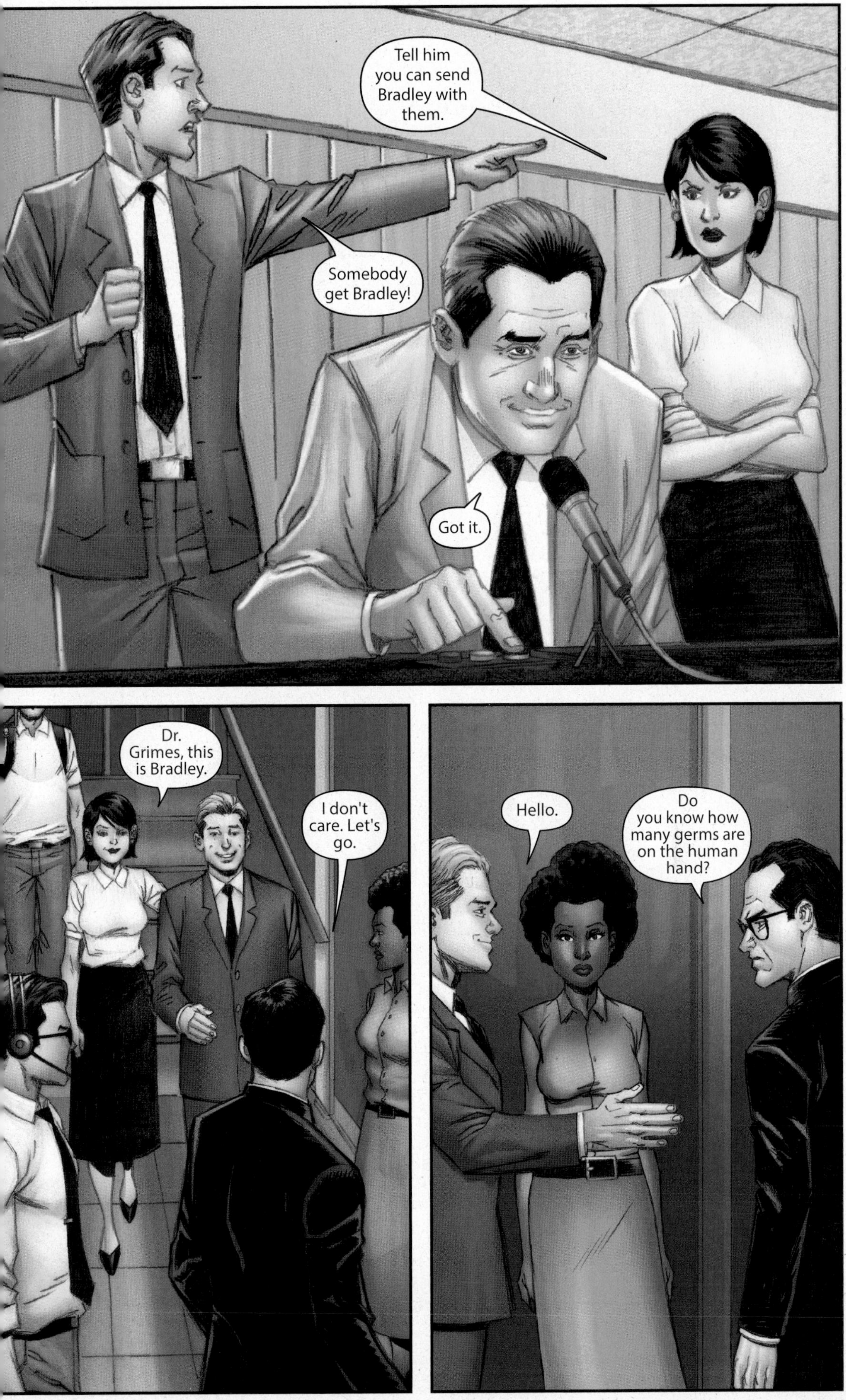
Tell him you can send Bradley with them.
Somebody get Bradley!
Got it.
Dr. Grimes, this is Bradley.
I don't care. Let's go.
Hello.
Do you know how many germs are on the human hand?

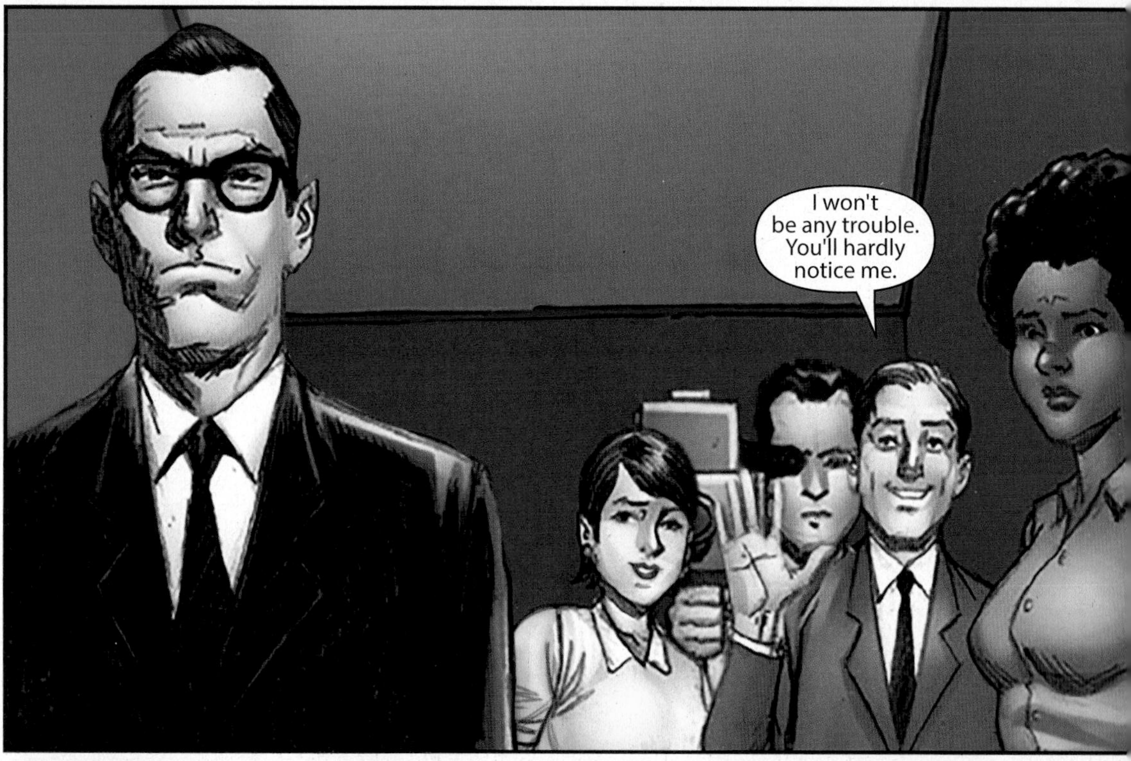
I won't be any trouble. You'll hardly notice me.

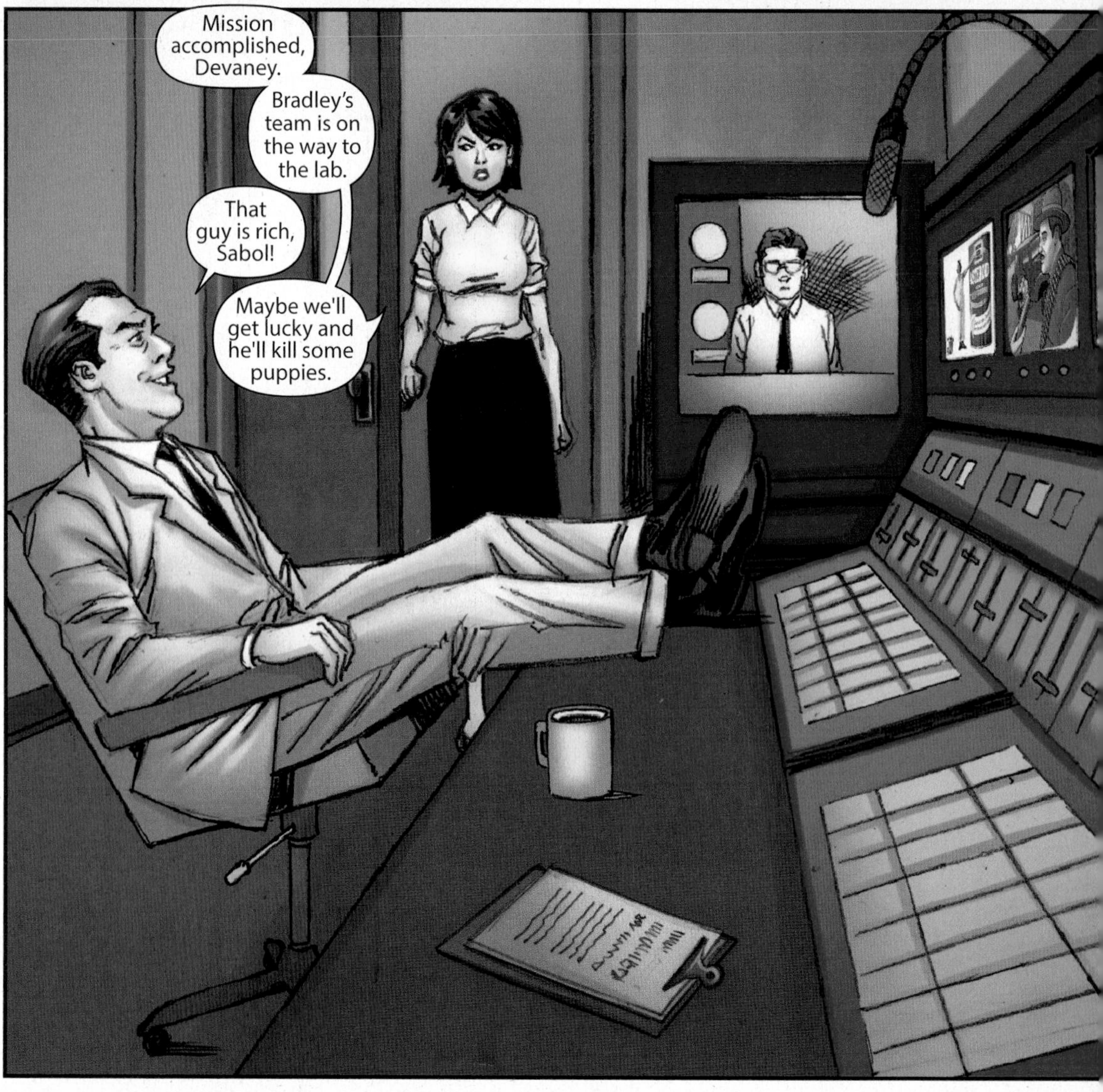
Mission accomplished, Devaney.
Bradley's team is on the way to the lab.
That guy is rich, Sabol!
Maybe we'll get lucky and he'll kill some puppies.

JLTIMATE TECHNOLOGY

Buyer's Guide

YOUR GUIDE TO THE BEST
TELEPHONES, TVs, CAMERAS, AND COMPUTERS
US A SNEAK PEEK AT THE SMARTEST CAR IN TOWN.

HONDA

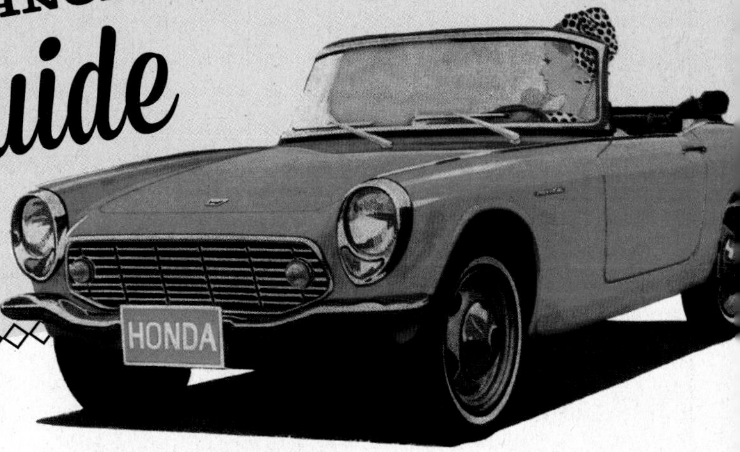

HONDA S-600

The smartest car in town for the family that has the latest high technology in their home. This car is smart in style with power to spare. It's easy to handle, easy to park, and has spacious luggage compartment for family trips.

$6500; at your local Honda dealership

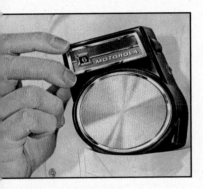

MOTOROLA

1OTOROLA POCKET RADIO

shirt-pocket radio with the power and sound ou'd expect from a larger set. A six-transistor hassis pinpoints stations and the speaker de-vers sound in rich, clear lows, and crisp highs. Vith battery life up to 100 hours, you can take on a trip in a custom carrying case.

4; mail order

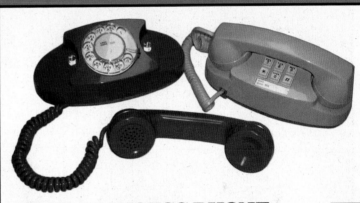

AT&T PRINCESS PHONE

America has fallen in love with the new Princess phone. It's little so it fits in those small places where you couldn't fit a telephone before. It's lovely and charms people with its graceful lines and color. It lights so you can find it easily in the dark.

$35; mail order

RCA
COLOR

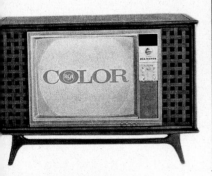

RCA COLOR TELEVISION

living color. Get a perfectly fine-tuned pic-re with brighter highlights every time you atch and circuitry that won't go haywire.

55; Kaufmann's

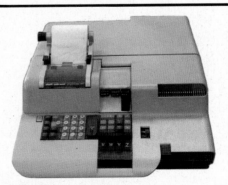

OLIVETTI PROGRAMMA 101

The first computer on your desk. Every company, university, department, laboratory, or institute can now have their own private electronic digital computer. It's only a little larger than a typewriter and doesn't require a skilled operator.

$75; mail order

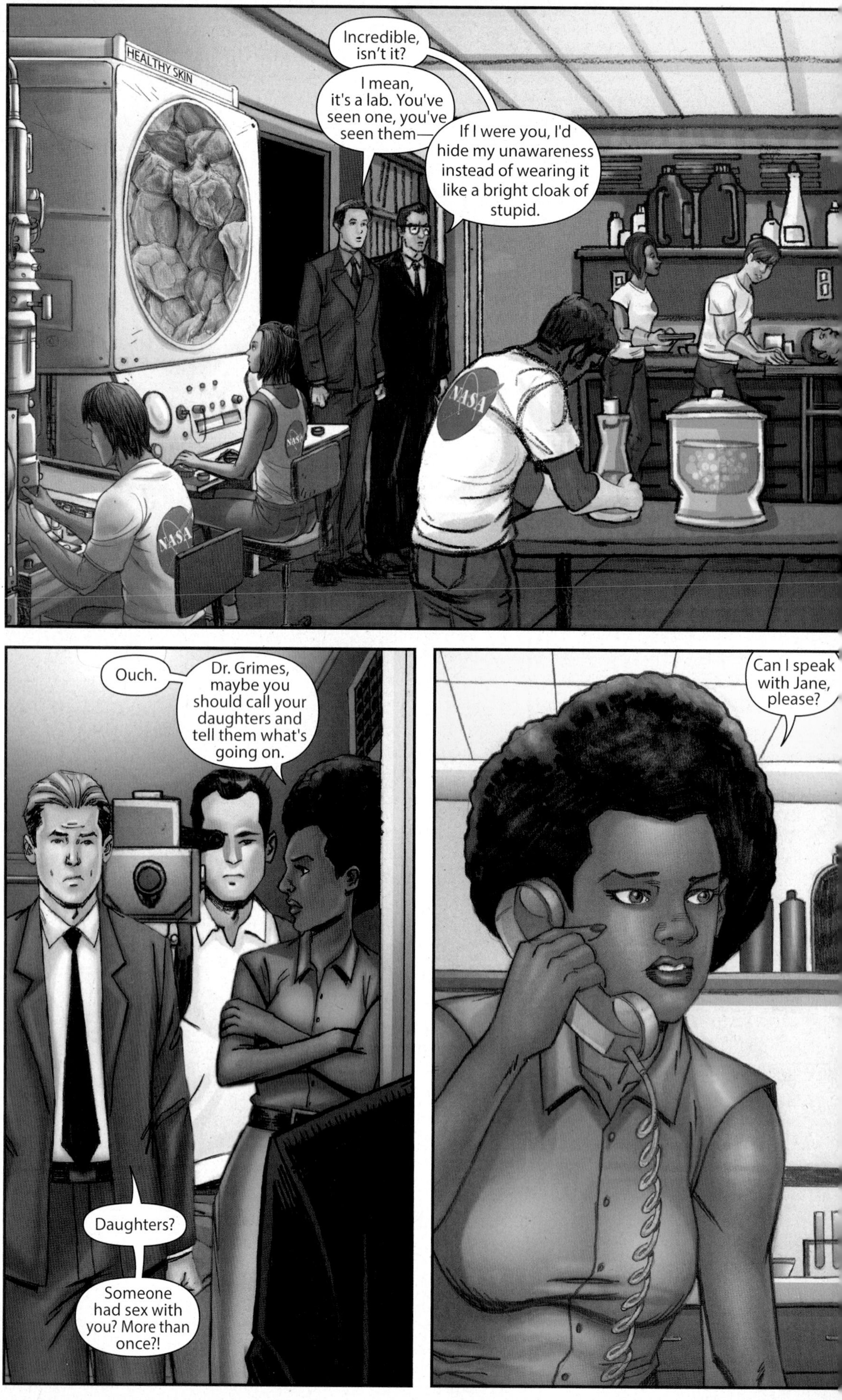
HEALTHY SKIN
Incredible, isn't it?
I mean, it's a lab. You've seen one, you've seen them—
If I were you, I'd hide my unawareness instead of wearing it like a bright cloak of stupid.
NASA
NASA
NASA
Ouch.
Dr. Grimes, maybe you should call your daughters and tell them what's going on.
Daughters?
Someone had sex with you? More than once?!
Can I speak with Jane, please?

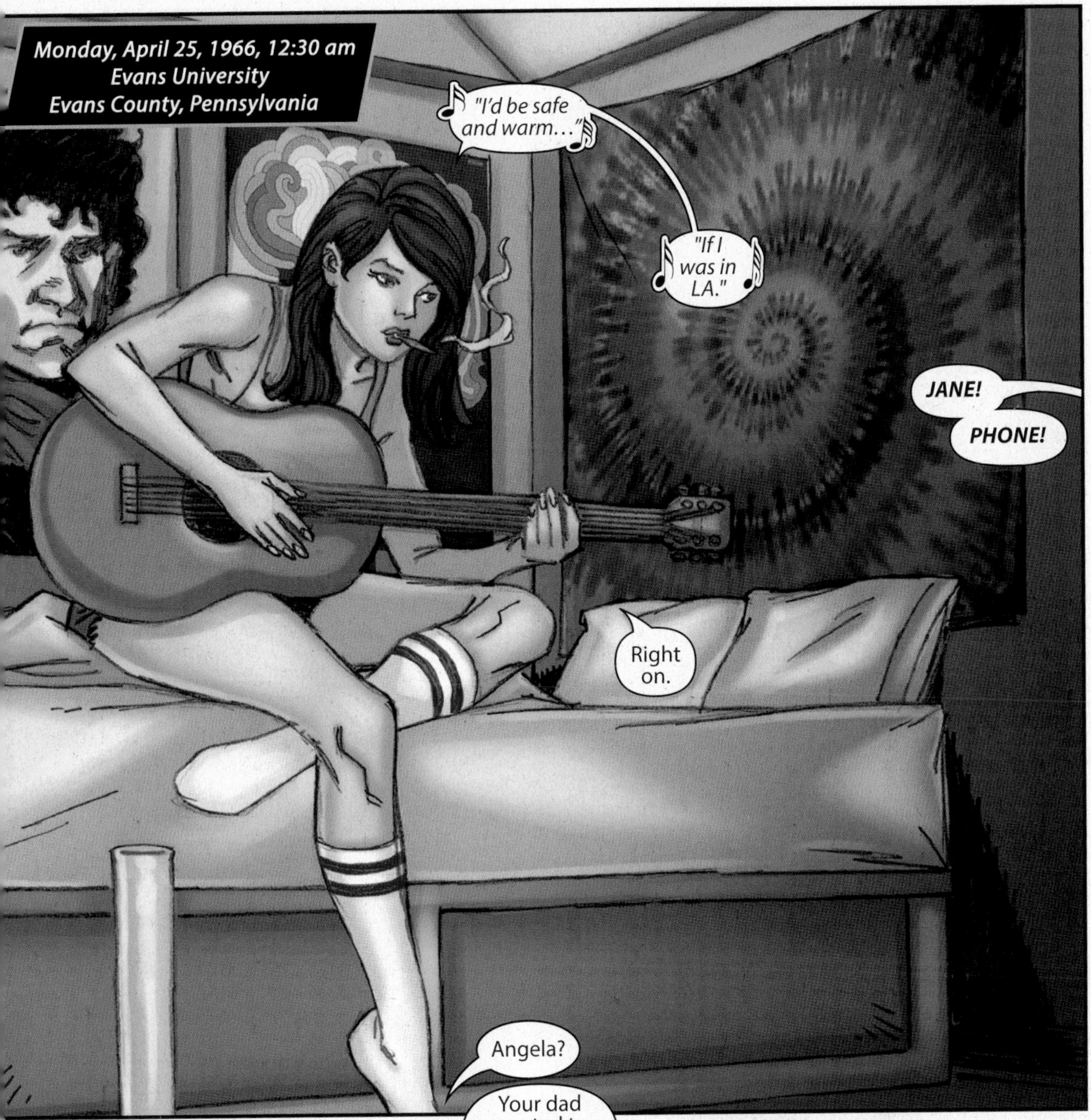
Monday, April 25, 1966, 12:30 am
Evans University
Evans County, Pennsylvania
"I'd be safe and warm…"
"If I was in LA."
JANE!
PHONE!
Right on.
Angela?

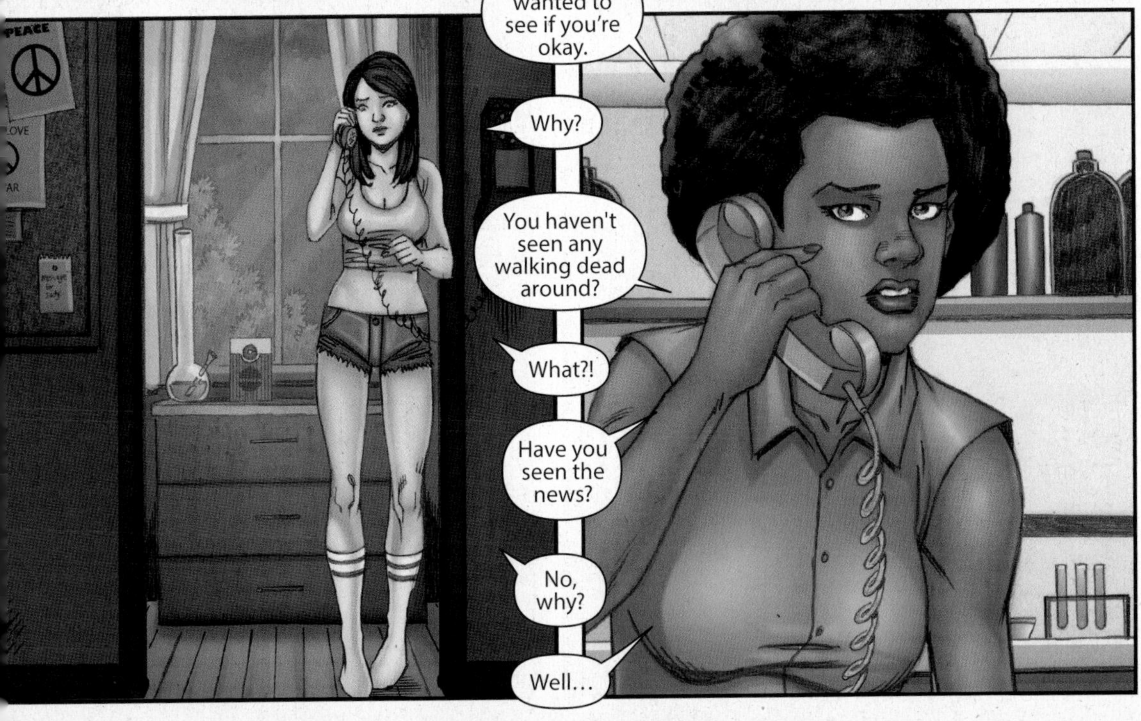
PEACE
Your dad wanted to see if you're okay.
Why?
You haven't seen any walking dead around?
What?!
Have you seen the news?
No, why?
Well…

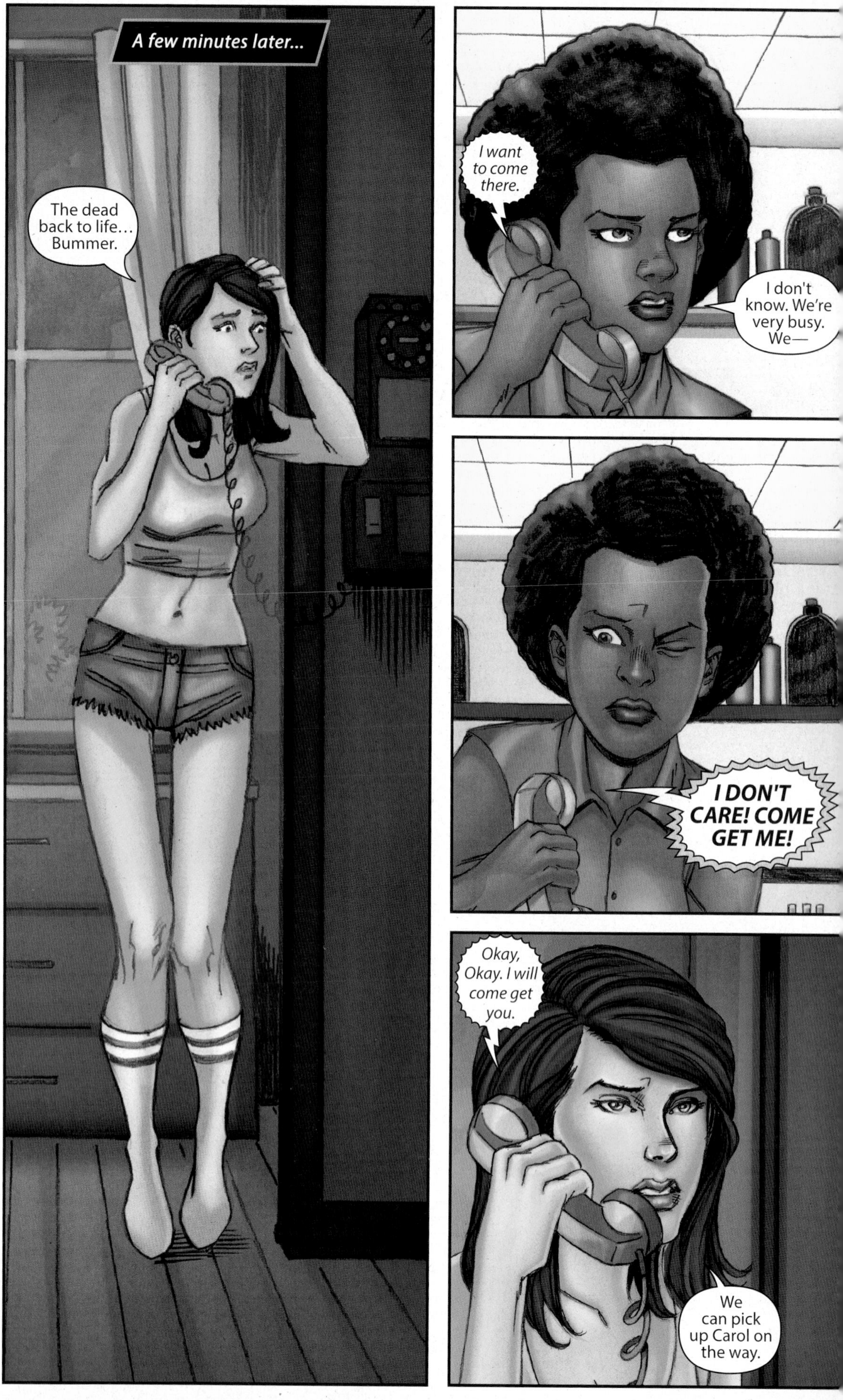

A few minutes later...
The dead back to life... Bummer.
I want to come there.
I don't know. We're very busy. We—
I DON'T CARE! COME GET ME!
Okay, Okay. I will come get you.
We can pick up Carol on the way.

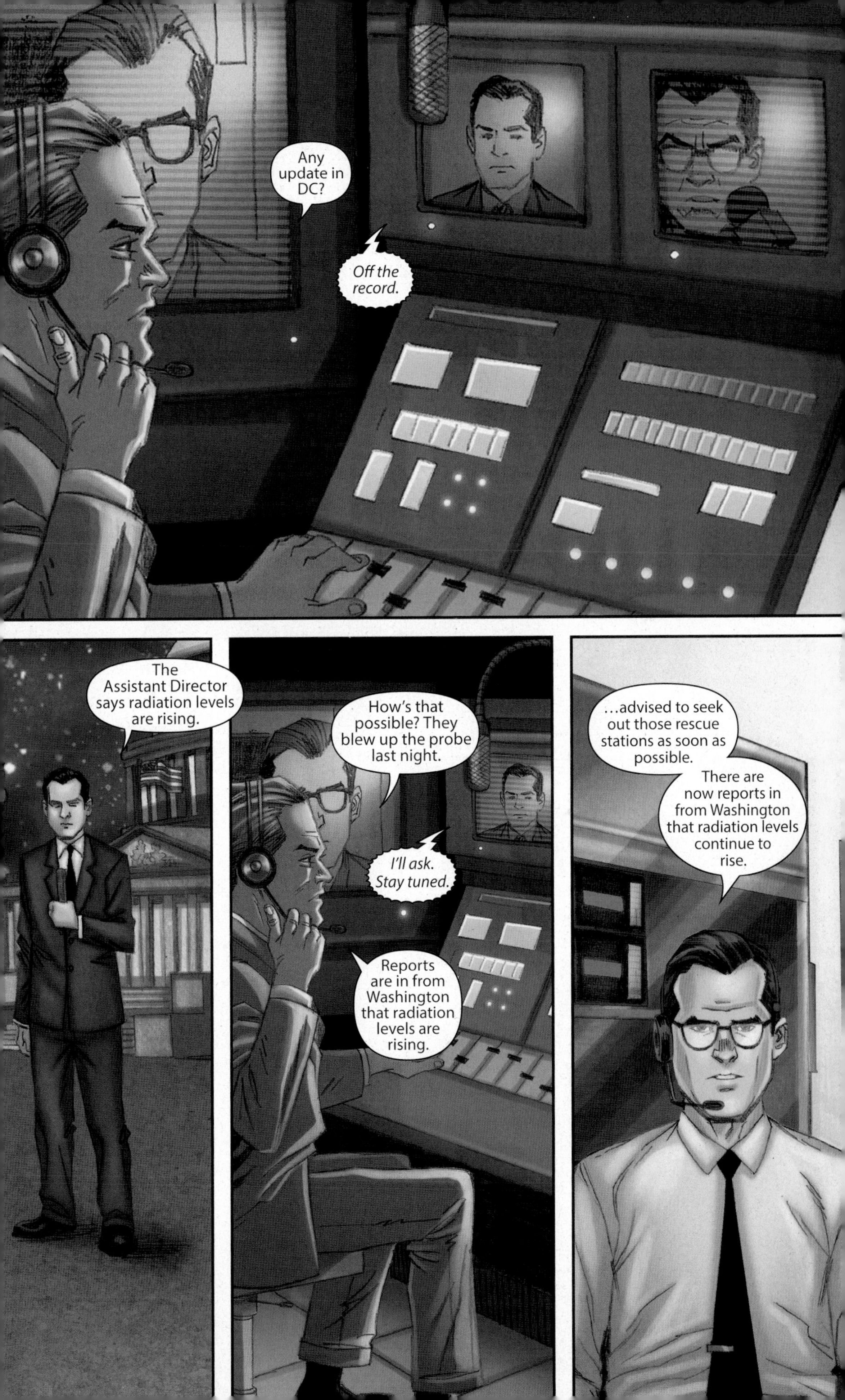
Any update in DC?
Off the record.
The Assistant Director says radiation levels are rising.
How's that possible? They blew up the probe last night.
I'll ask. Stay tuned.
Reports are in from Washington that radiation levels are rising.
…advised to seek out those rescue stations as soon as possible.
There are now reports in from Washington that radiation levels continue to rise.

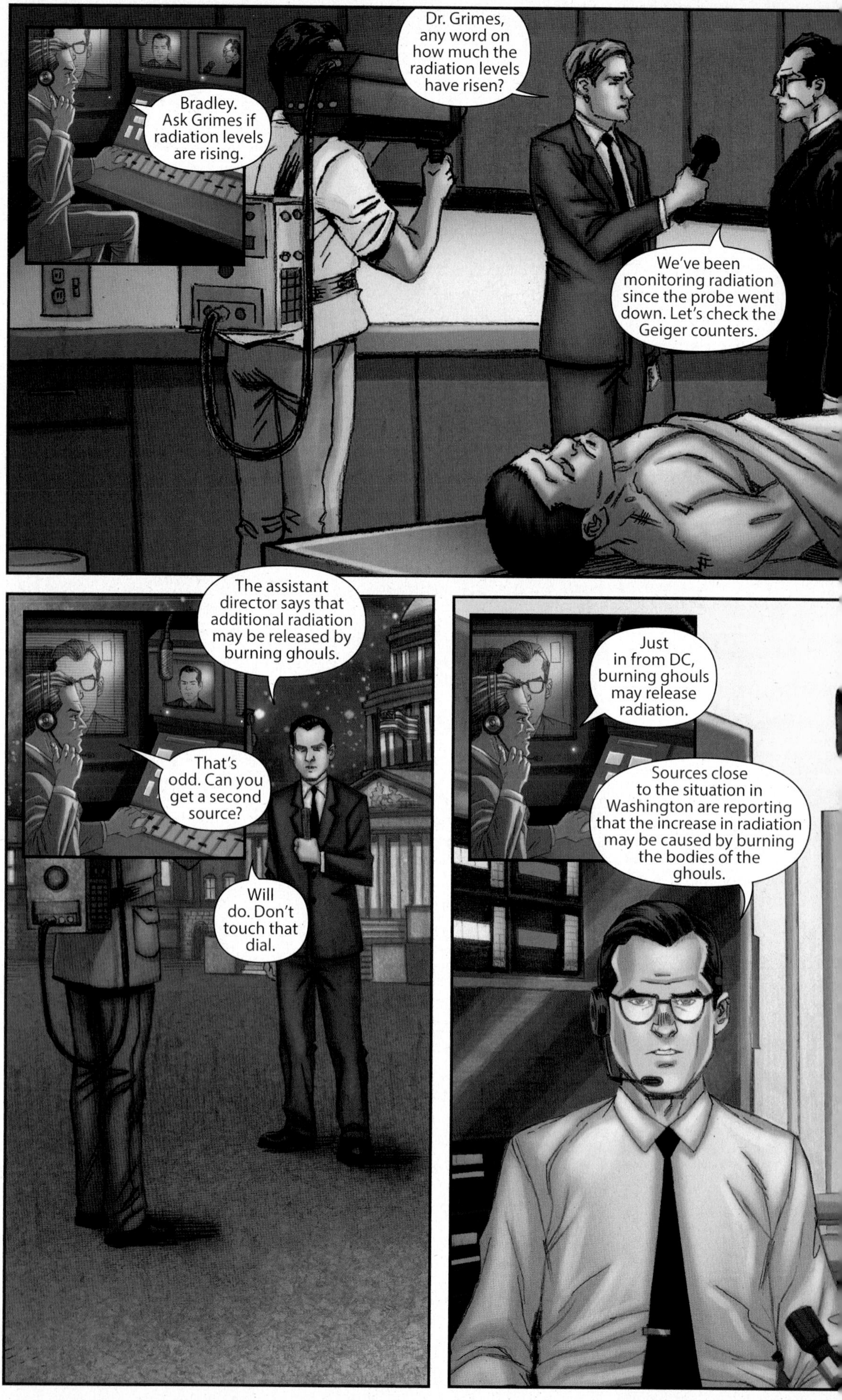
Bradley. Ask Grimes if radiation levels are rising.
Dr. Grimes, any word on how much the radiation levels have risen?
We've been monitoring radiation since the probe went down. Let's check the Geiger counters.
The assistant director says that additional radiation may be released by burning ghouls.
That's odd. Can you get a second source?
Will do. Don't touch that dial.
Just in from DC, burning ghouls may release radiation.
Sources close to the situation in Washington are reporting that the increase in radiation may be caused by burning the bodies of the ghouls.

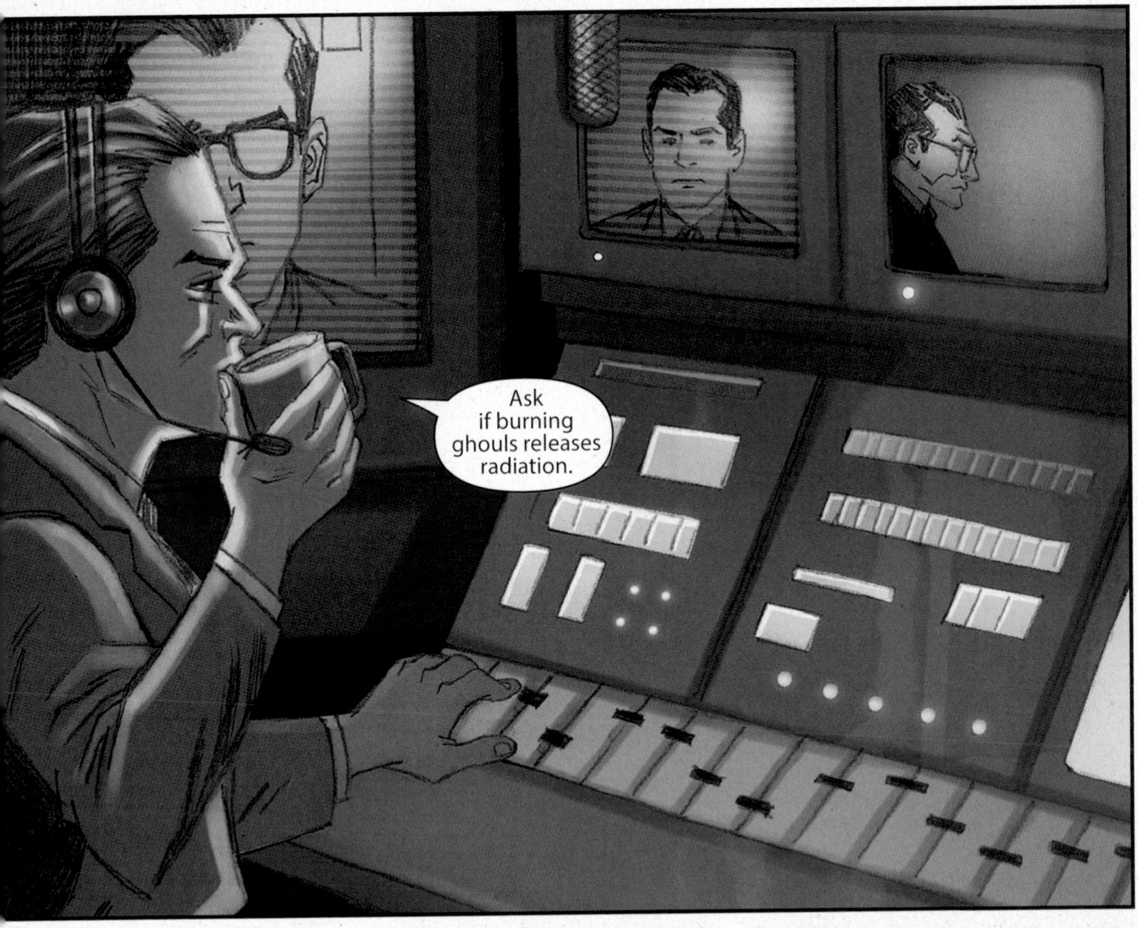
Ask if burning ghouls releases radiation.

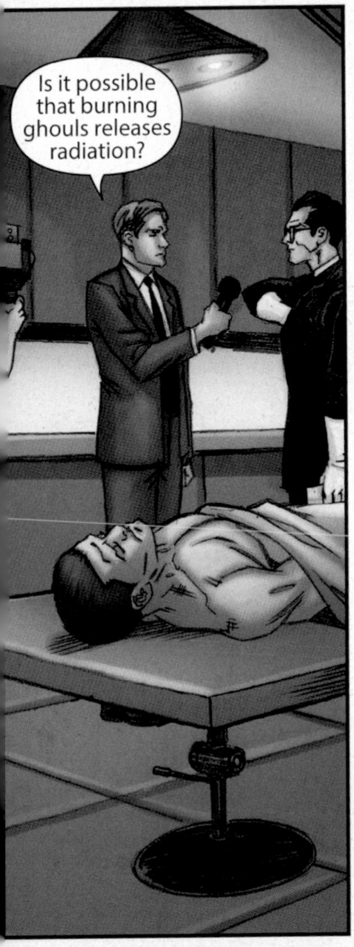
Is it possible that burning ghouls releases radiation?

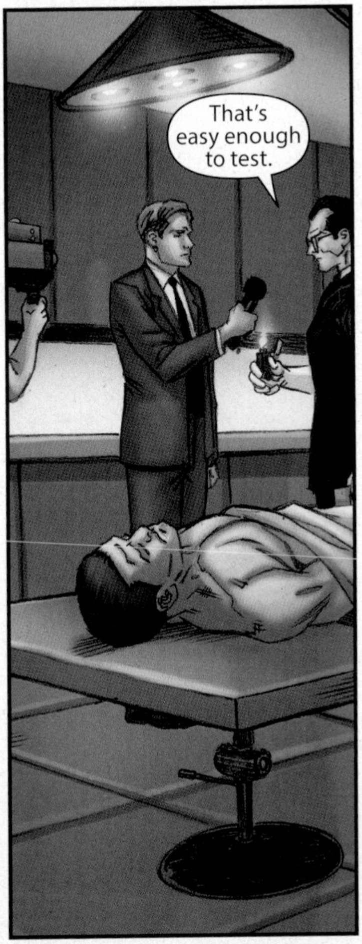
That's easy enough to test.

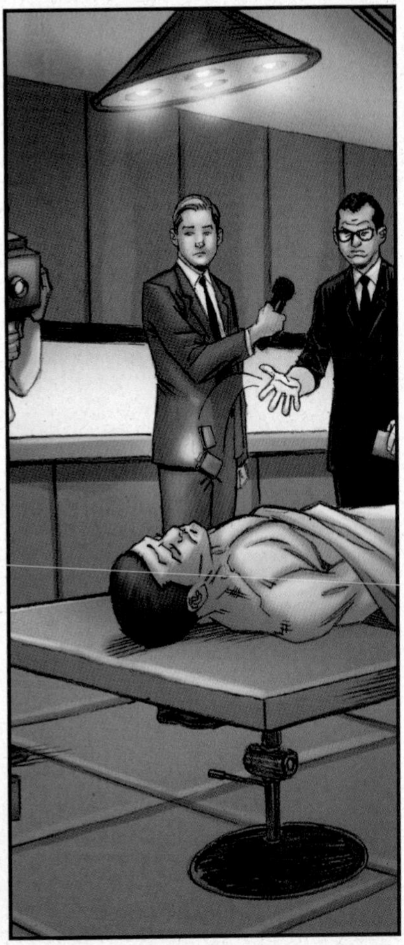

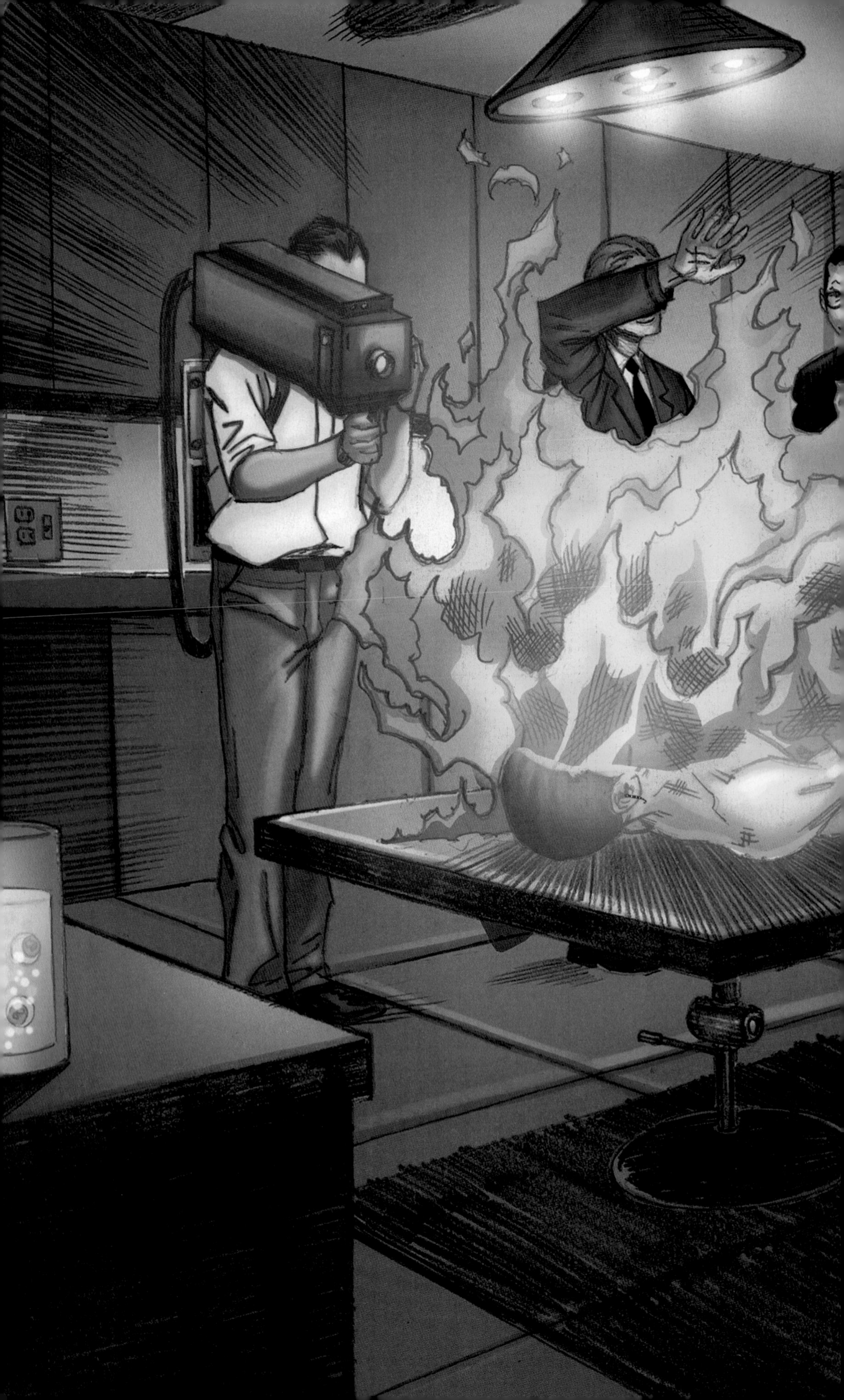

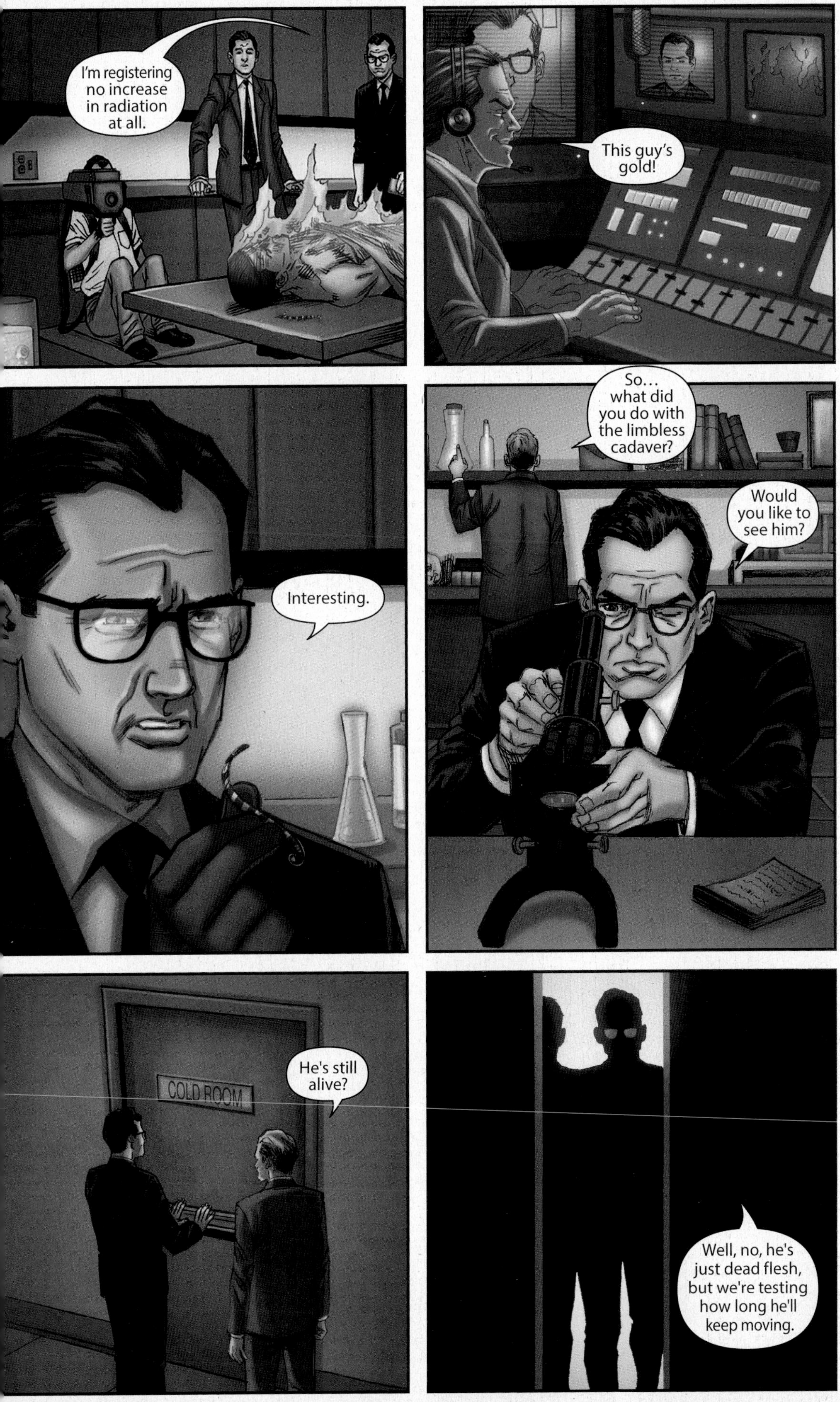
I'm registering no increase in radiation at all.
This guy's gold!
Interesting.
So... what did you do with the limbless cadaver?
Would you like to see him?
COLD ROOM
He's still alive?
Well, no, he's just dead flesh, but we're testing how long he'll keep moving.

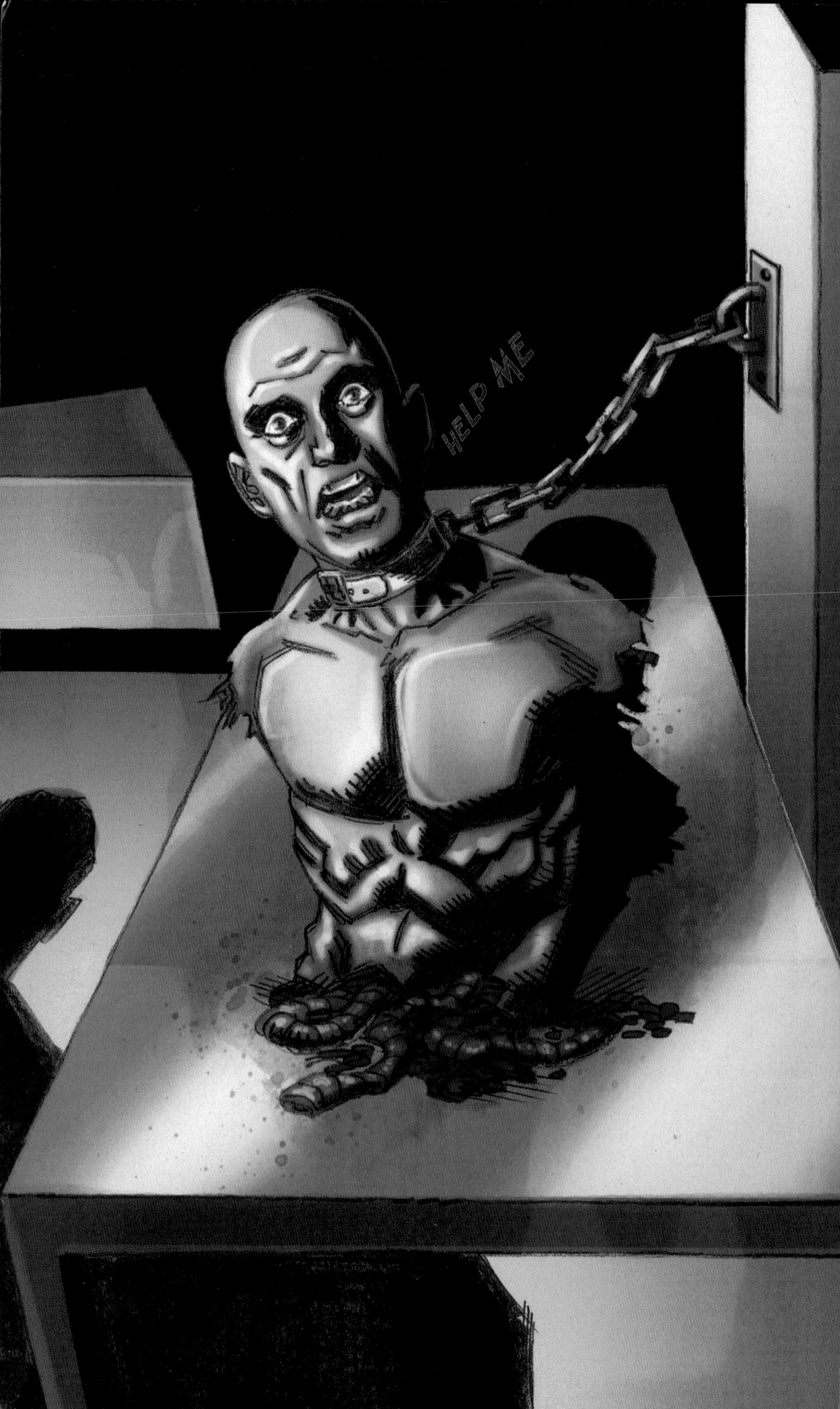
HELP ME

Interesting.

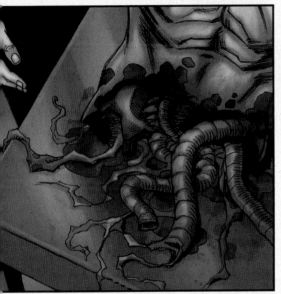

I smell a Pulitzer.

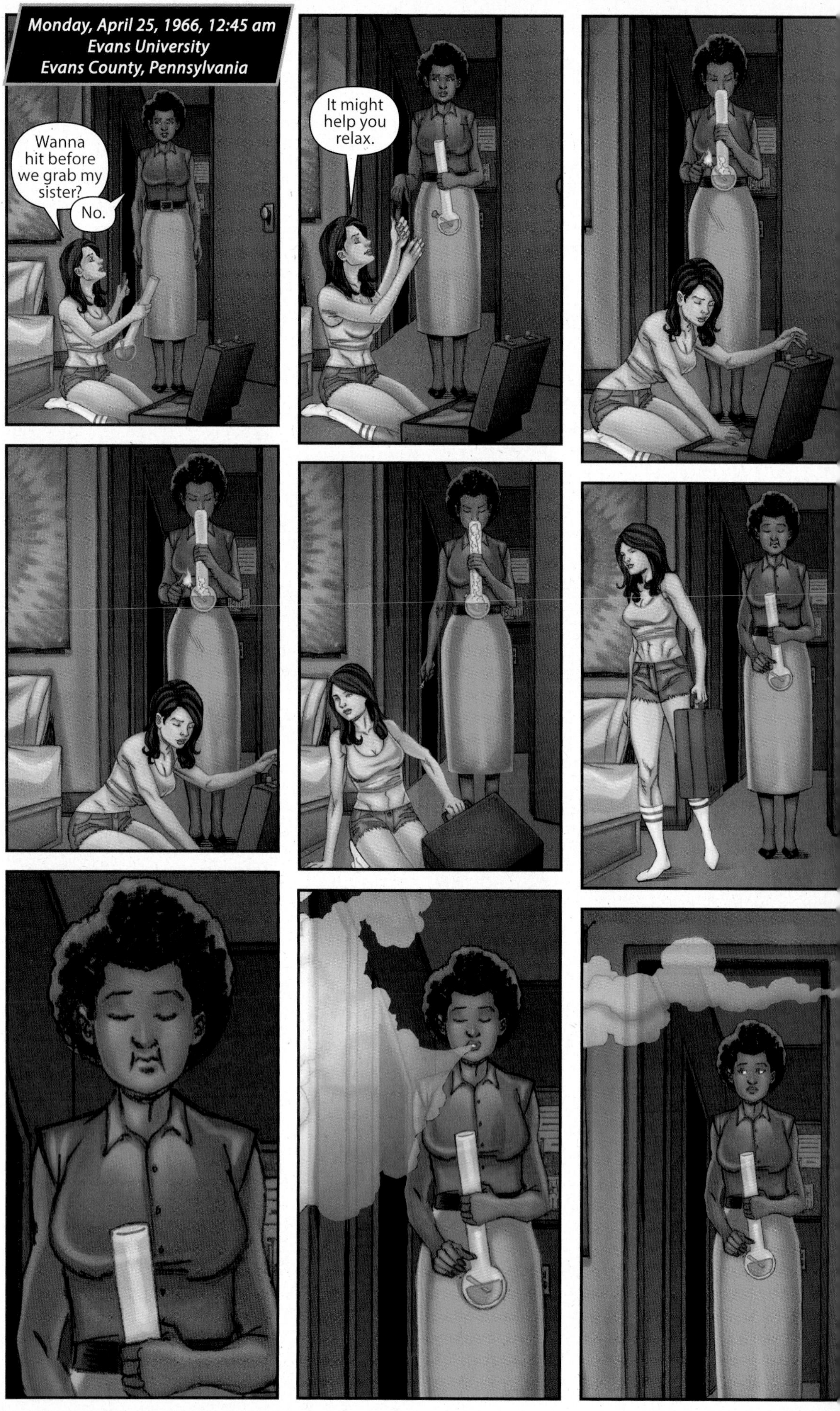

Monday, April 25, 1966, 12:45 am
Evans University
Evans County, Pennsylvania
Wanna hit before we grab my sister?
No.
It might help you relax.

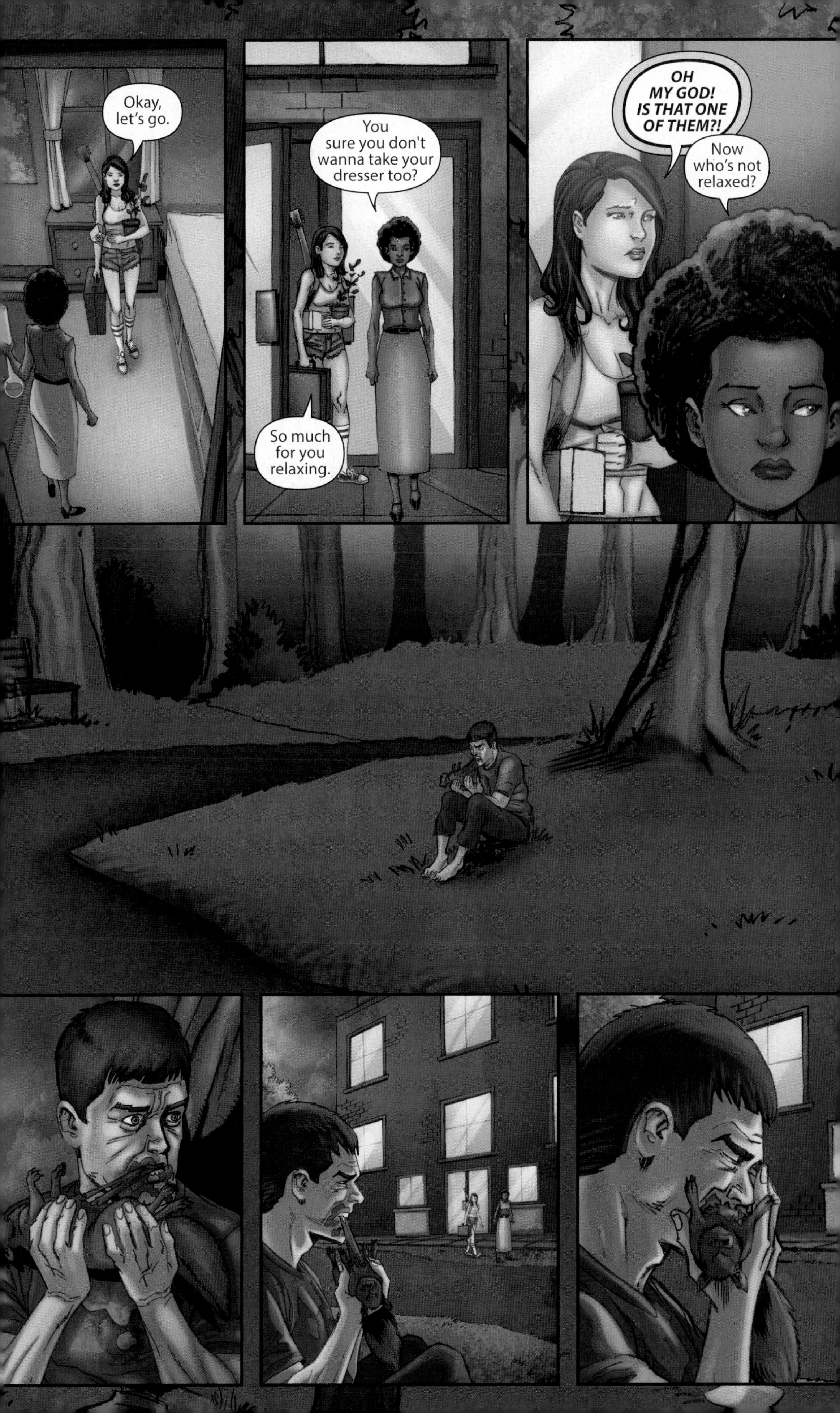
Okay, let's go.
You sure you don't wanna take your dresser too?
So much for you relaxing.
OH MY GOD! IS THAT ONE OF THEM?!
Now who's not relaxed?

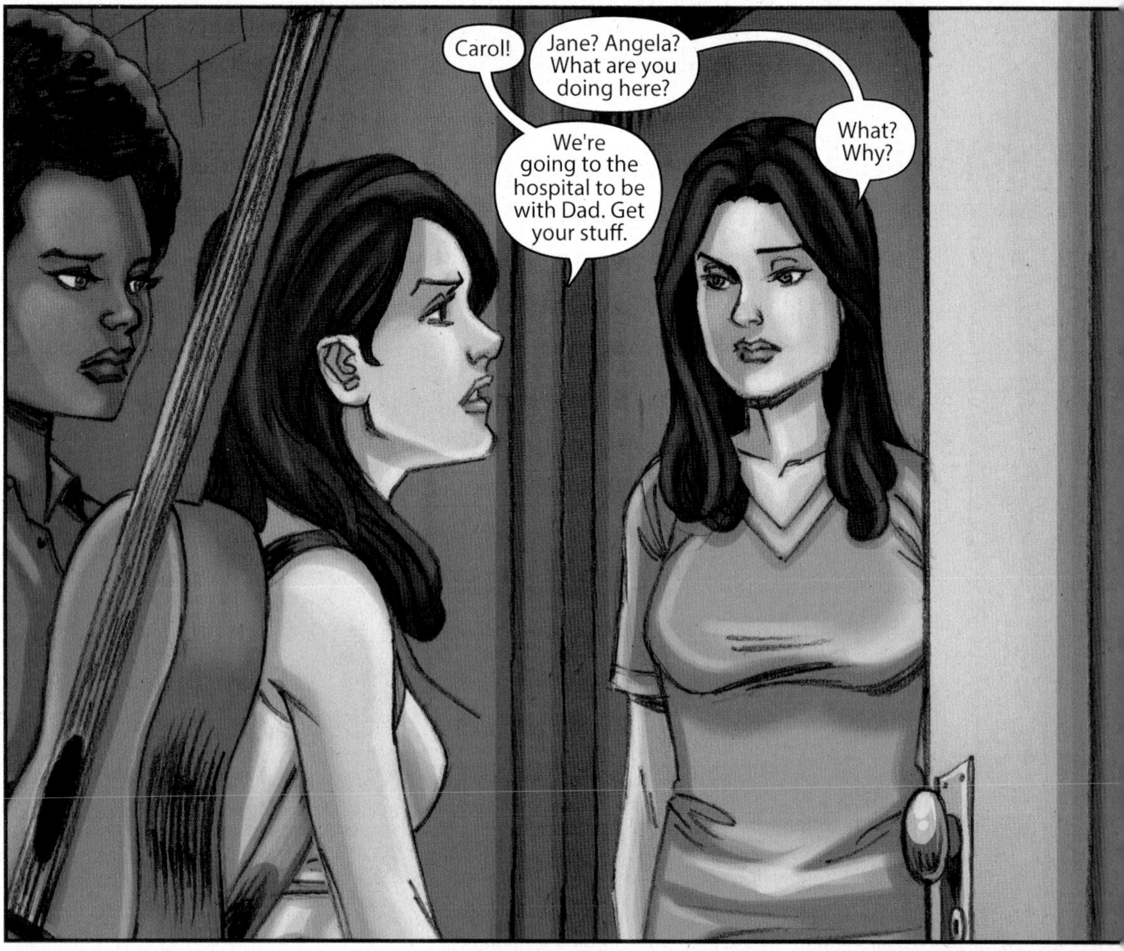
Carol!
Jane? Angela? What are you doing here?
We're going to the hospital to be with Dad. Get your stuff.
What? Why?

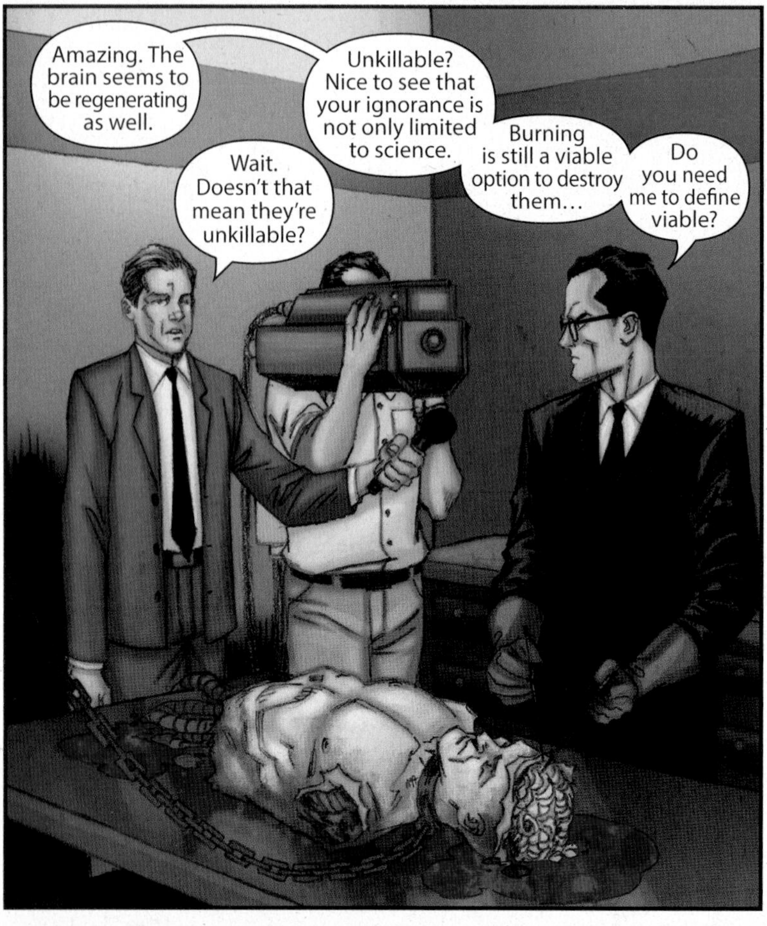
Amazing. The brain seems to be regenerating as well.
Wait. Doesn't that mean they're unkillable?
Unkillable? Nice to see that your ignorance is not only limited to science.
Burning is still a viable option to destroy them…
Do you need me to define viable?

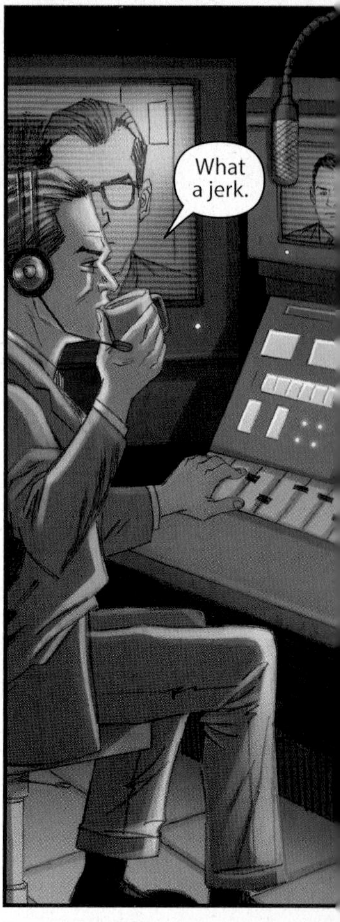
What a jerk.

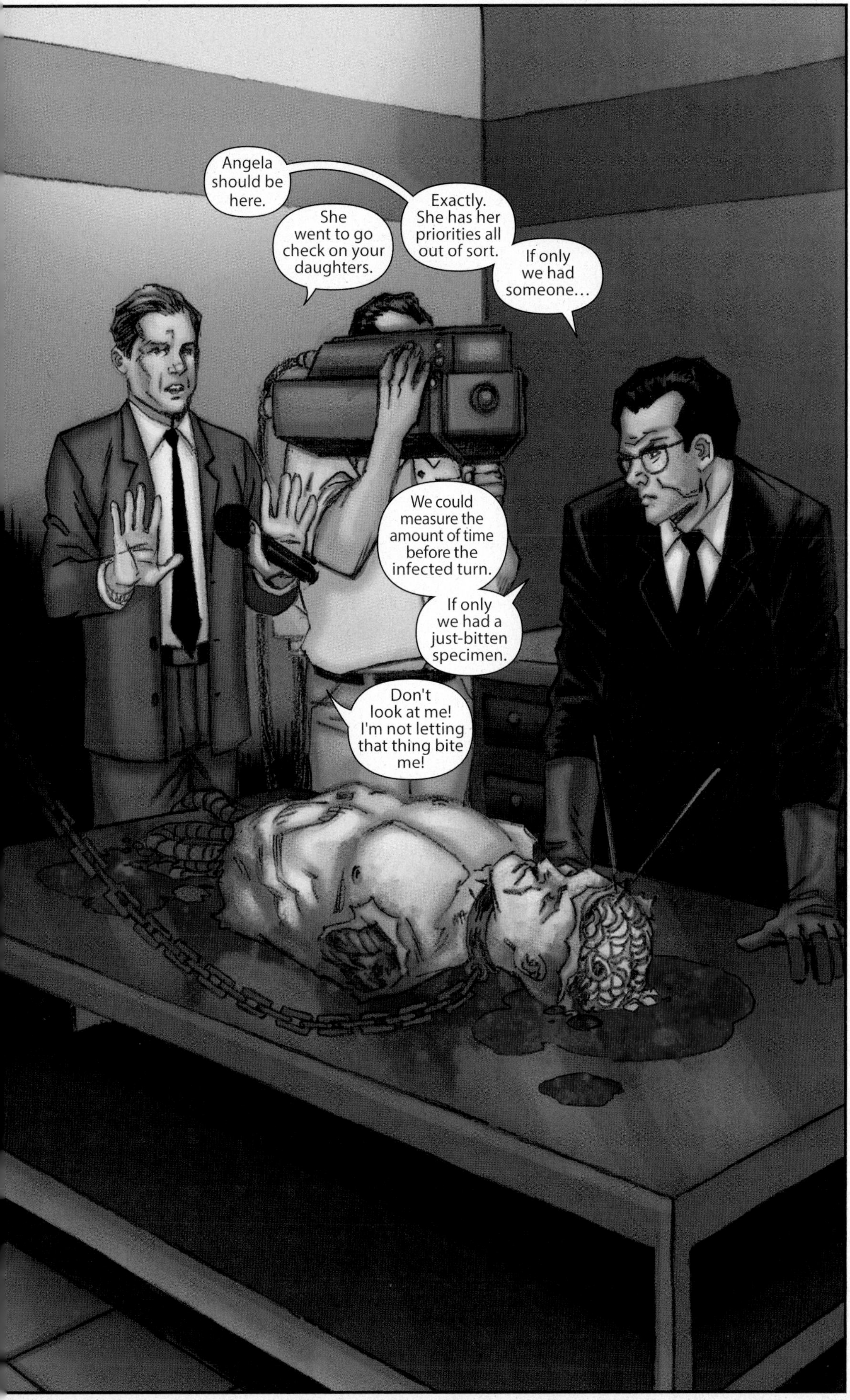
Angela should be here.
She went to go check on your daughters.
Exactly. She has her priorities all out of sort.
If only we had someone…
We could measure the amount of time before the infected turn.
If only we had a just-bitten specimen.
Don't look at me! I'm not letting that thing bite me!

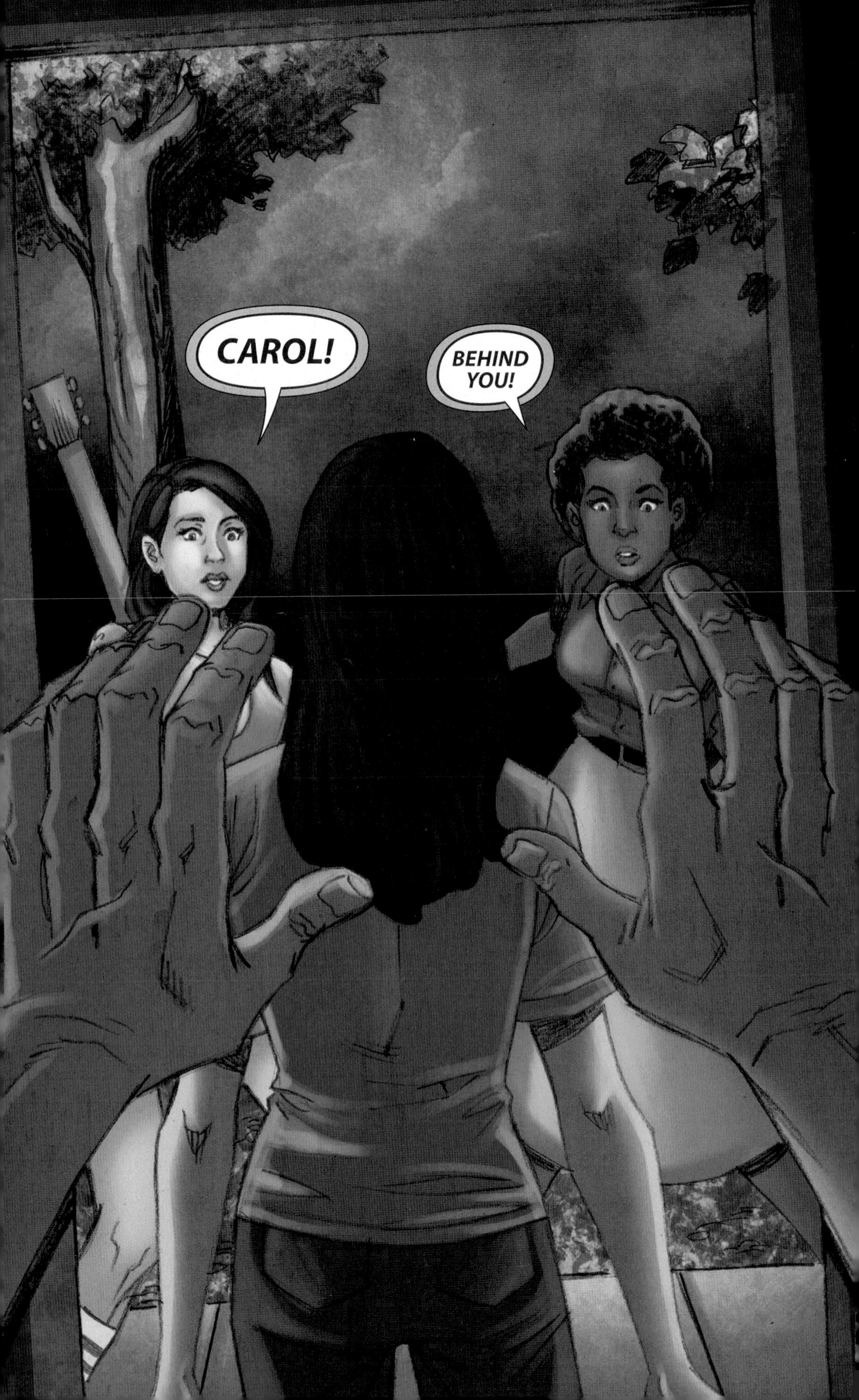
CAROL!
BEHIND YOU!

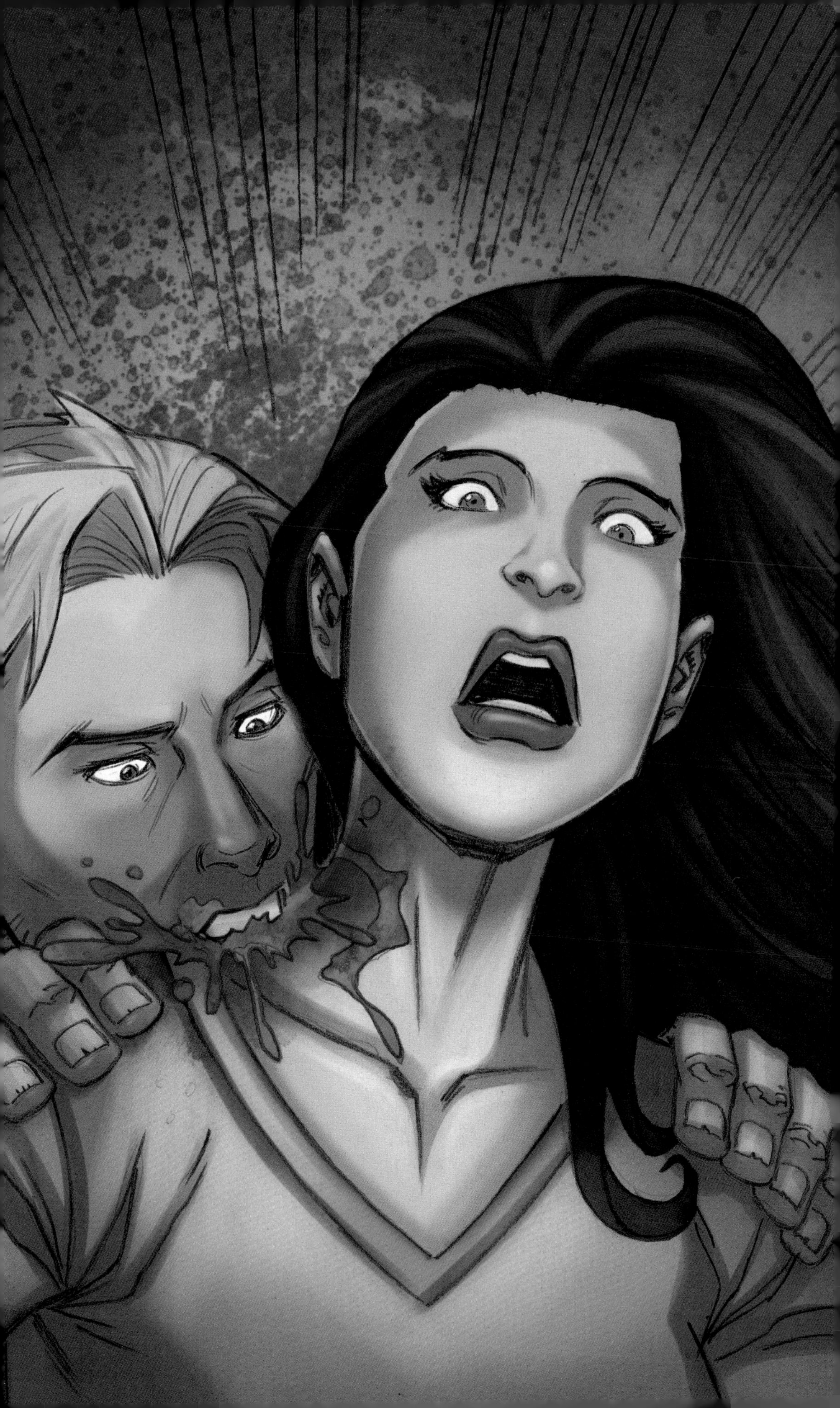

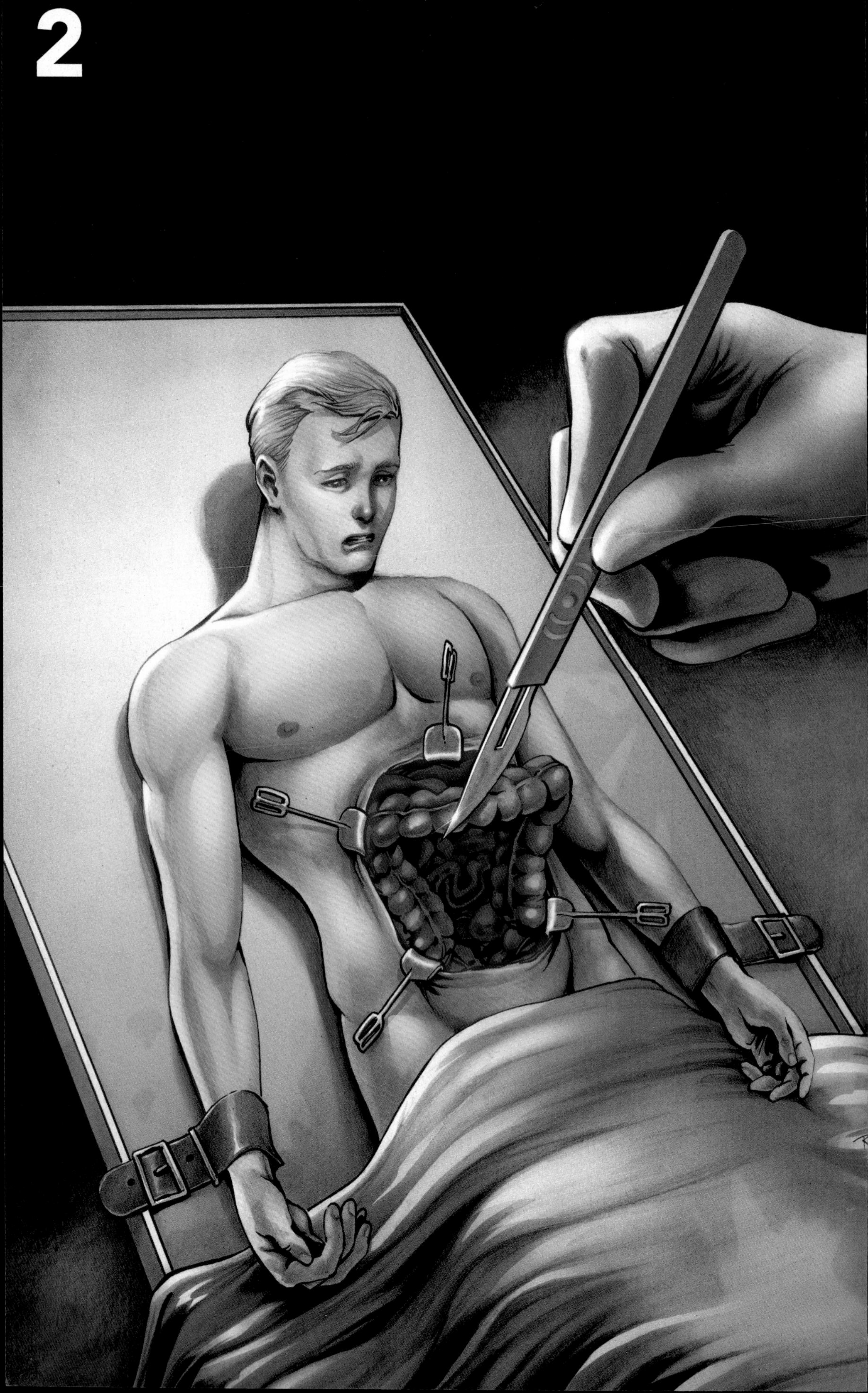
2

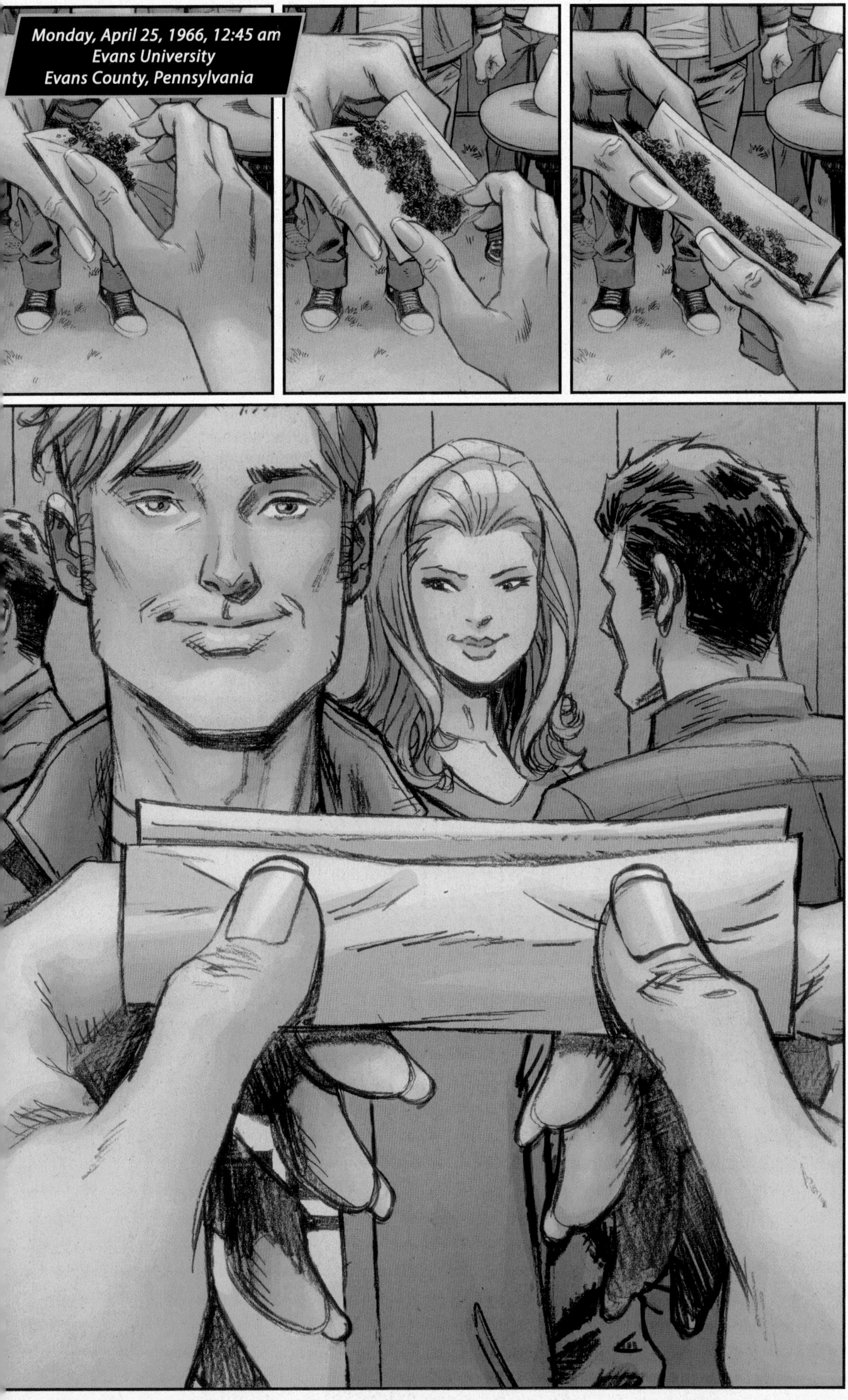
Monday, April 25, 1966, 12:45 am
Evans University
Evans County, Pennsylvania

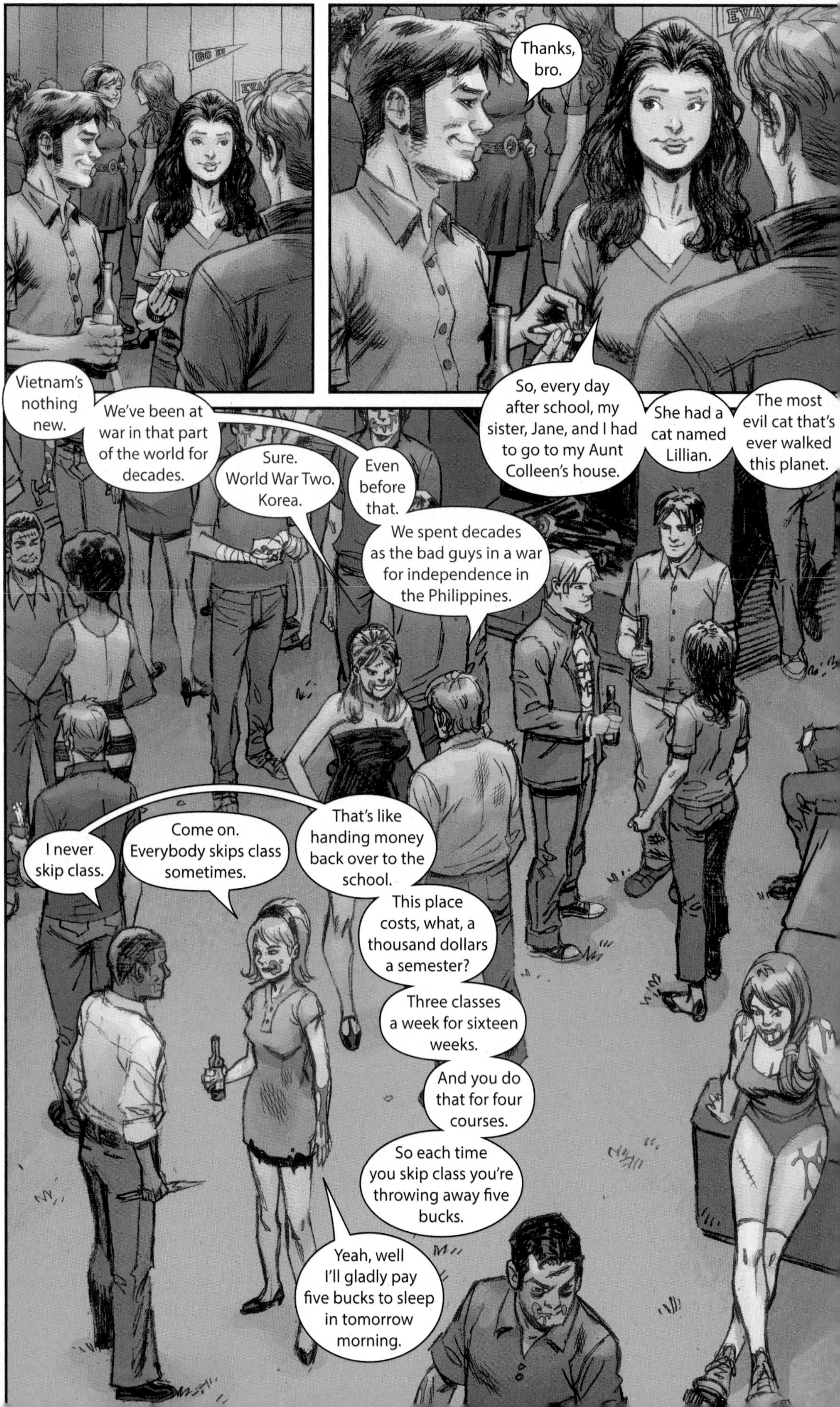
GO E
EVA
Thanks, bro.
So, every day after school, my sister, Jane, and I had to go to my Aunt Colleen's house.
She had a cat named Lillian.
The most evil cat that's ever walked this planet.
Vietnam's nothing new.
We've been at war in that part of the world for decades.
Sure. World War Two. Korea.
Even before that.
We spent decades as the bad guys in a war for independence in the Philippines.
I never skip class.
Come on. Everybody skips class sometimes.
That's like handing money back over to the school.
This place costs, what, a thousand dollars a semester?
Three classes a week for sixteen weeks.
And you do that for four courses.
So each time you skip class you're throwing away five bucks.
Yeah, well I'll gladly pay five bucks to sleep in tomorrow morning.

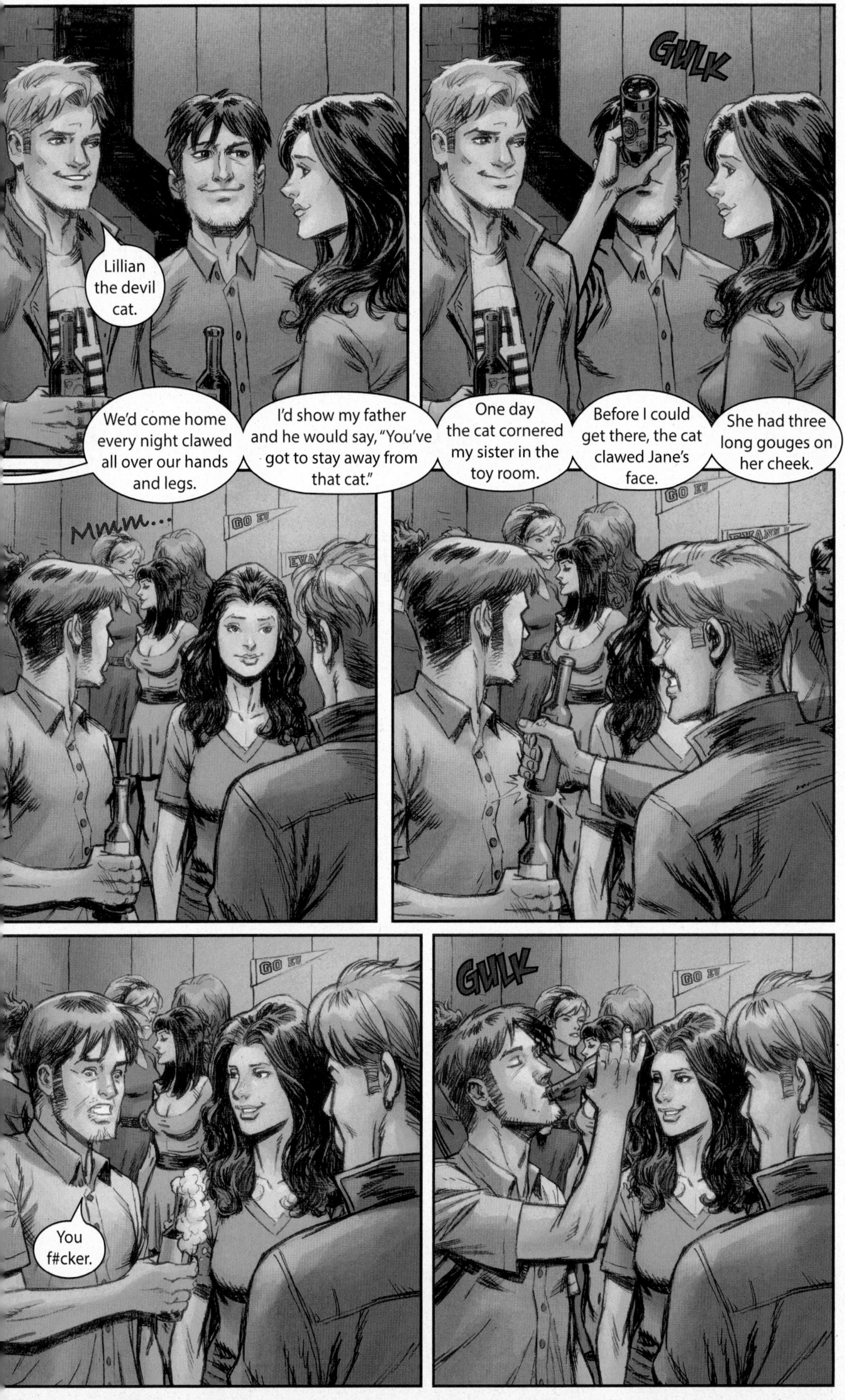

Lillian the devil cat.
GULK
We'd come home every night clawed all over our hands and legs.
I'd show my father and he would say, "You've got to stay away from that cat."
One day the cat cornered my sister in the toy room.
Before I could get there, the cat clawed Jane's face.
She had three long gouges on her cheek.
MMM...
GO EU
GO EU
You f#cker.
GULK
GO EU

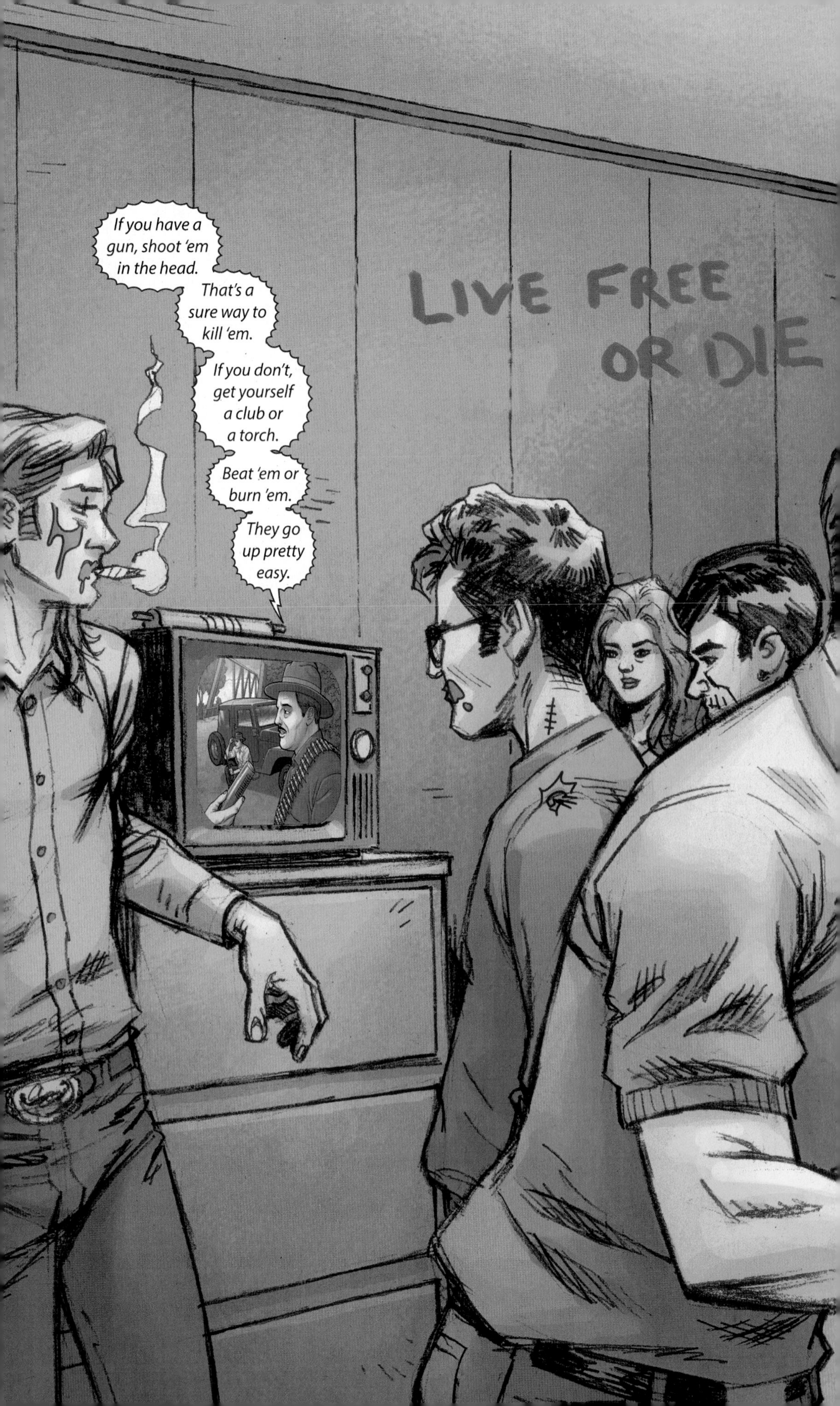
If you have a gun, shoot 'em in the head.
That's a sure way to kill 'em.
If you don't, get yourself a club or a torch.
Beat 'em or burn 'em.
They go up pretty easy.
LIVE FREE OR DIE

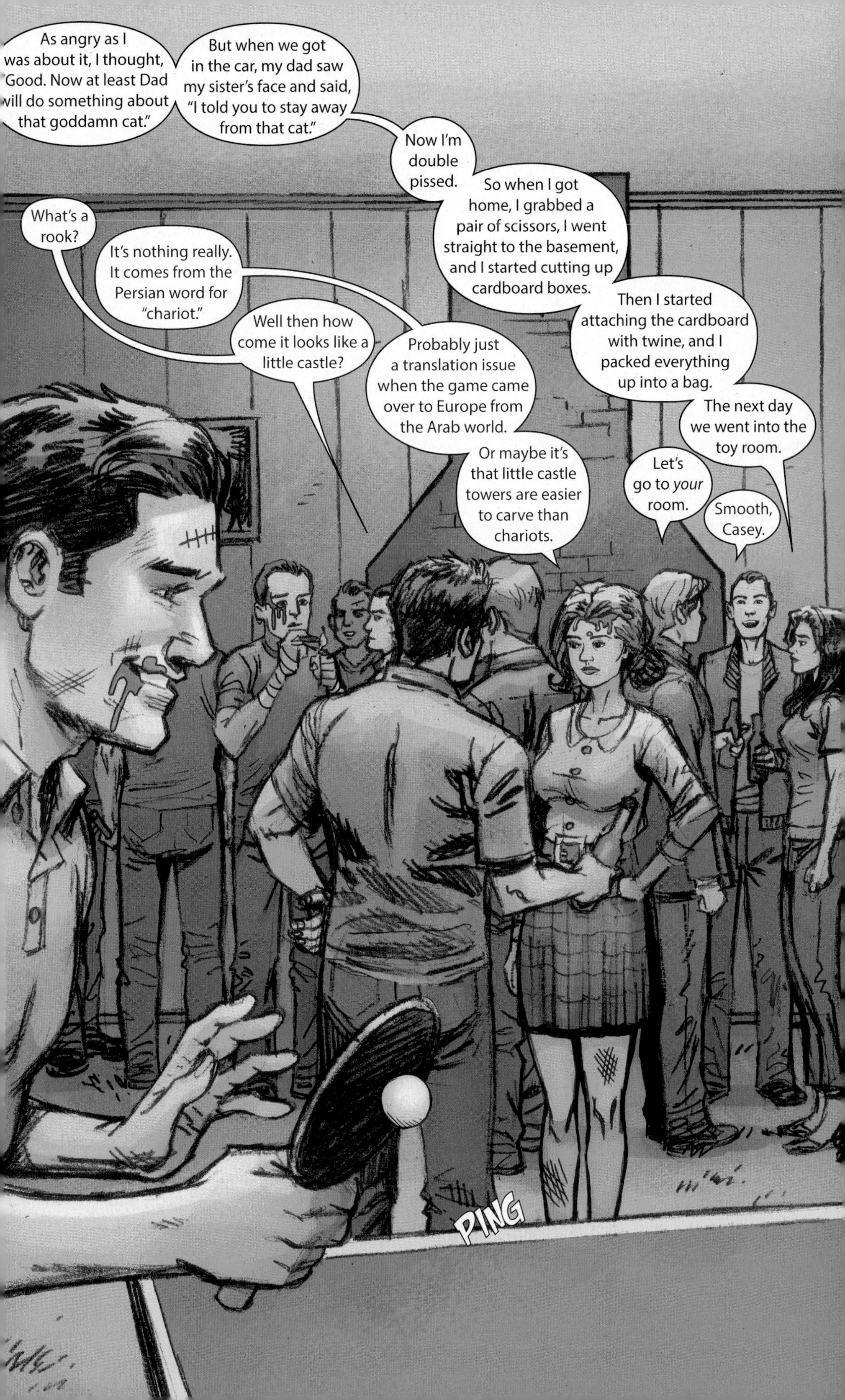
As angry as I was about it, I thought, "Good. Now at least Dad will do something about that goddamn cat."
But when we got in the car, my dad saw my sister's face and said, "I told you to stay away from that cat."
Now I'm double pissed.
So when I got home, I grabbed a pair of scissors, I went straight to the basement, and I started cutting up cardboard boxes.
What's a rook?
It's nothing really. It comes from the Persian word for "chariot."
Well then how come it looks like a little castle?
Probably just a translation issue when the game came over to Europe from the Arab world.
Or maybe it's that little castle towers are easier to carve than chariots.
Then I started attaching the cardboard with twine, and I packed everything up into a bag.
The next day we went into the toy room.
Let's go to *your* room.
Smooth, Casey.
PING

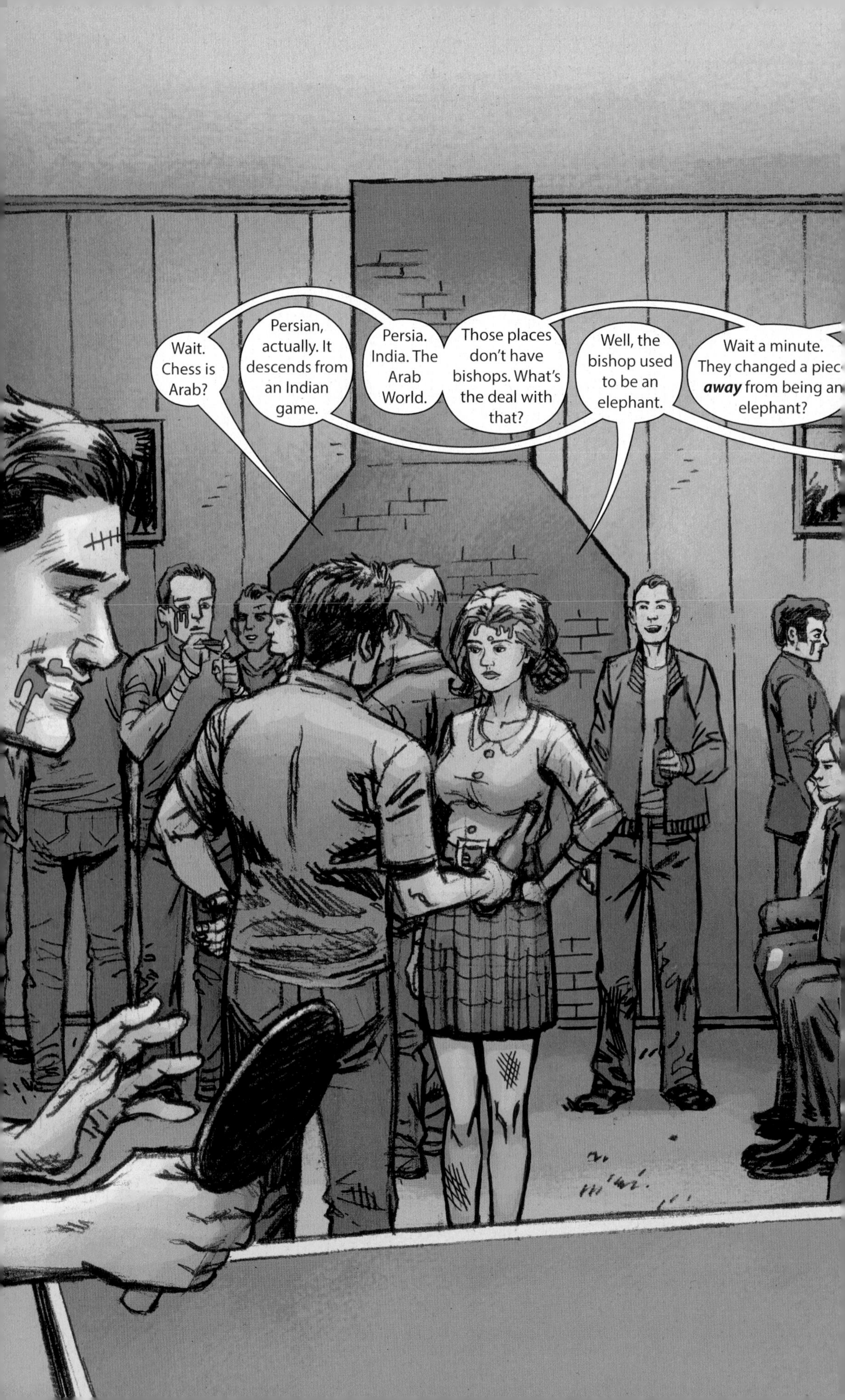
Wait. Chess is Arab?
Persian, actually. It descends from an Indian game.
Persia. India. The Arab World.
Those places don't have bishops. What's the deal with that?
Well, the bishop used to be an elephant.
Wait a minute. They changed a piec
away from being an
elephant?

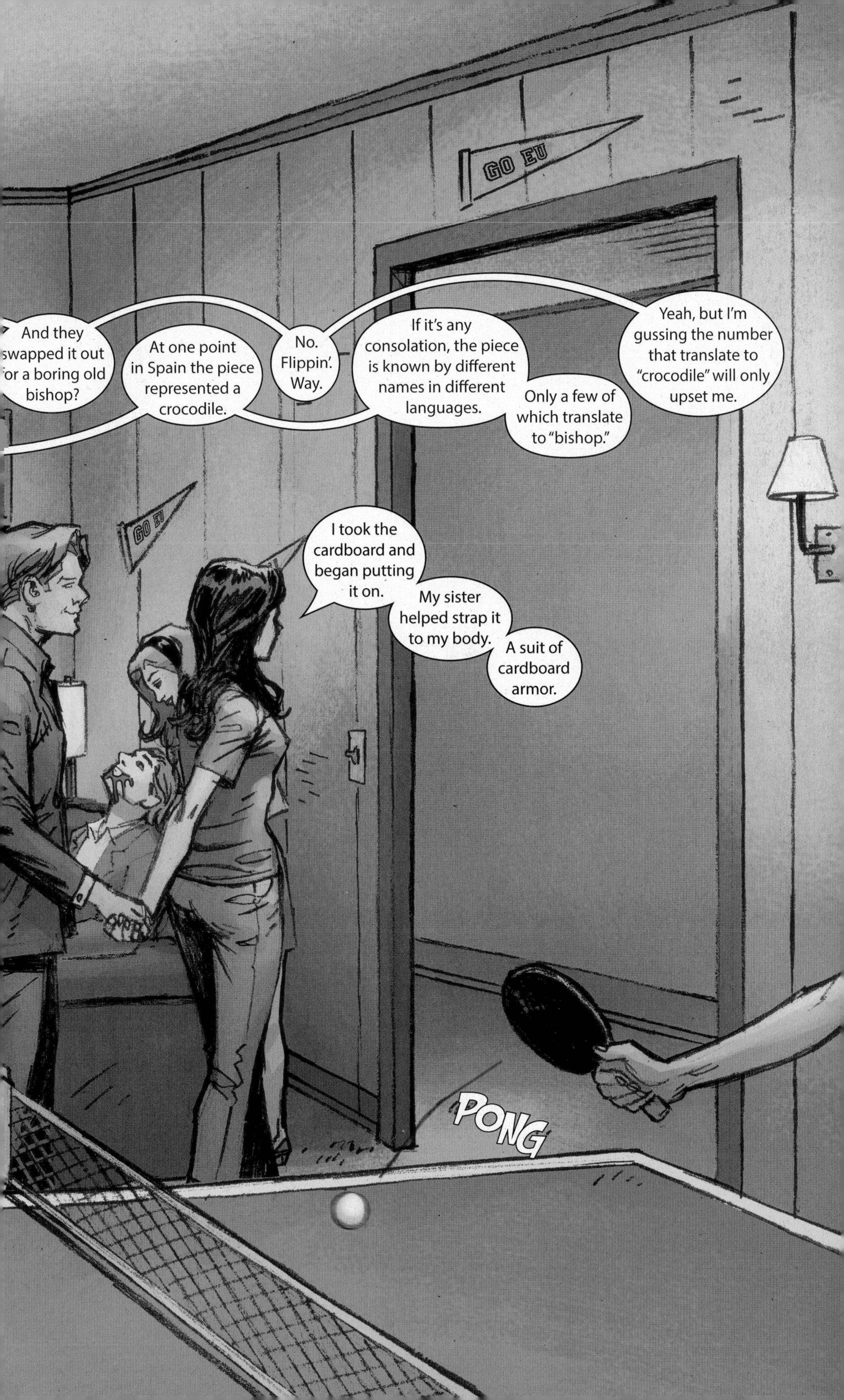
And they swapped it out for a boring old bishop?
At one point in Spain the piece represented a crocodile.
No. Flippin'. Way.
If it's any consolation, the piece is known by different names in different languages.
Only a few of which translate to "bishop."
Yeah, but I'm gussing the number that translate to "crocodile" will only upset me.
GO EU
GO EU
I took the cardboard and began putting it on.
My sister helped strap it to my body.
A suit of cardboard armor.
PONG

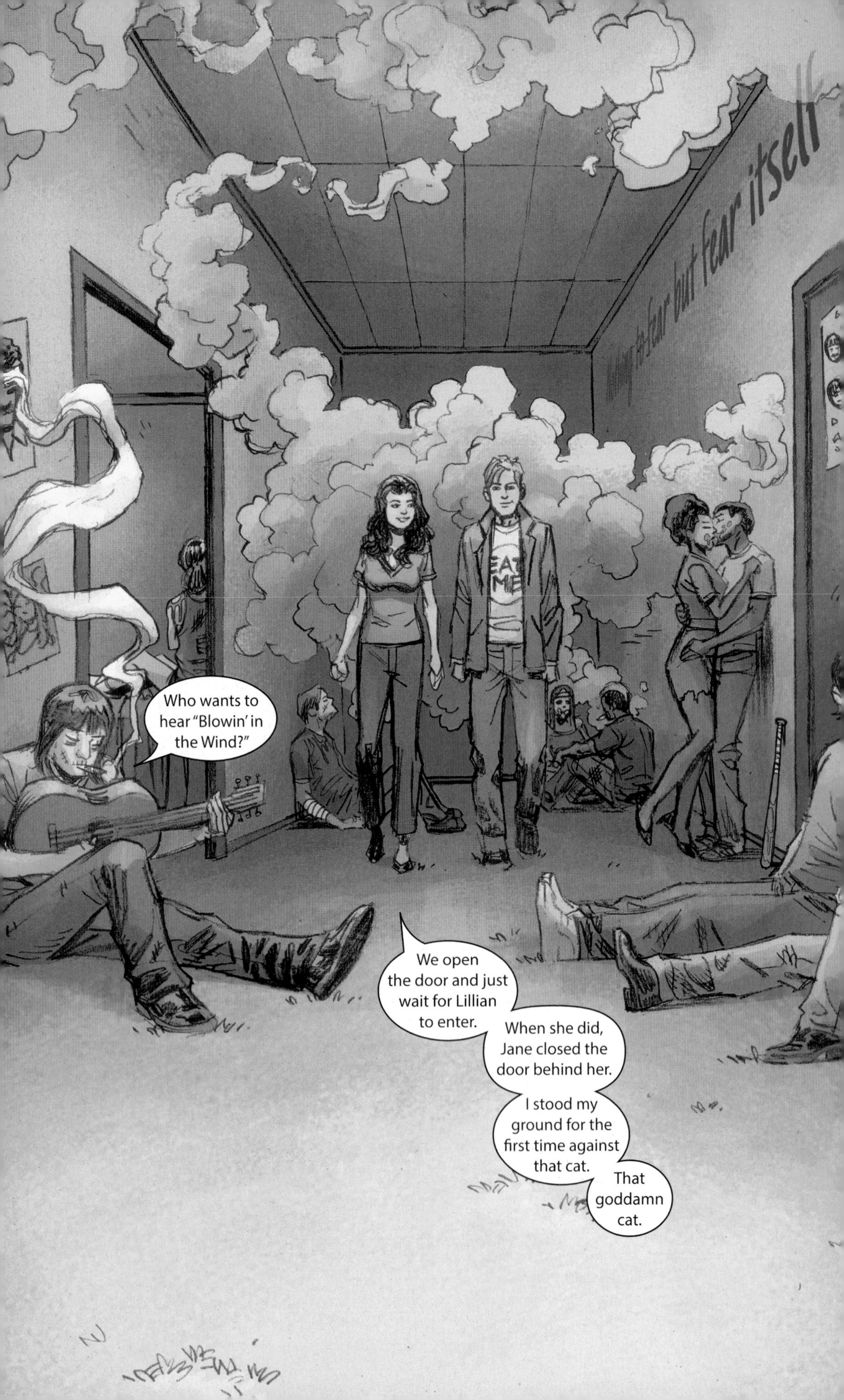
fear but fear itself
EAT ME
Who wants to hear "Blowin' in the Wind?"
We open the door and just wait for Lillian to enter.
When she did, Jane closed the door behind her.
I stood my ground for the first time against that cat.
That goddamn cat.

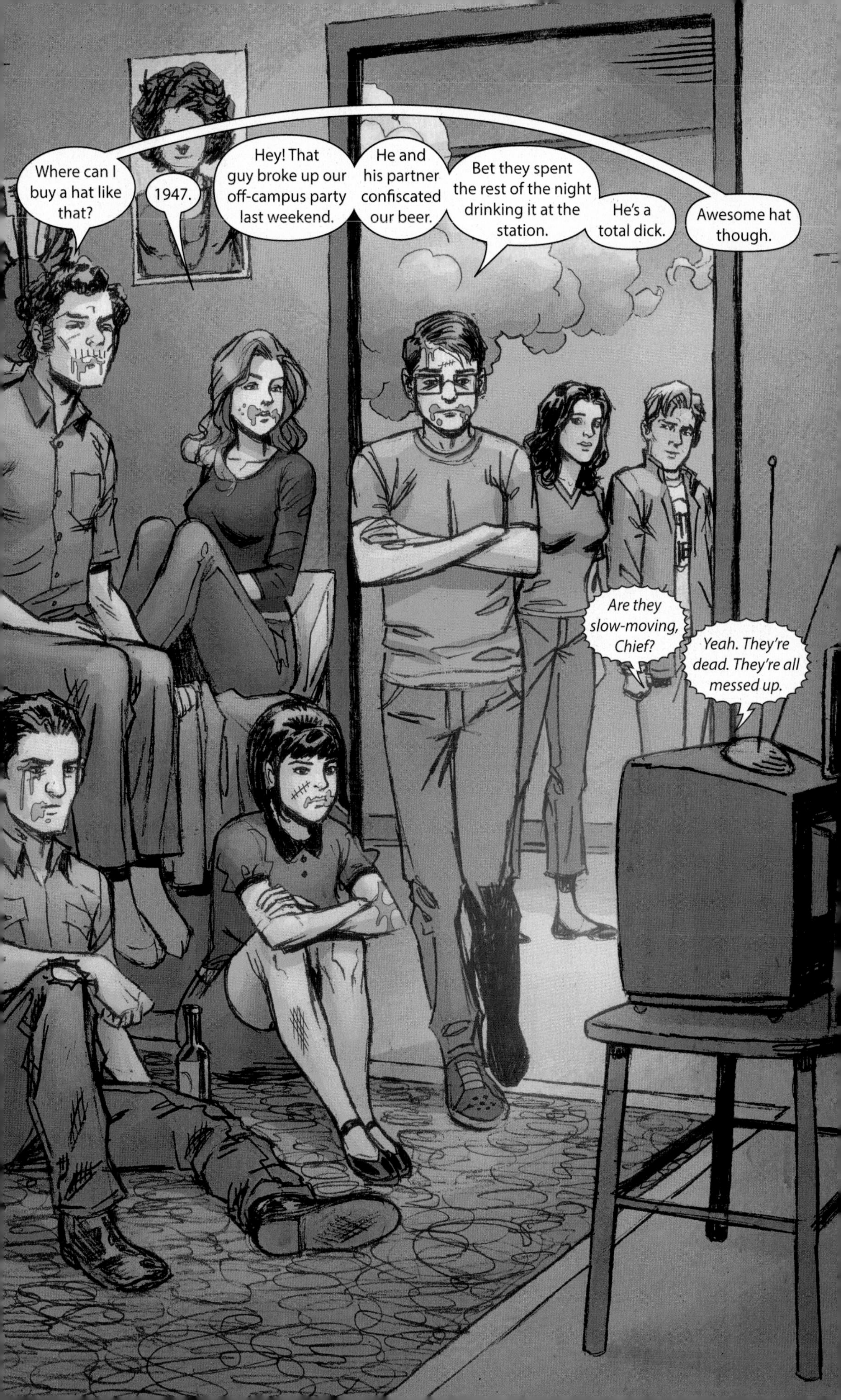
Where can I buy a hat like that?
1947.
Hey! That guy broke up our off-campus party last weekend.
He and his partner confiscated our beer.
Bet they spent the rest of the night drinking it at the station.
He's a total dick.
Awesome hat though.
Are they slow-moving, Chief?
Yeah. They're dead. They're all messed up.

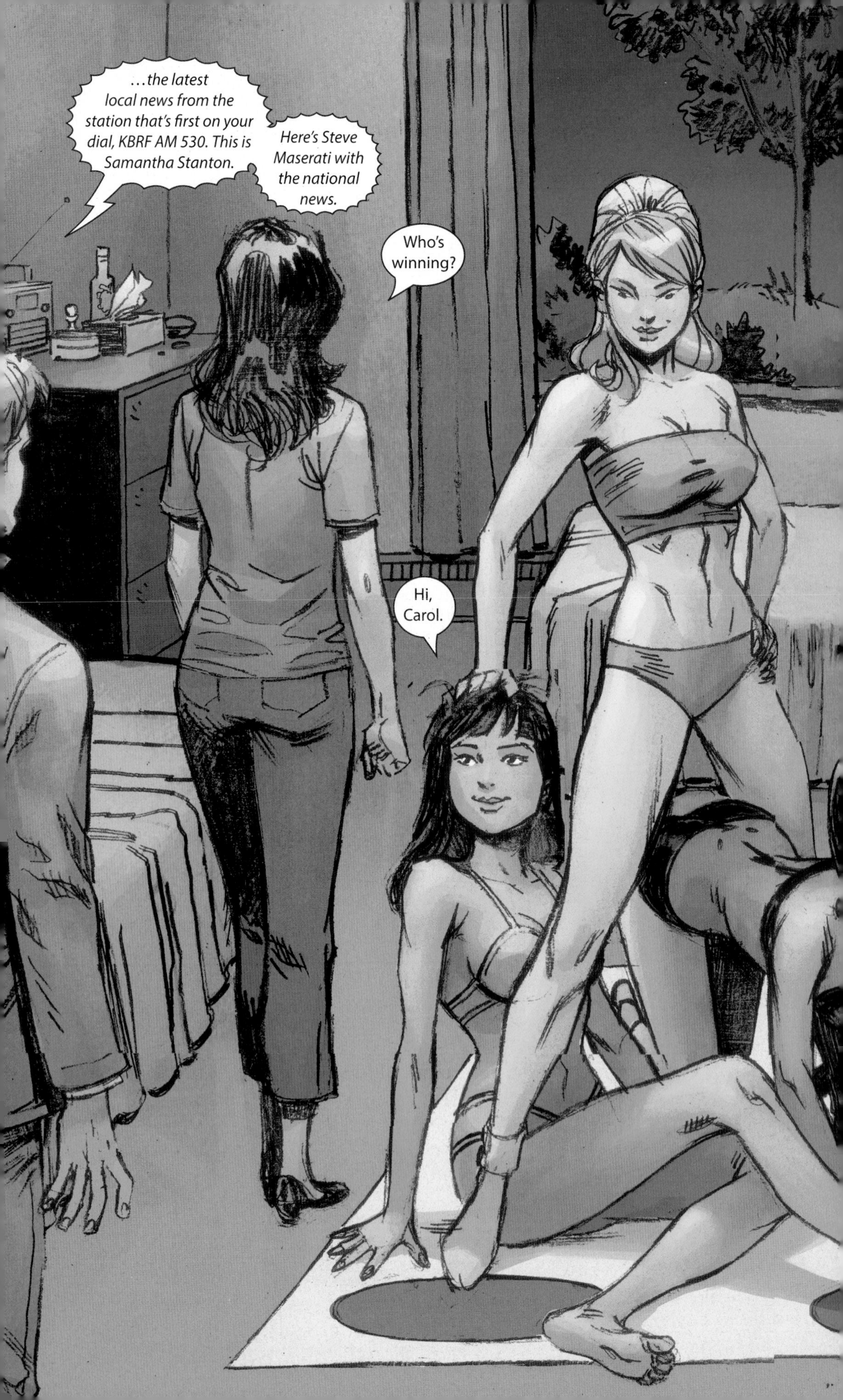
…the latest local news from the station that's first on your dial, KBRF AM 530. This is Samantha Stanton.
Here's Steve Maserati with the national news.
Who's winning?
Hi, Carol.

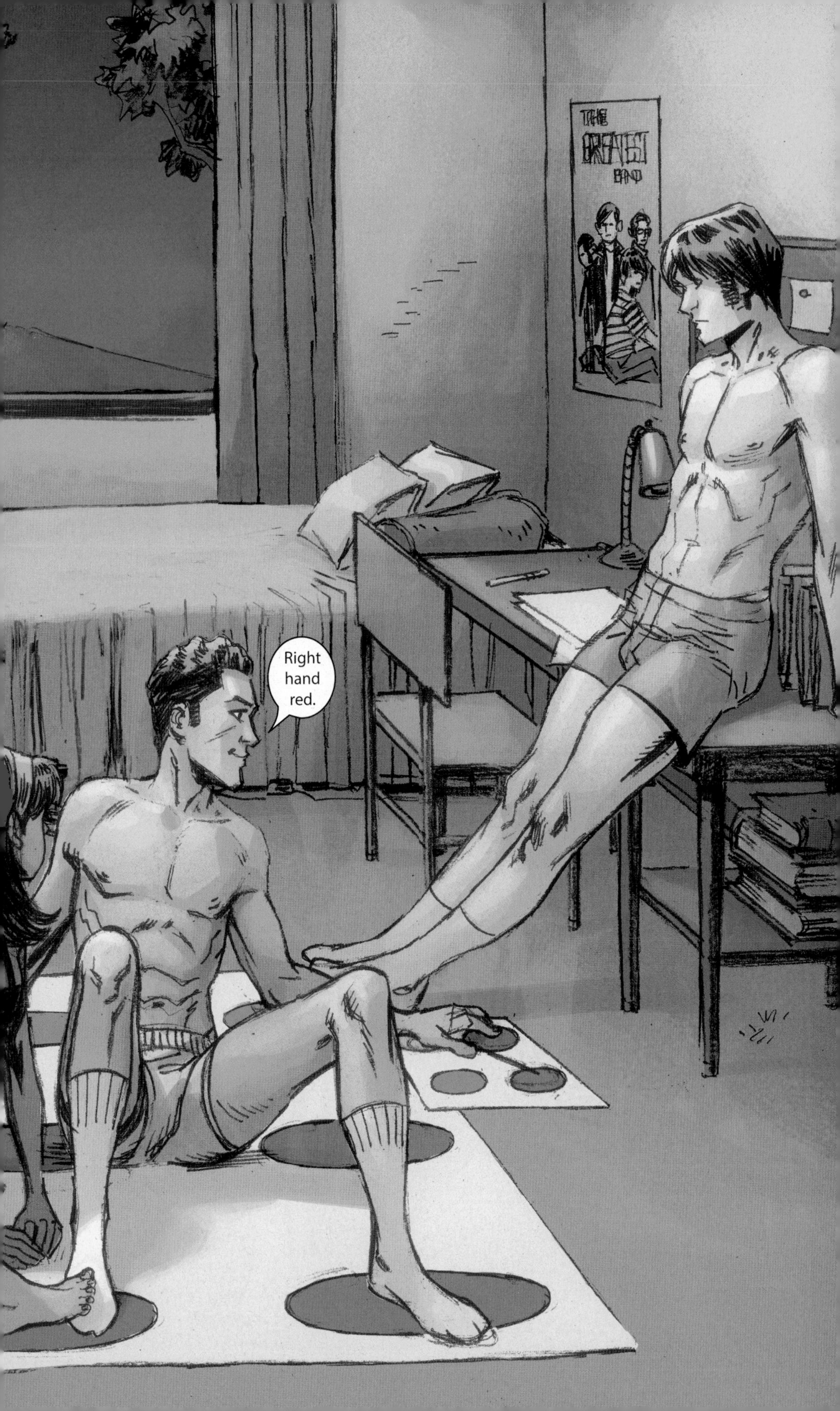
THE GREATEST BAND
Right hand red.

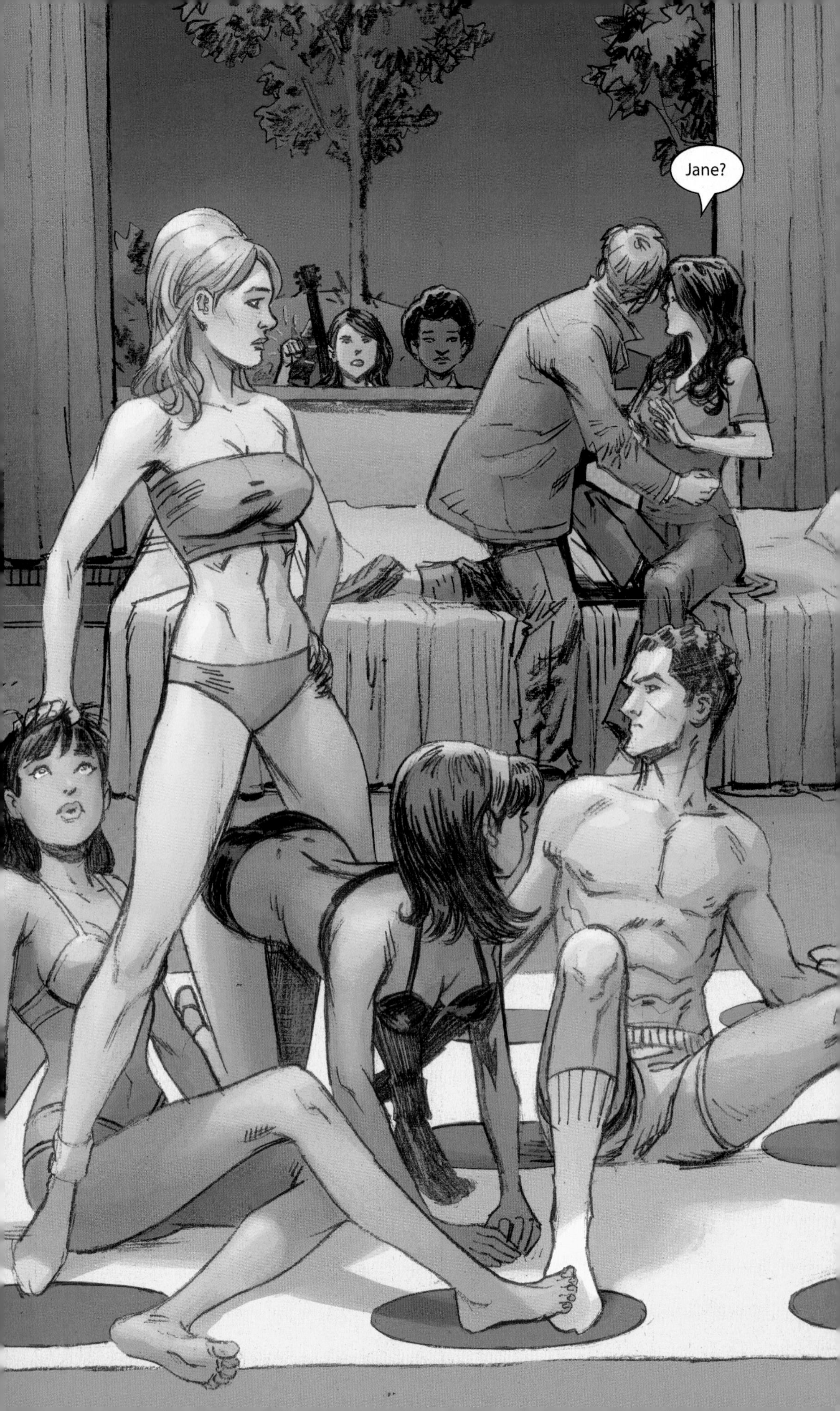
Jane?

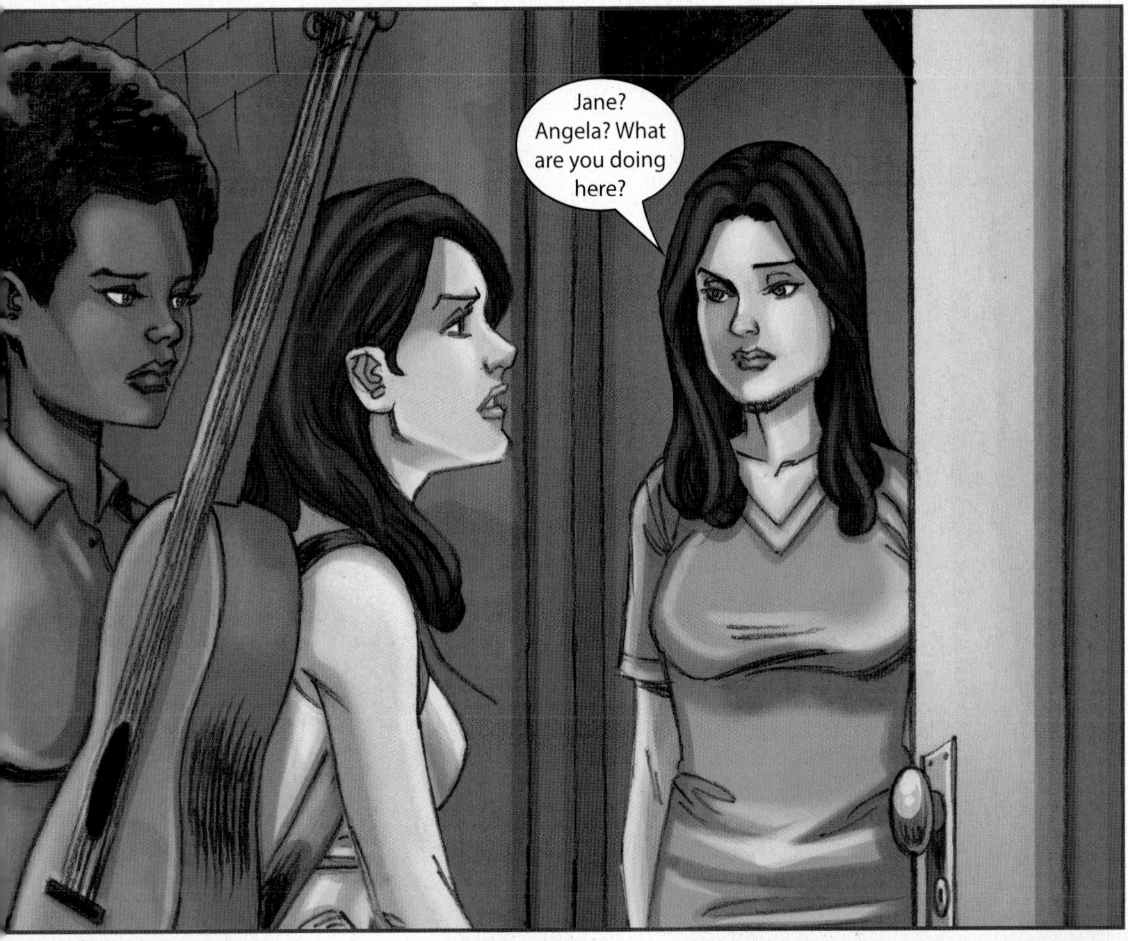
Jane? Angela? What are you doing here?

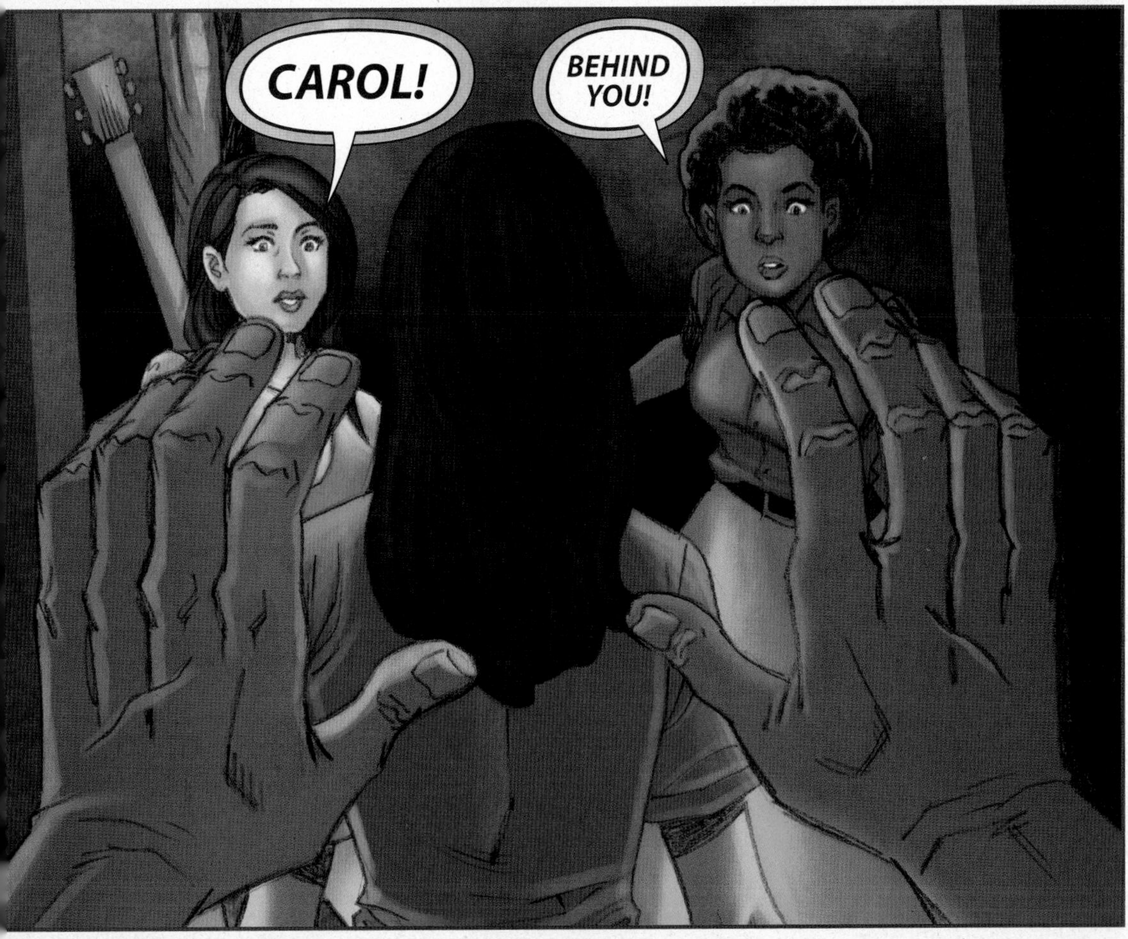
CAROL!
BEHIND YOU!

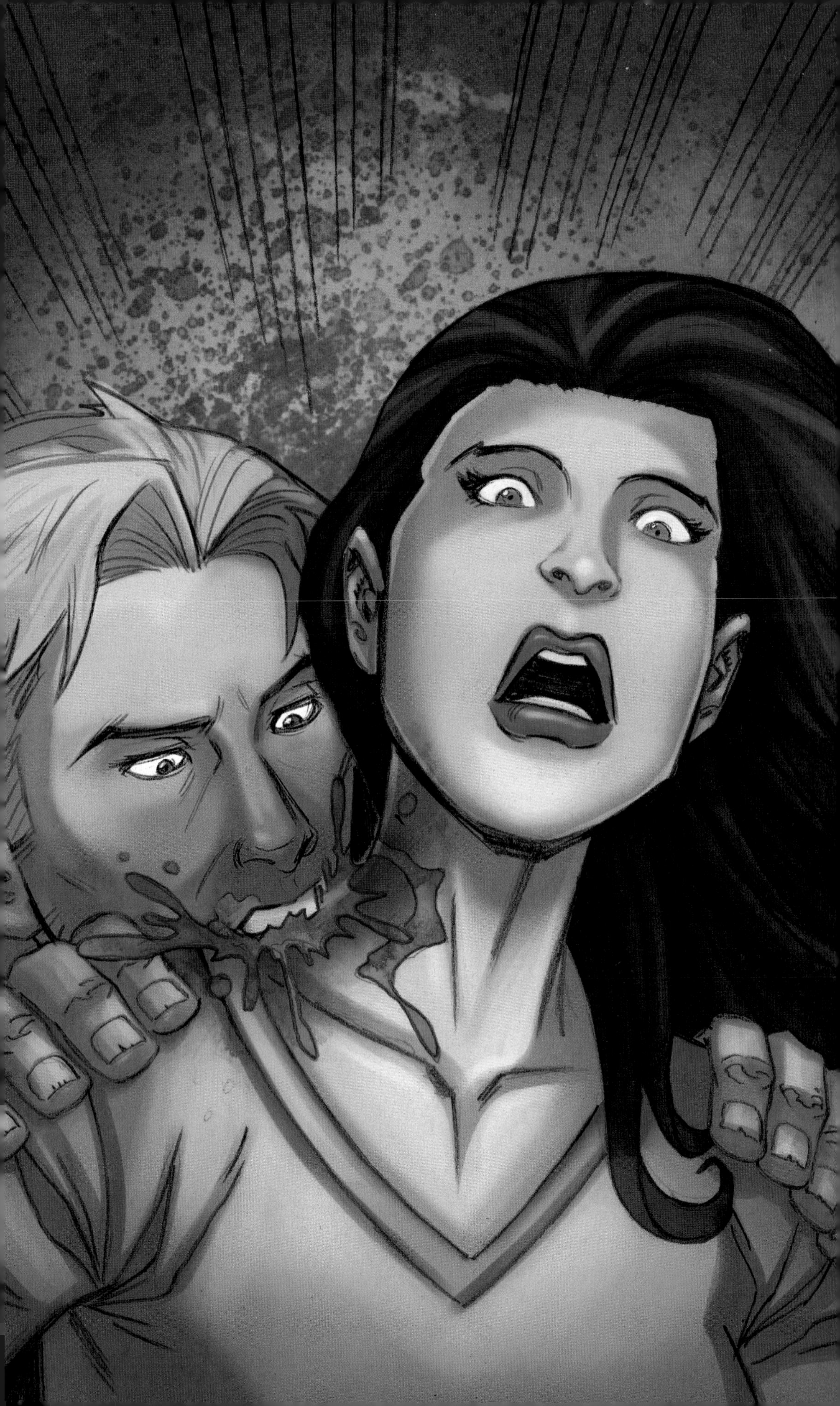

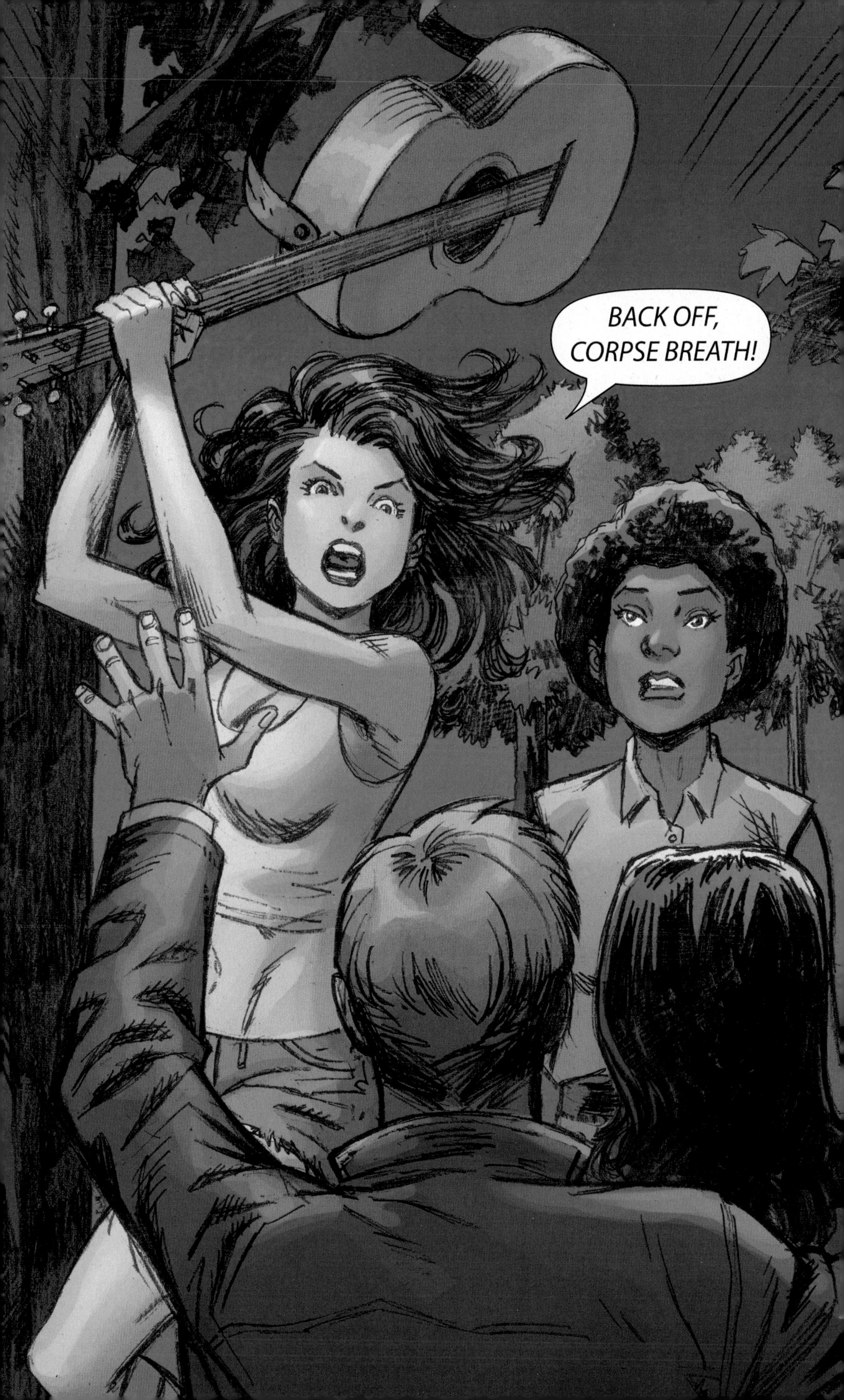
BACK OFF, CORPSE BREATH!

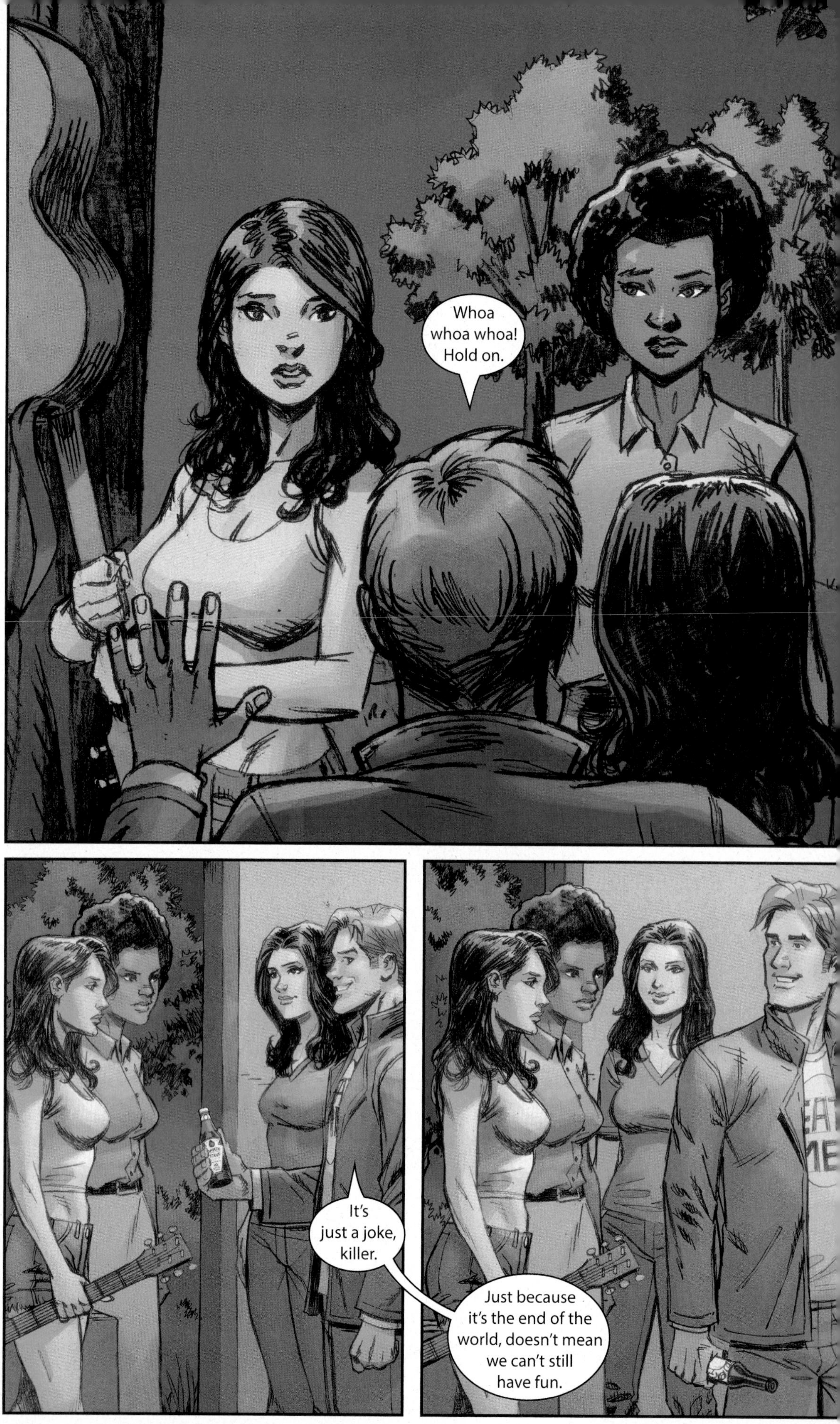
Whoa whoa whoa! Hold on.
It's just a joke, killer.
Just because it's the end of the world, doesn't mean we can't still have fun.

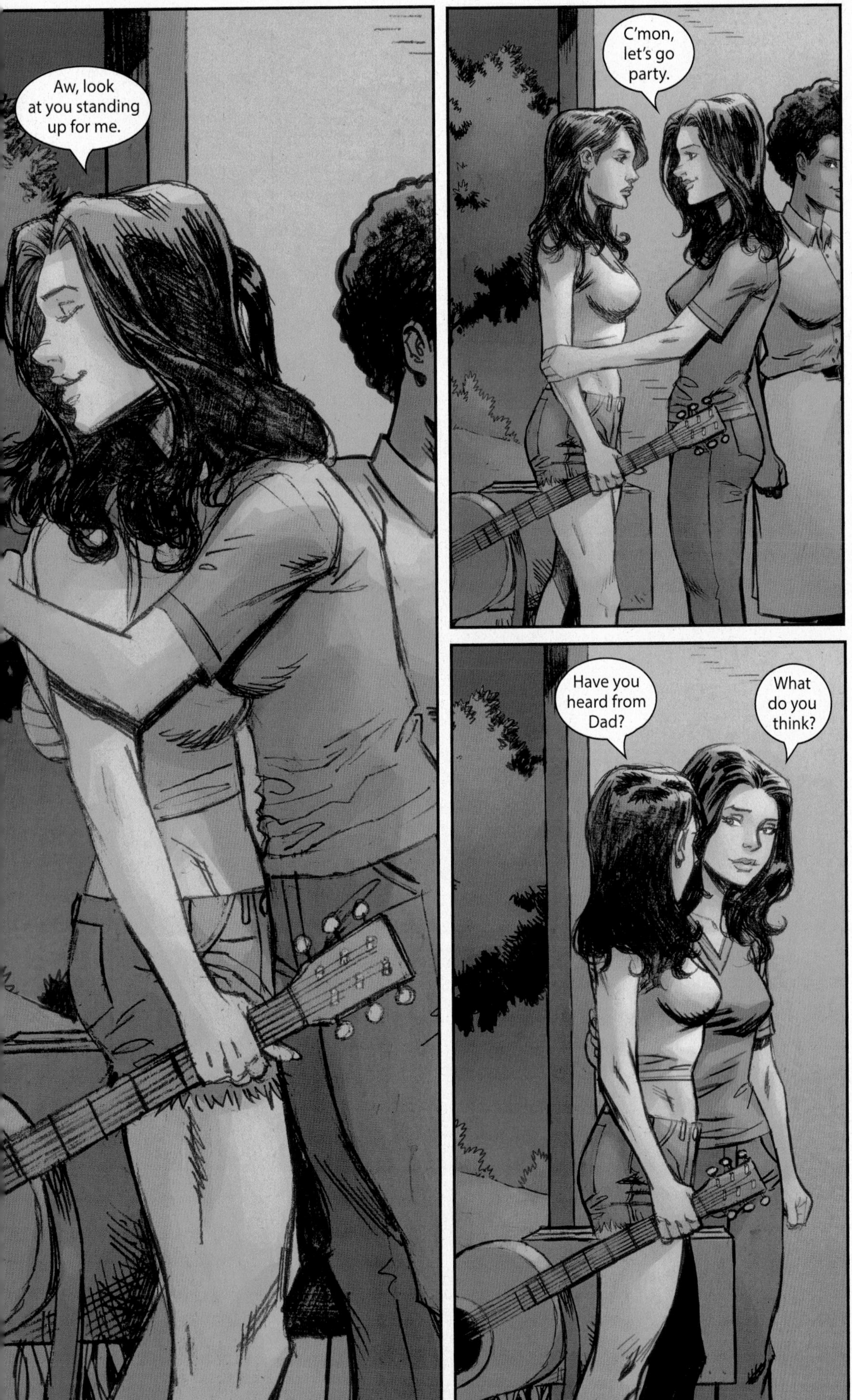
Aw, look at you standing up for me.
C'mon, let's go party.
Have you heard from Dad?
What do you think?

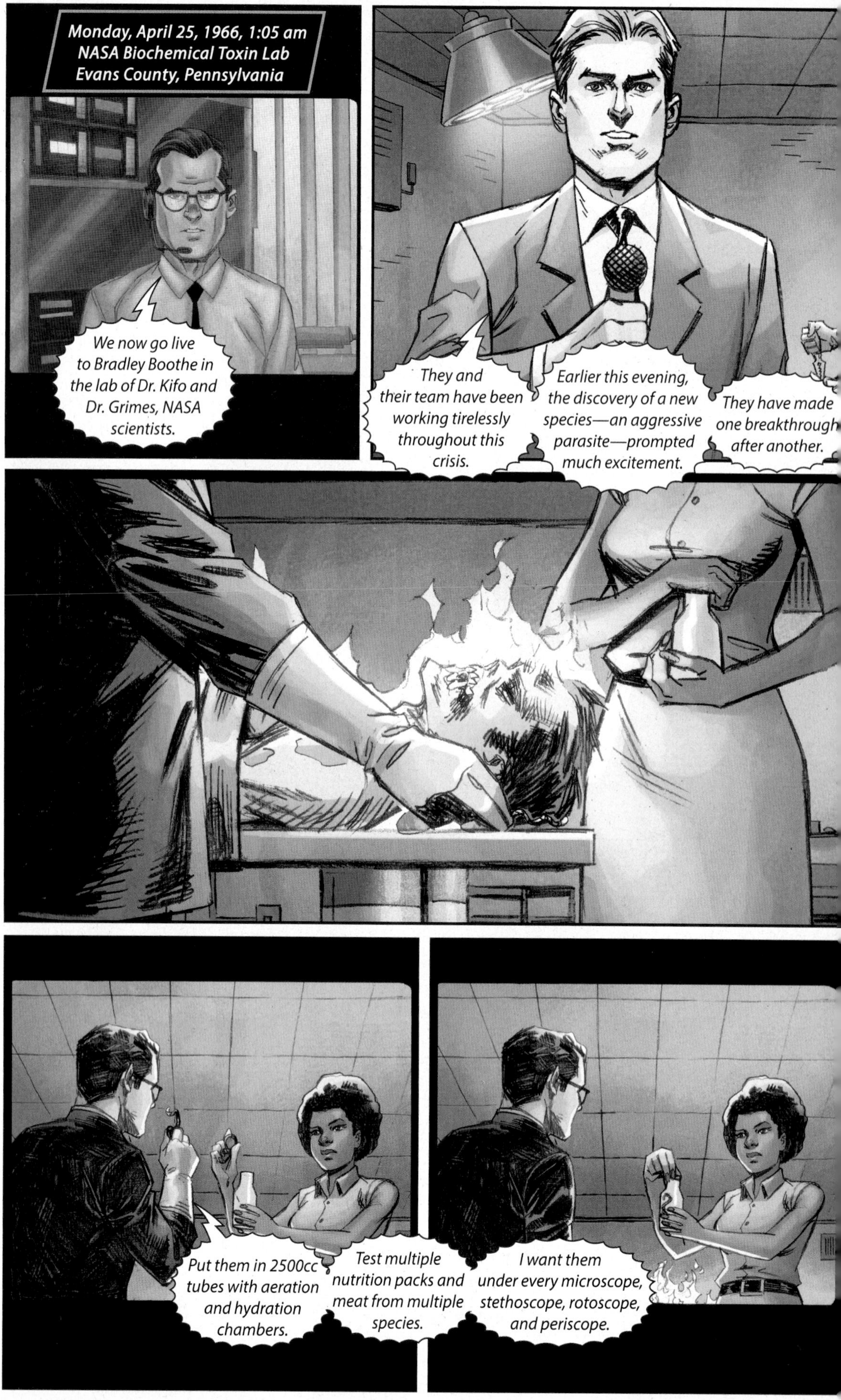

Monday, April 25, 1966, 1:05 am
NASA Biochemical Toxin Lab
Evans County, Pennsylvania
We now go live to Bradley Boothe in the lab of Dr. Kifo and Dr. Grimes, NASA scientists.
They and their team have been working tirelessly throughout this crisis.
Earlier this evening, the discovery of a new species—an aggressive parasite—prompted much excitement.
They have made one breakthrough after another.
Put them in 2500cc tubes with aeration and hydration chambers.
Test multiple nutrition packs and meat from multiple species.
I want them under every microscope, stethoscope, rotoscope, and periscope.

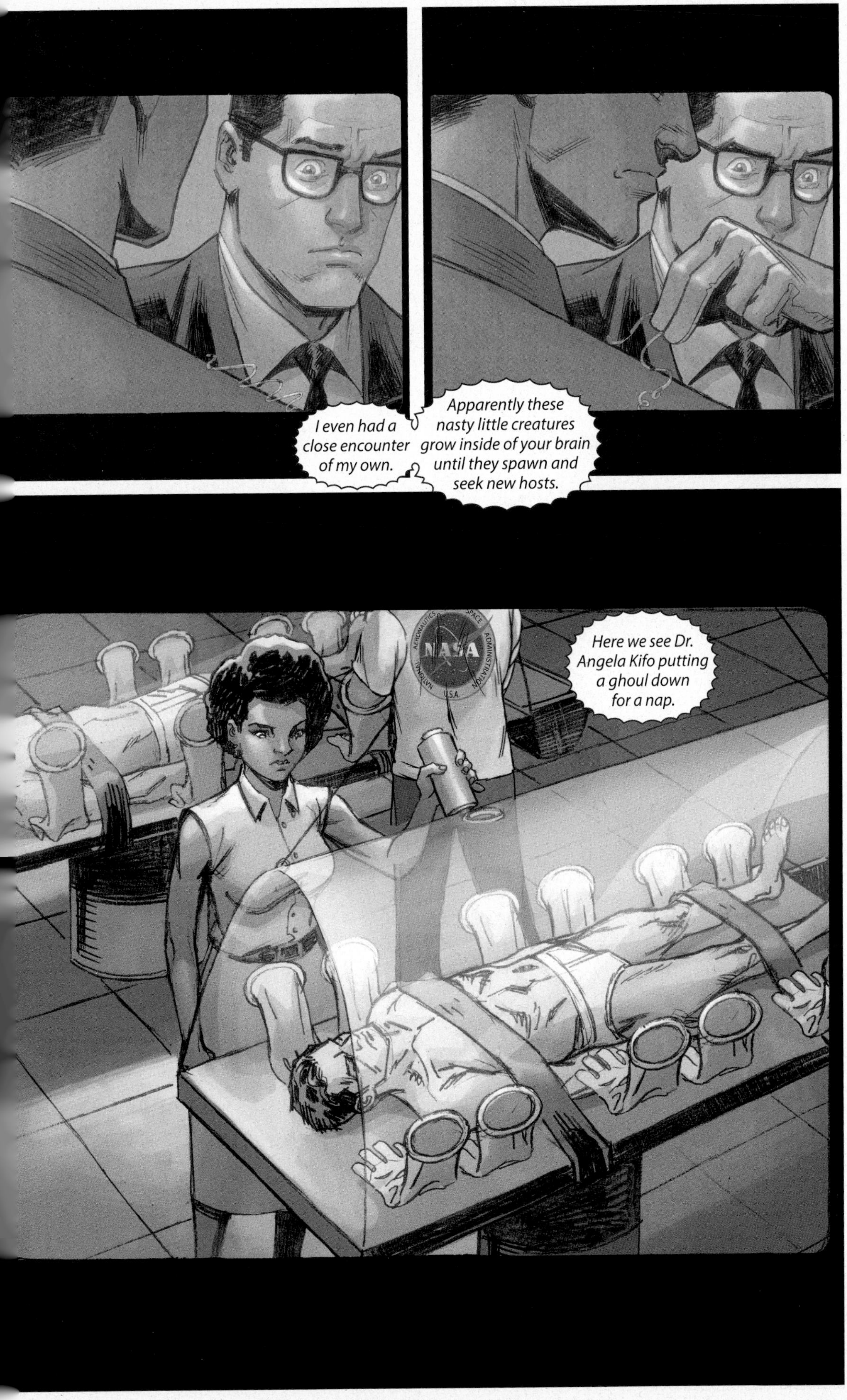
I even had a close encounter of my own.
Apparently these nasty little creatures grow inside of your brain until they spawn and seek new hosts.
NASA
Here we see Dr. Angela Kifo putting a ghoul down for a nap.

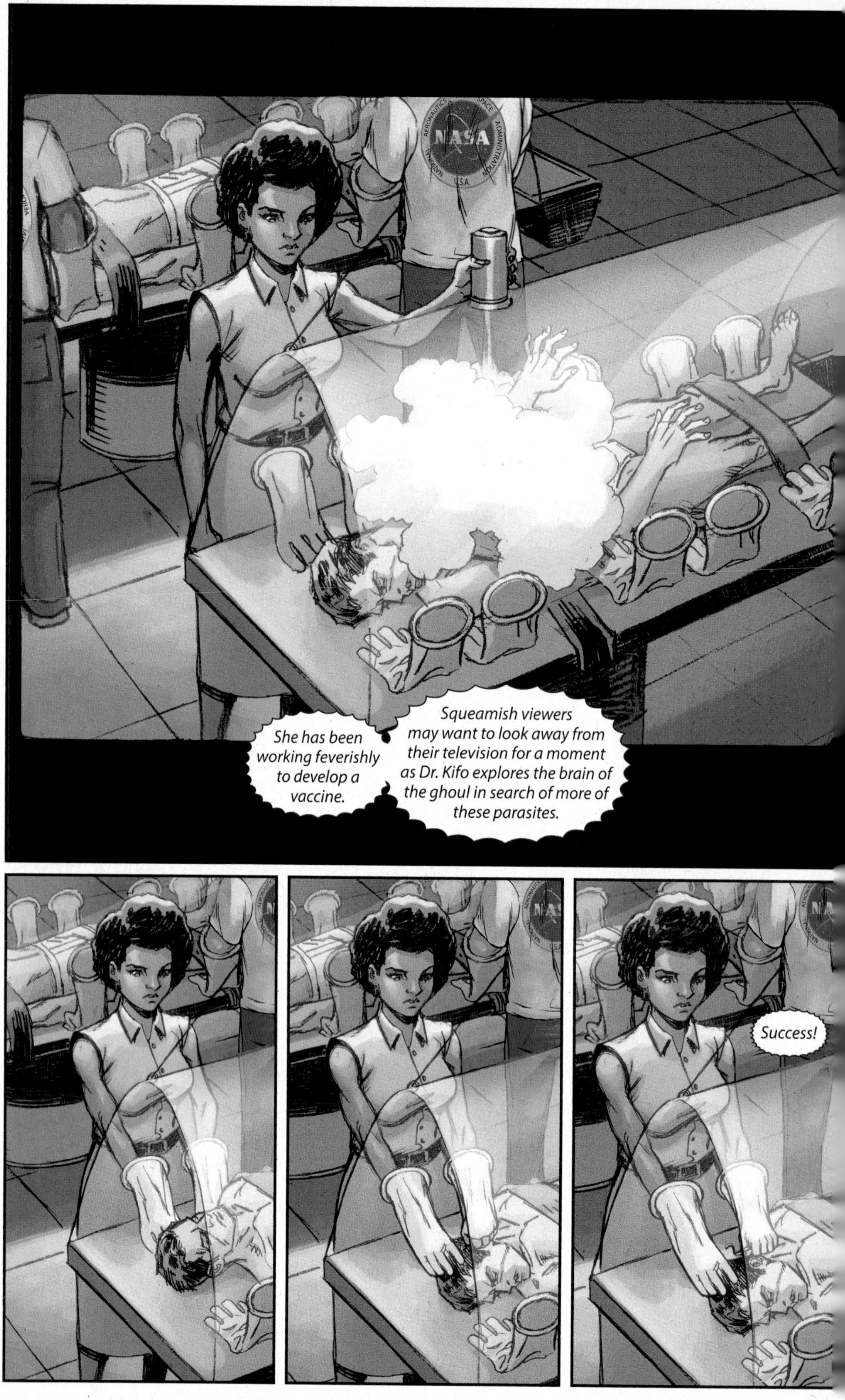
She has been working feverishly to develop a vaccine.
Squeamish viewers may want to look away from their television for a moment as Dr. Kifo explores the brain of the ghoul in search of more of these parasites.
Success!

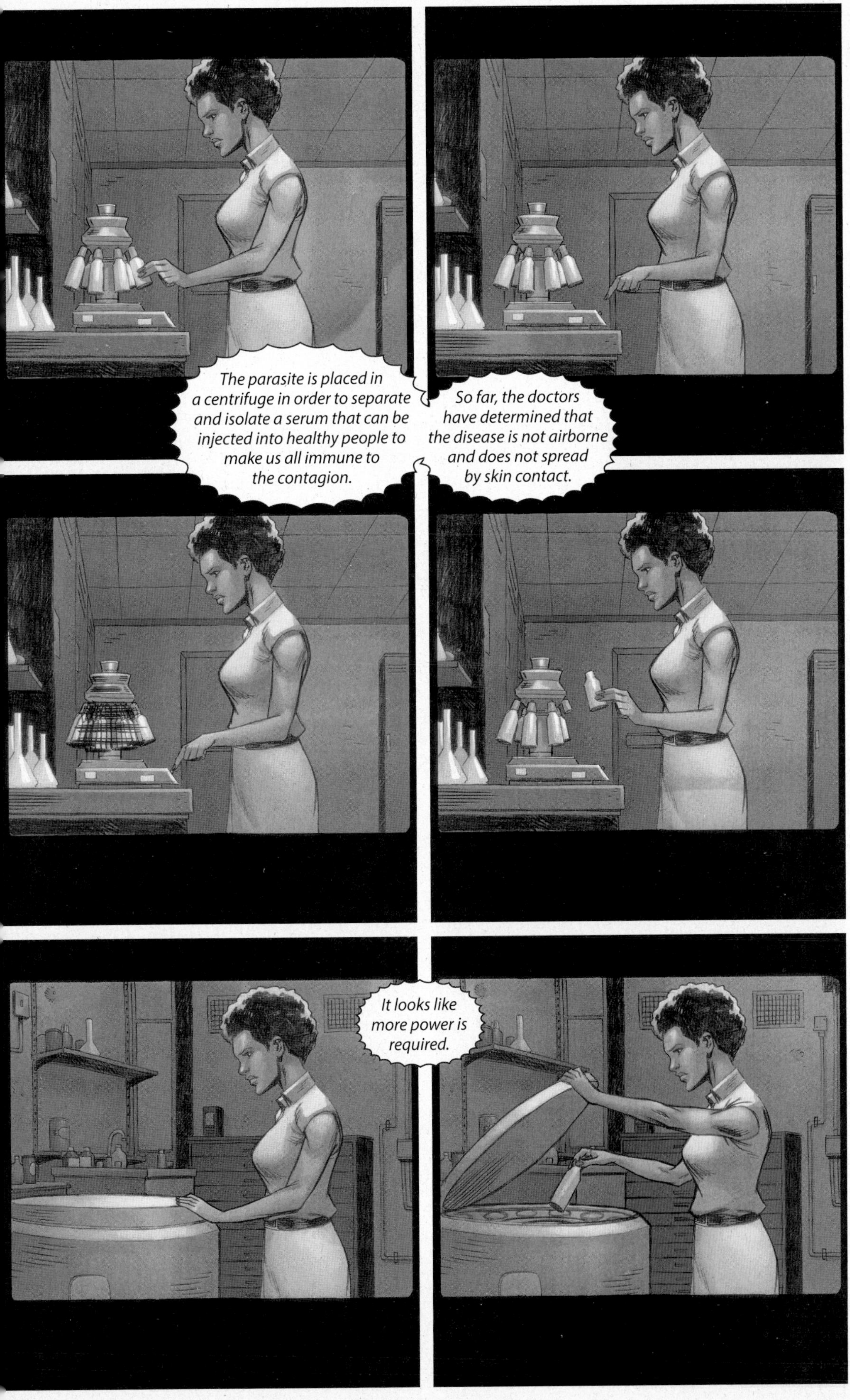
The parasite is placed in a centrifuge in order to separate and isolate a serum that can be injected into healthy people to make us all immune to the contagion.
So far, the doctors have determined that the disease is not airborne and does not spread by skin contact.
It looks like more power is required.

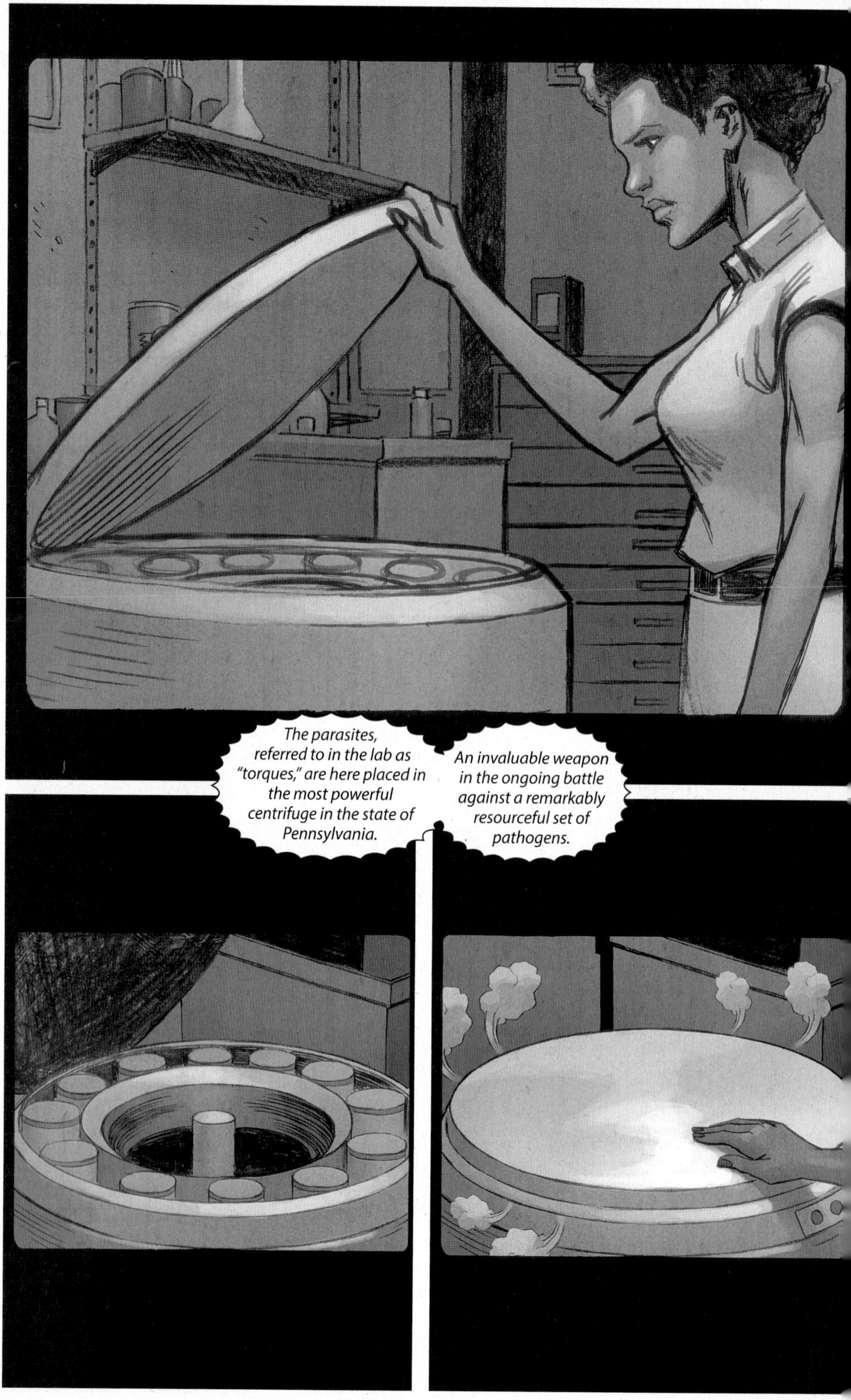
The parasites, referred to in the lab as "torques," are here placed in the most powerful centrifuge in the state of Pennsylvania.
An invaluable weapon in the ongoing battle against a remarkably resourceful set of pathogens.

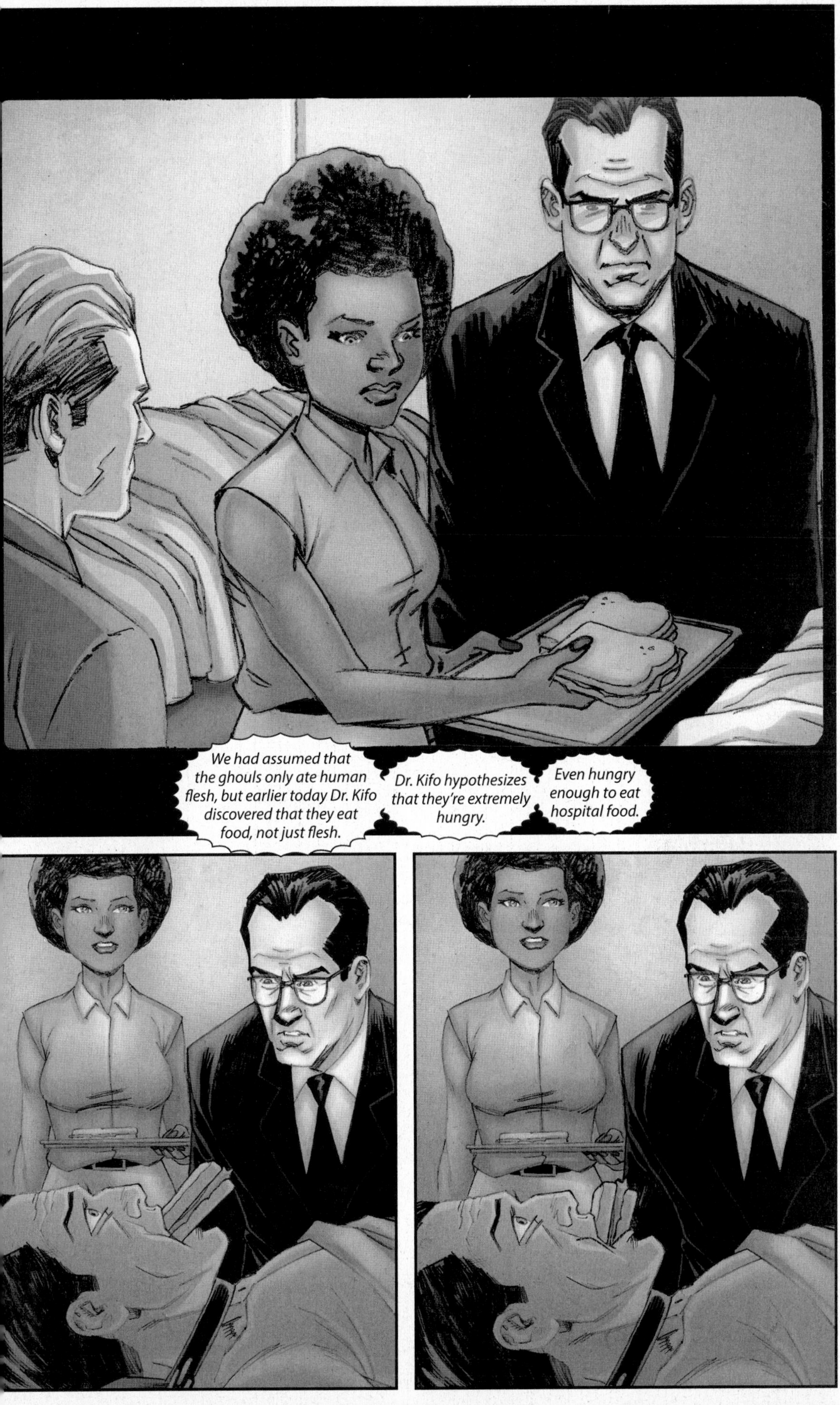
We had assumed that the ghouls only ate human flesh, but earlier today Dr. Kifo discovered that they eat food, not just flesh.
Dr. Kifo hypothesizes that they're extremely hungry.
Even hungry enough to eat hospital food.

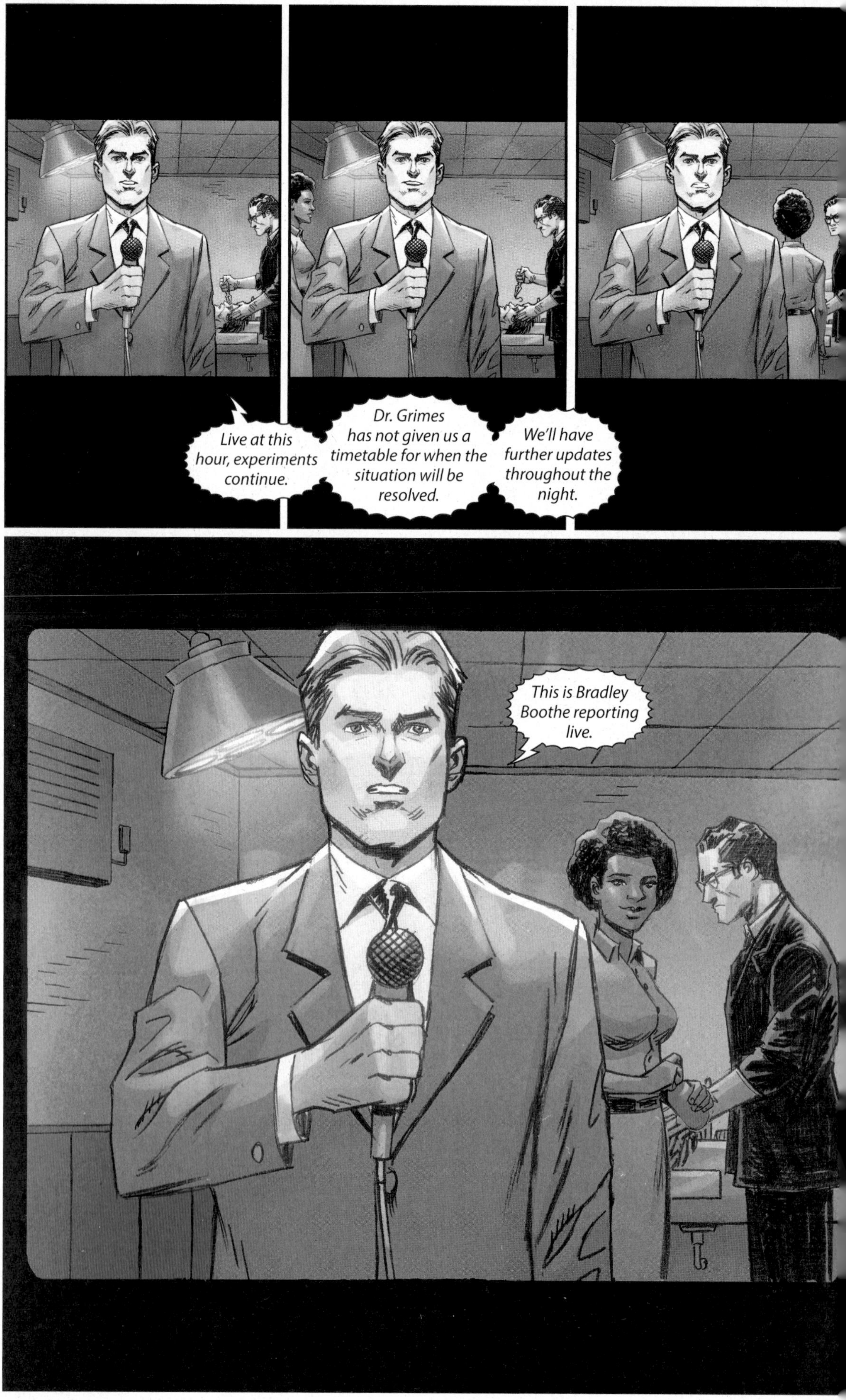
Live at this hour, experiments continue.
Dr. Grimes has not given us a timetable for when the situation will be resolved.
We'll have further updates throughout the night.
This is Bradley Boothe reporting live.

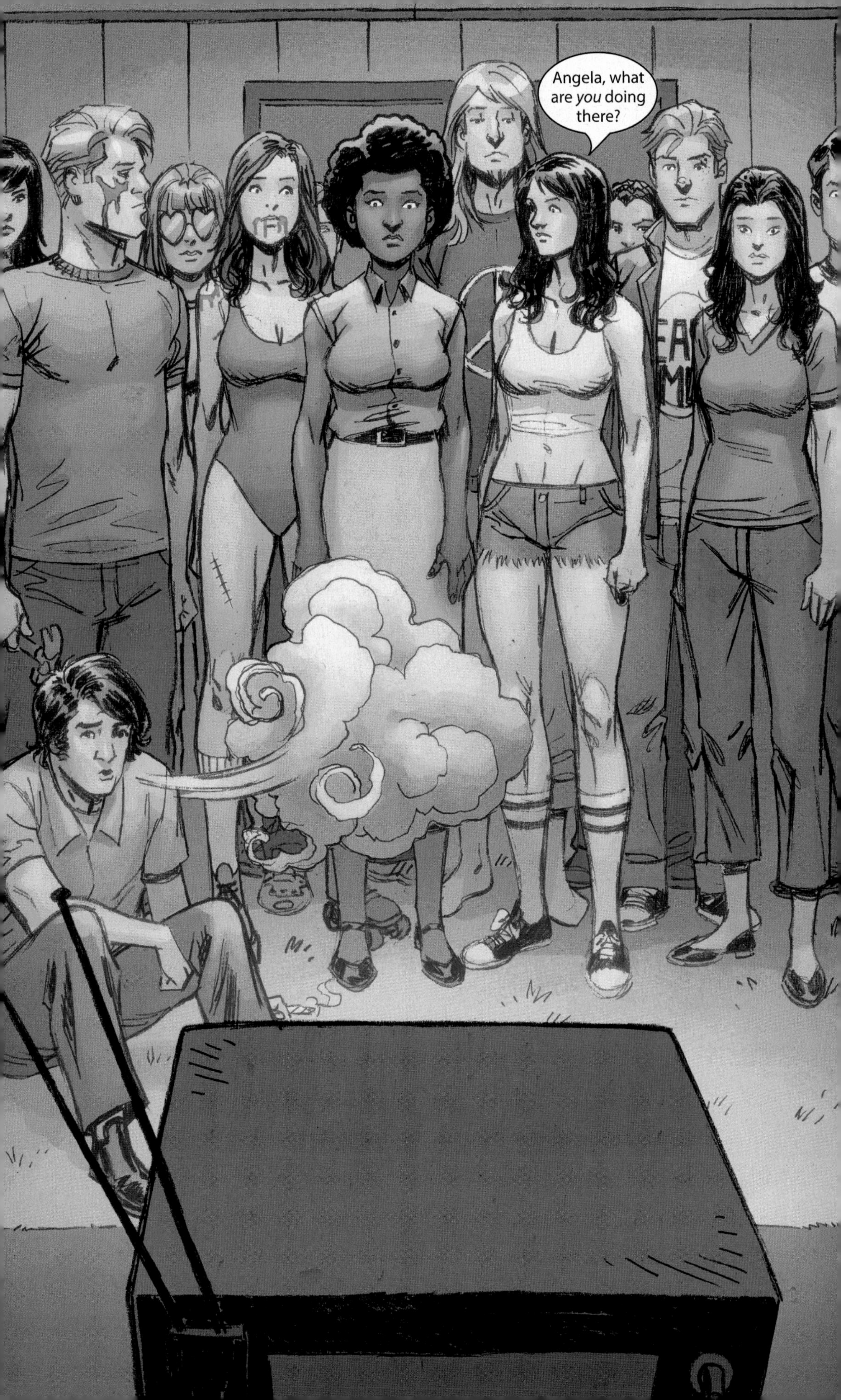
Angela, what are *you* doing there?

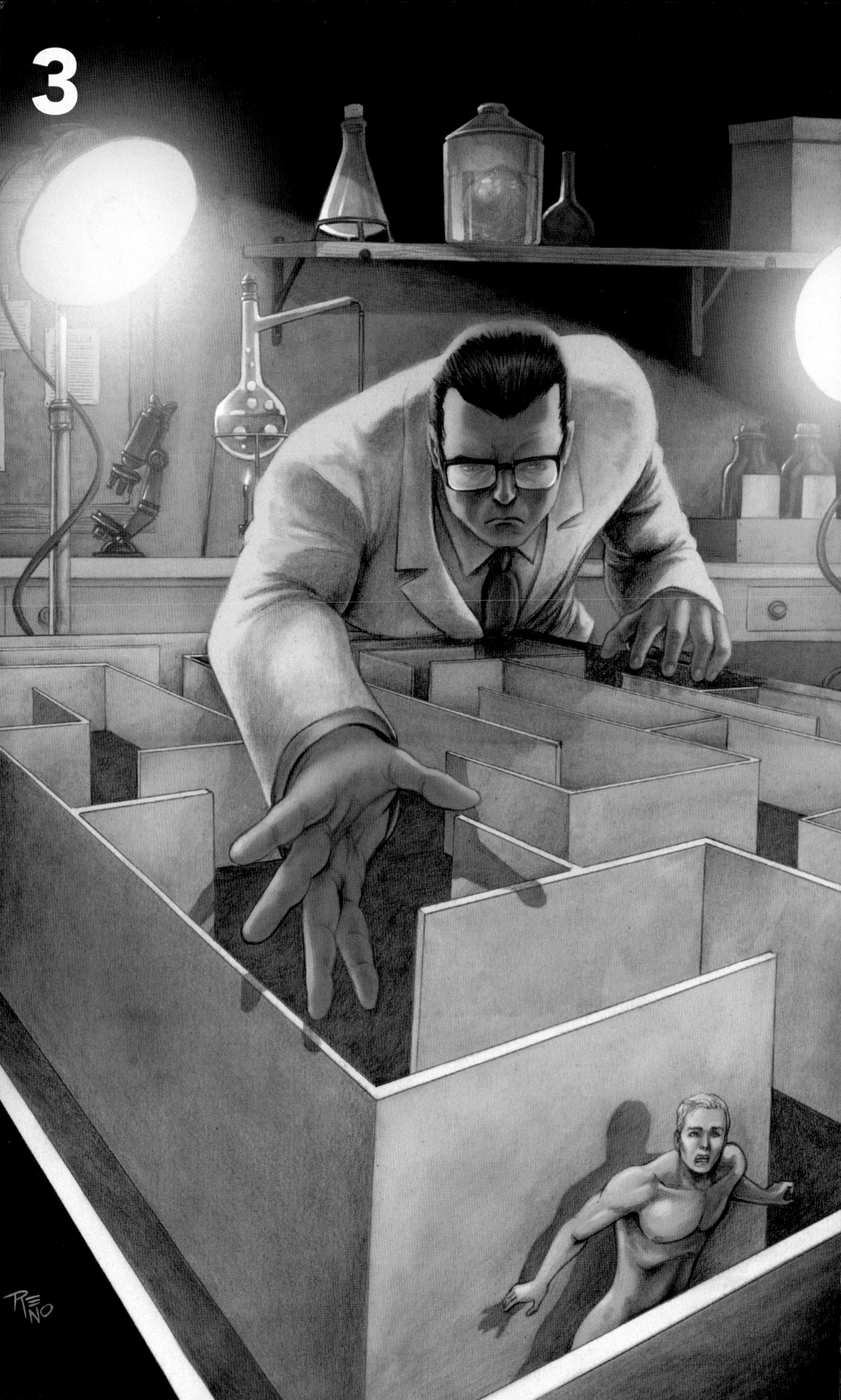
3
RENO

This is Dr. Oswald Grimes, head of the NASA Research Center located at Evans University Hospital.

This is Dr. Angela Kifo.

She is the one who really runs the show at the NASA Research Center located at the Evans University Hospital.

  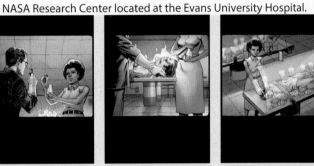 

This is Ron and Emily Stevens, recent guests of Evans University Hospital.

Ron died angry, then aroused, then terrified, then in pain.

He and Emily recently checked out of their own volition.

This is Fred Sproles. Fred is the one who sent Ron and Emily to the Evans University Hospital.

Fred died exultant, then terrified. He's an excellent candidate for leadership.

This is Chief Connor McClelland and Officer Penny Long.

This is footage of them using deadly force against reanimated corpses in the morgue of the Evans University Hopital.

This is footage captured by security cameras at the NASA Research Center located at the Evans University Hospital but unnoticed so far by staff.

    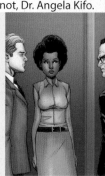

These are Dr. Angela Kifo's stolen clothes draped around a person who appears to be, but is not, Dr. Angela Kifo.

This is, once again, Dr. Oswald Grimes.

Dr. Grimes has been convinced to make a television appearance by a person who appears to be, but is not, Dr. Angela Kifo.

This is Jane. This is Carol.
Carol and Jane are the daughters of Dr. Oswald Grimes.

This is a man eating a squirrel.

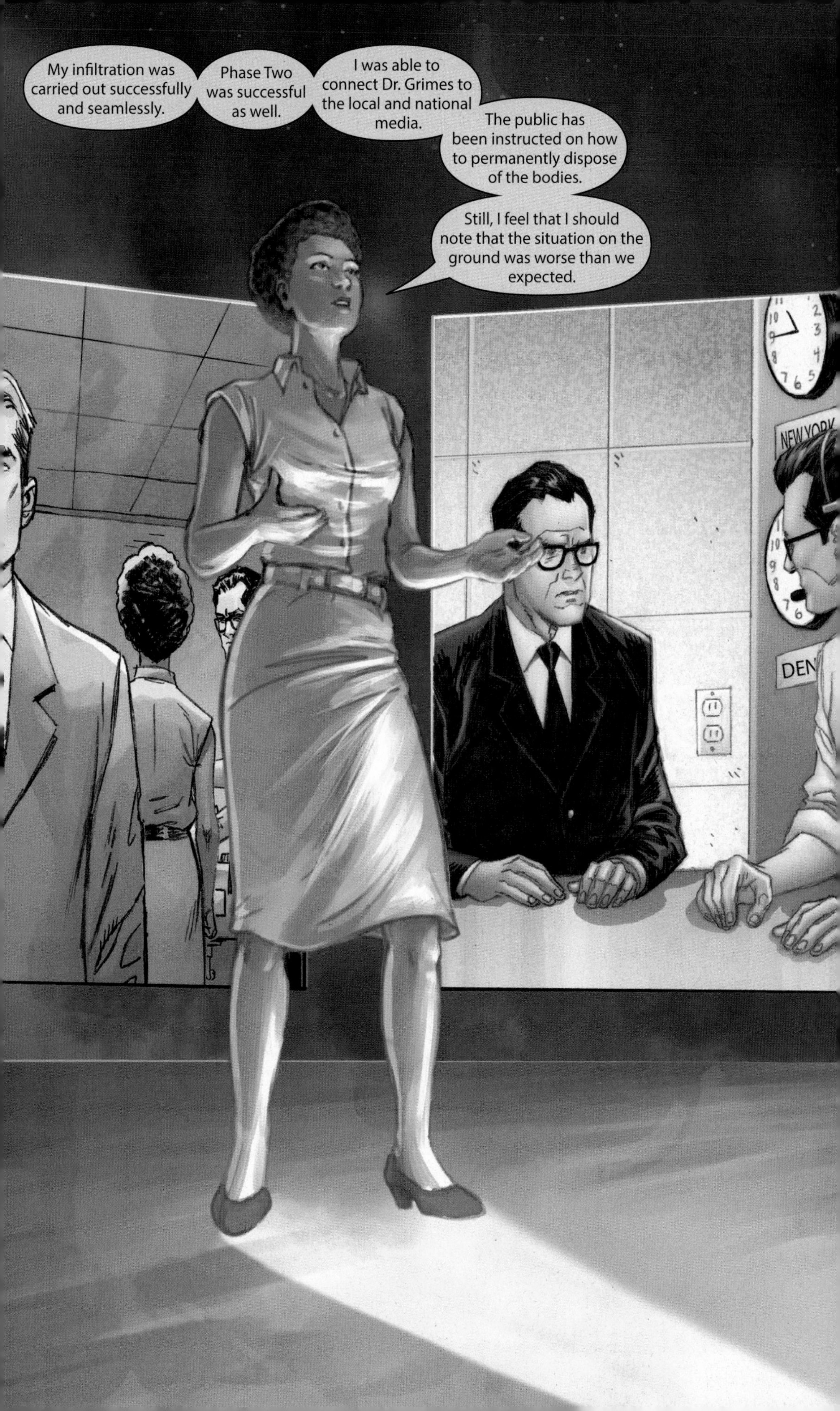

My infiltration was carried out successfully and seamlessly.
Phase Two was successful as well.
I was able to connect Dr. Grimes to the local and national media.
The public has been instructed on how to permanently dispose of the bodies.
Still, I feel that I should note that the situation on the ground was worse than we expected.
NEW YORK
DEN

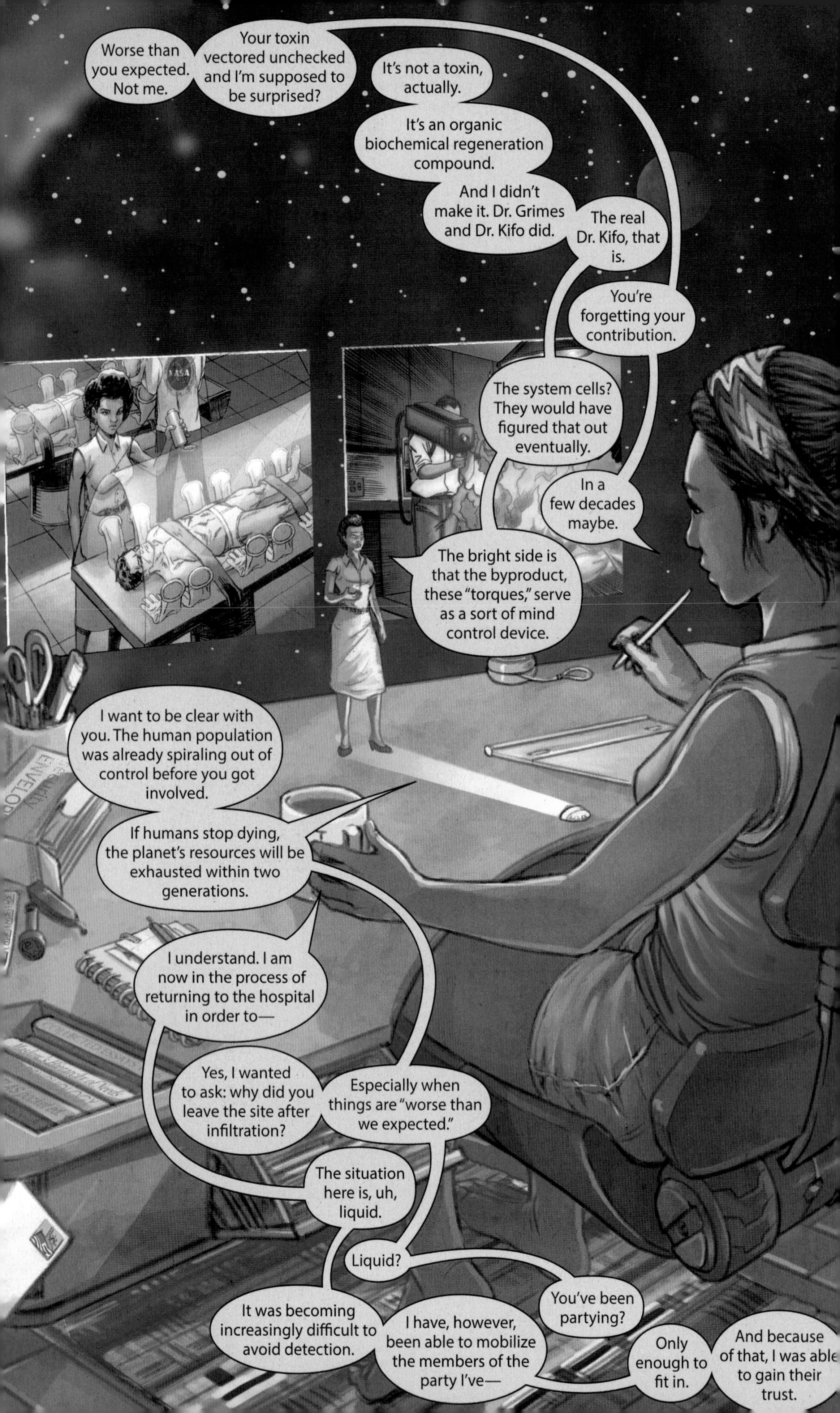
Worse than you expected. Not me.
Your toxin vectored unchecked and I'm supposed to be surprised?
It's not a toxin, actually.
It's an organic biochemical regeneration compound.
And I didn't make it. Dr. Grimes and Dr. Kifo did.
The real Dr. Kifo, that is.
You're forgetting your contribution.
The system cells? They would have figured that out eventually.
In a few decades maybe.
The bright side is that the byproduct, these "torques," serve as a sort of mind control device.
I want to be clear with you. The human population was already spiraling out of control before you got involved.
If humans stop dying, the planet's resources will be exhausted within two generations.
I understand. I am now in the process of returning to the hospital in order to—
Yes, I wanted to ask: why did you leave the site after infiltration?
Especially when things are "worse than we expected."
The situation here is, uh, liquid.
Liquid?
You've been partying?
It was becoming increasingly difficult to avoid detection.
I have, however, been able to mobilize the members of the party I've—
Only enough to fit in.
And because of that, I was able to gain their trust.

1960s Movements

CIVIL RIGHTS

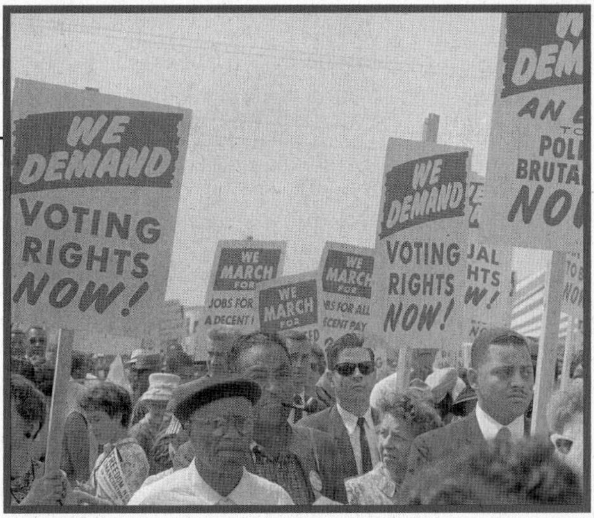
WE DEMAND VOTING RIGHTS NOW!
WE MARCH FOR JOBS FOR A DECENT
WE MARCH FOR
WE DEMAND VOTING RIGHTS NOW!
POLICE BRUTALITY

POPULAR SLOGANS

“We shall overcome”

“Keep your eyes on the prize and hold on”

“Say it loud: I’m Black and proud”

“Ain’t going to let nobody turn me round”

“Black is beautiful”

“Black power”

WOMEN’S LIBERATION

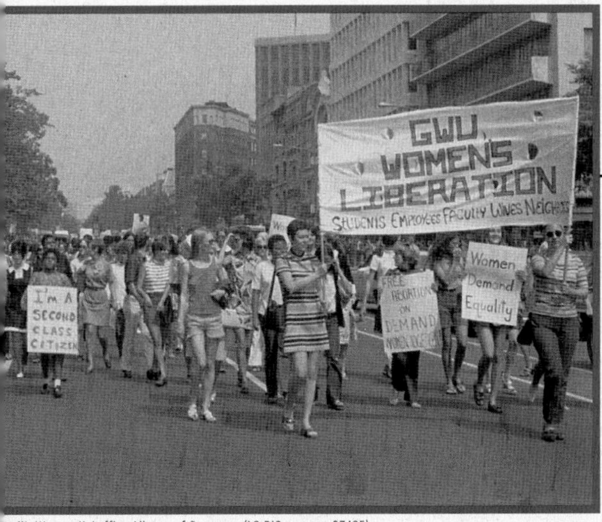
GWU WOMENS LIBERATION
STUDENTS EMPLOYEES FACULTY WIVES NEIGHBORS
I'M A SECOND CLASS CITIZEN
FREE ABORTION ON DEMAND
Women Demand Equality

Credit: Warren K. Leffler, Library of Congress (LC-DIG-ppmsca-03425)

POPULAR SLOGANS

“The Personal is Political”

“Sisterhood is Powerful”

“Equal Pay for Equal Work”

“Women Demand Equality”

“We’re not beautiful. We’re not ugly. We’re angry.”

ANTI WAR

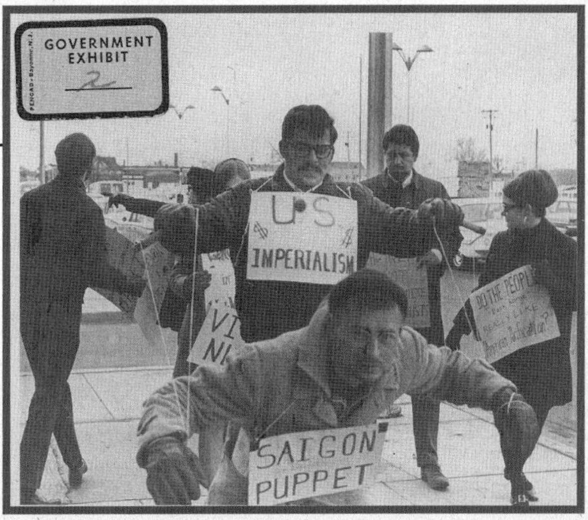
GOVERNMENT EXHIBIT
U.S. IMPERIALISM
SAIGON PUPPET

POPULAR SLOGANS

“Hey, hey, LBJ,
how many kids did you kill today?”

“Draft beer, not boys”

“Hell no, we won’t go”

“Make love, not war”

“Eighteen today, dead tomorrow”

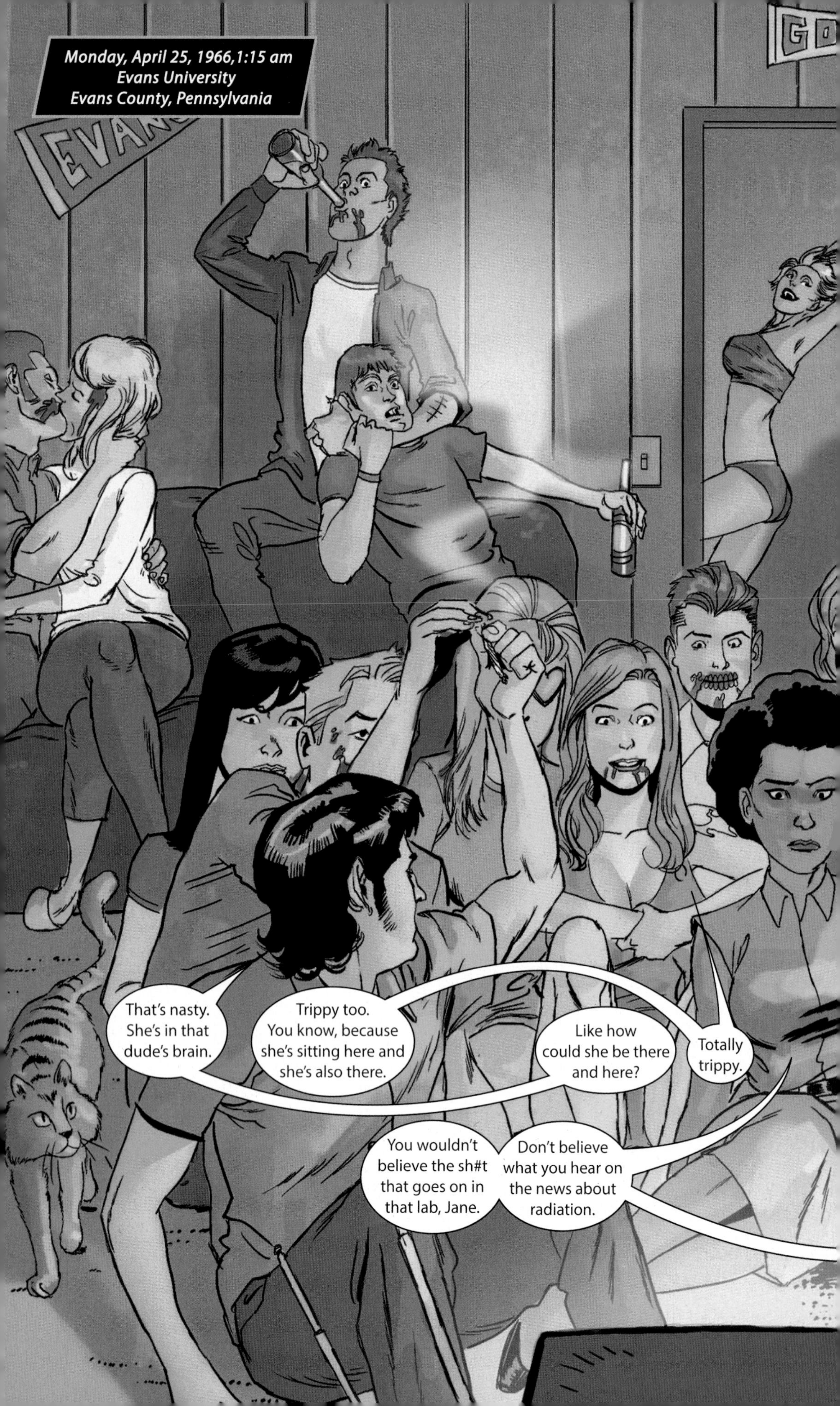
Monday, April 25, 1966,1:15 am
Evans University
Evans County, Pennsylvania
EVANS
That's nasty. She's in that dude's brain.
Trippy too. You know, because she's sitting here and she's also there.
Like how could she be there and here?
Totally trippy.
You wouldn't believe the sh#t that goes on in that lab, Jane.
Don't believe what you hear on the news about radiation.

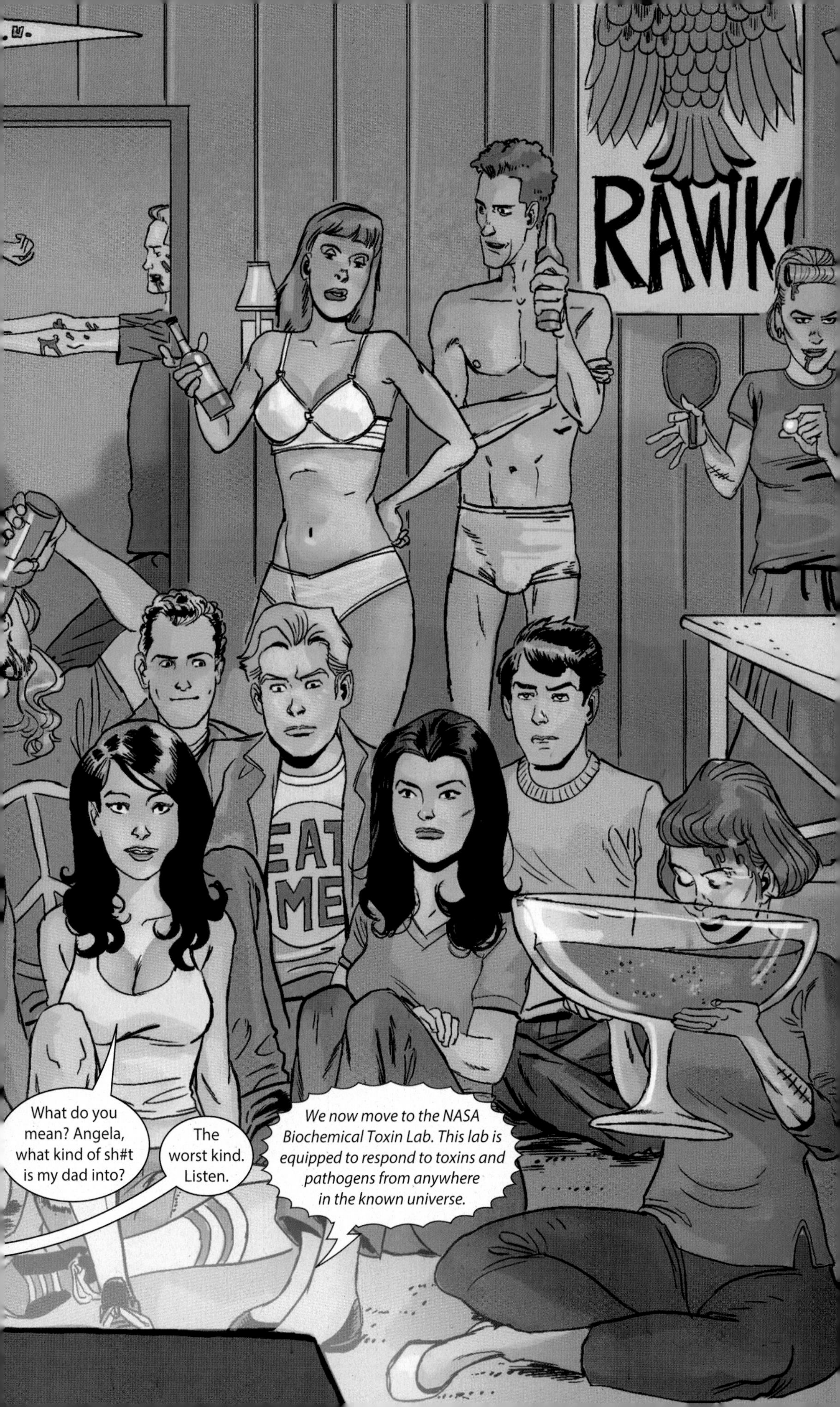
RAWK!
EAT ME
What do you mean? Angela, what kind of sh#t is my dad into?
The worst kind. Listen.
We now move to the NASA Biochemical Toxin Lab. This lab is equipped to respond to toxins and pathogens from anywhere in the known universe.

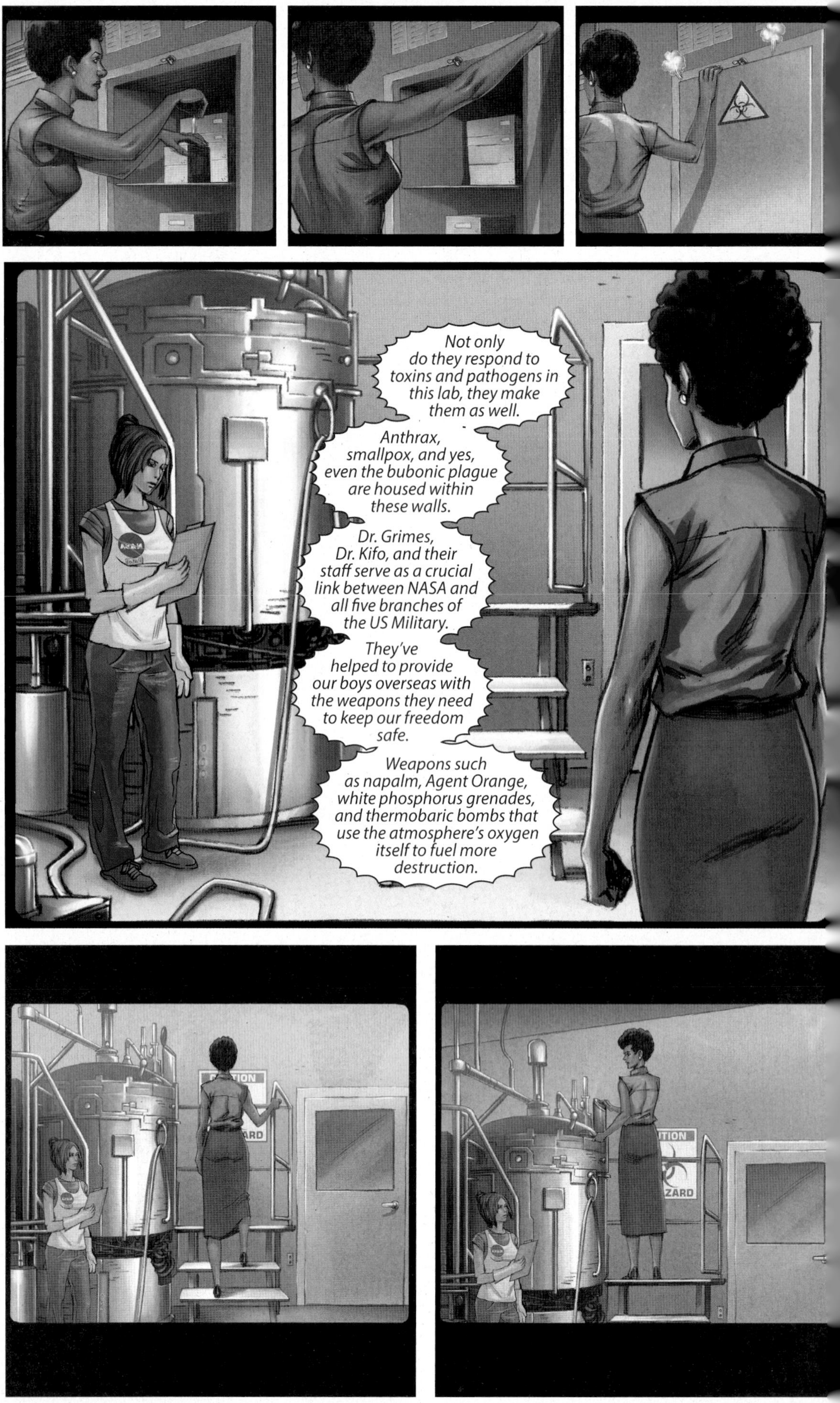
Not only do they respond to toxins and pathogens in this lab, they make them as well.
Anthrax, smallpox, and yes, even the bubonic plague are housed within these walls.
Dr. Grimes, Dr. Kifo, and their staff serve as a crucial link between NASA and all five branches of the US Military.
They've helped to provide our boys overseas with the weapons they need to keep our freedom safe.
Weapons such as napalm, Agent Orange, white phosphorus grenades, and thermobaric bombs that use the atmosphere's oxygen itself to fuel more destruction.

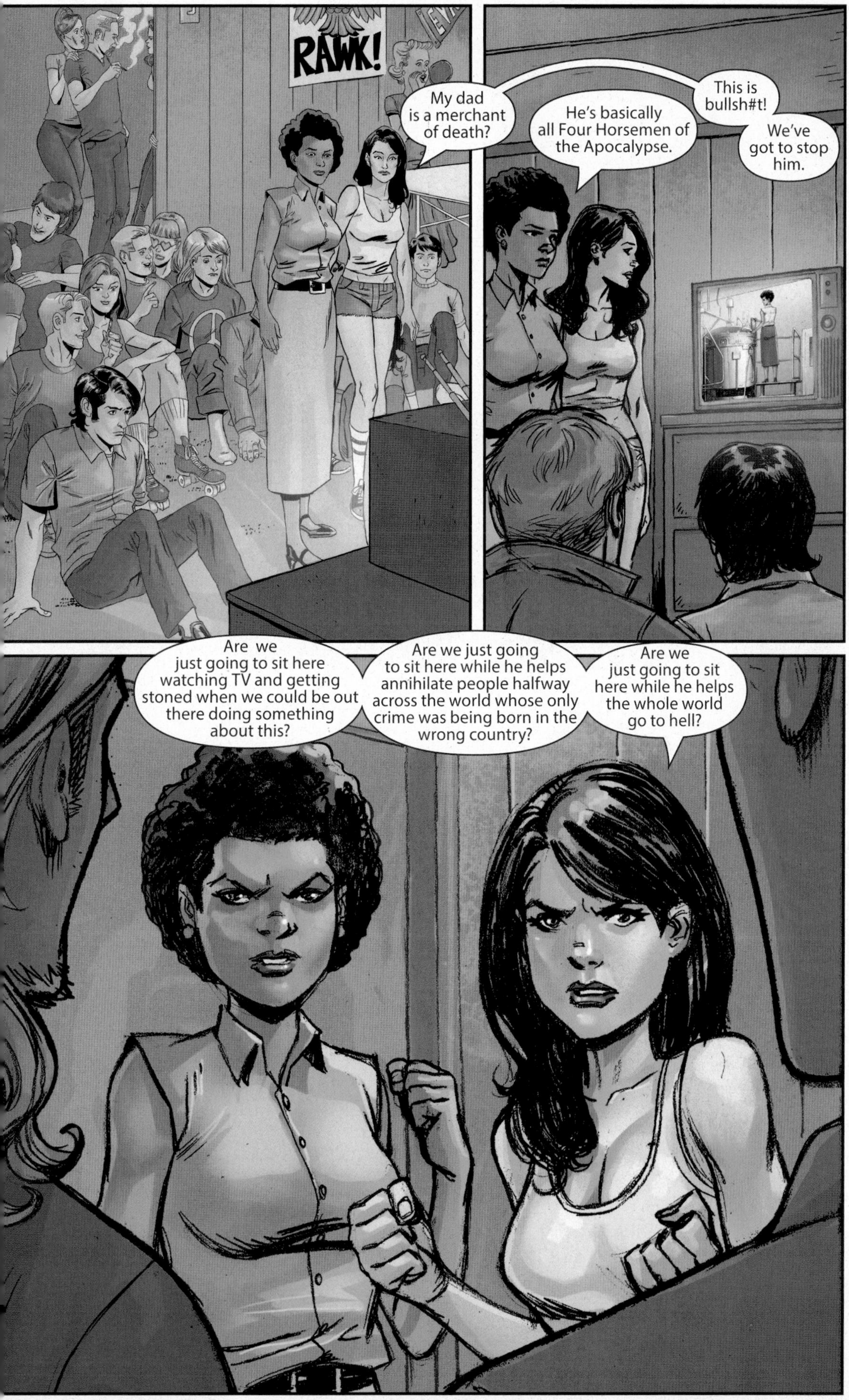
RAWK!
My dad is a merchant of death?
He's basically all Four Horsemen of the Apocalypse.
This is bullsh#t!
We've got to stop him.
Are we just going to sit here watching TV and getting stoned when we could be out there doing something about this?
Are we just going to sit here while he helps annihilate people halfway across the world whose only crime was being born in the wrong country?
Are we just going to sit here while he helps the whole world go to hell?

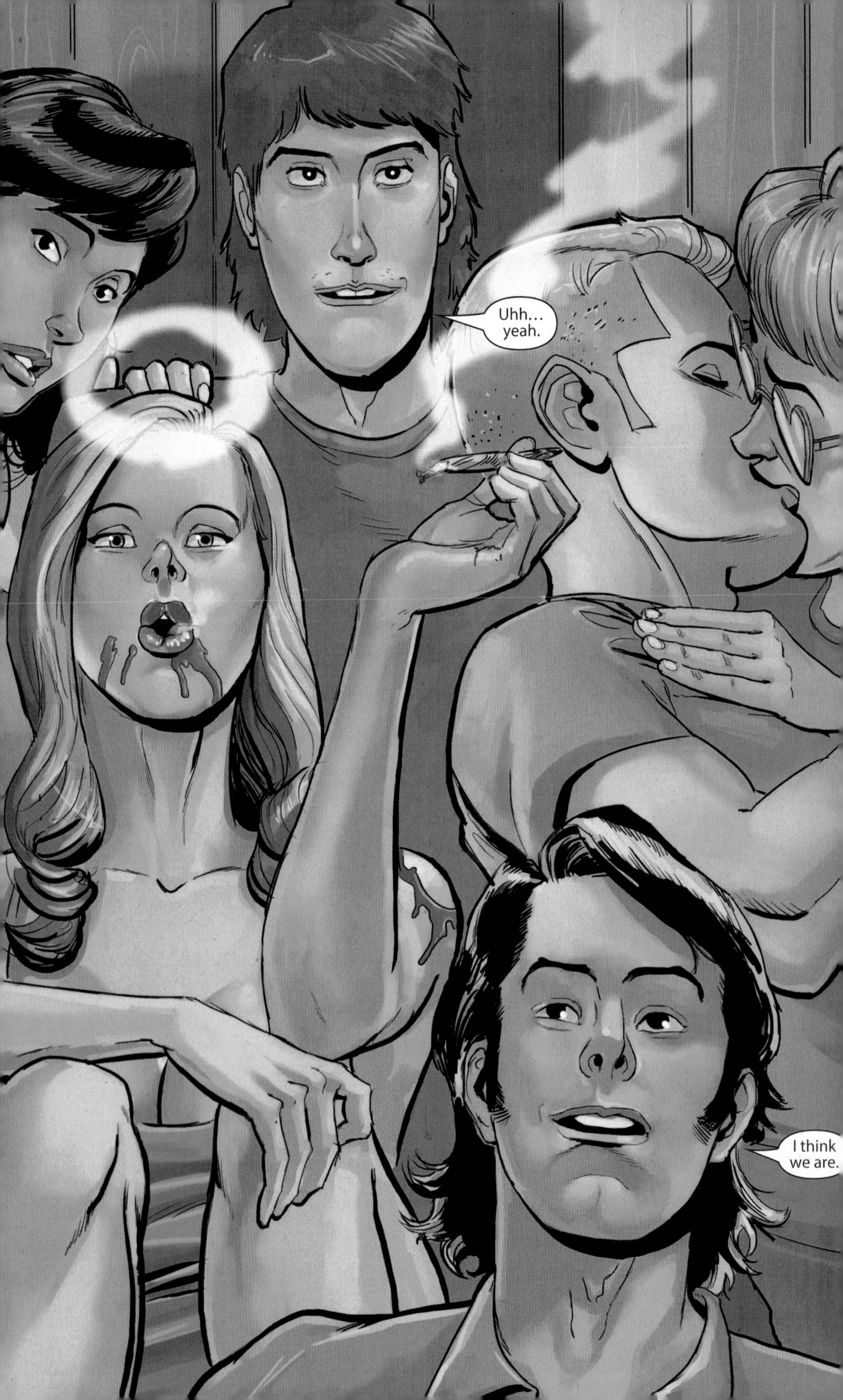
Uhh… yeah.
I think we are.

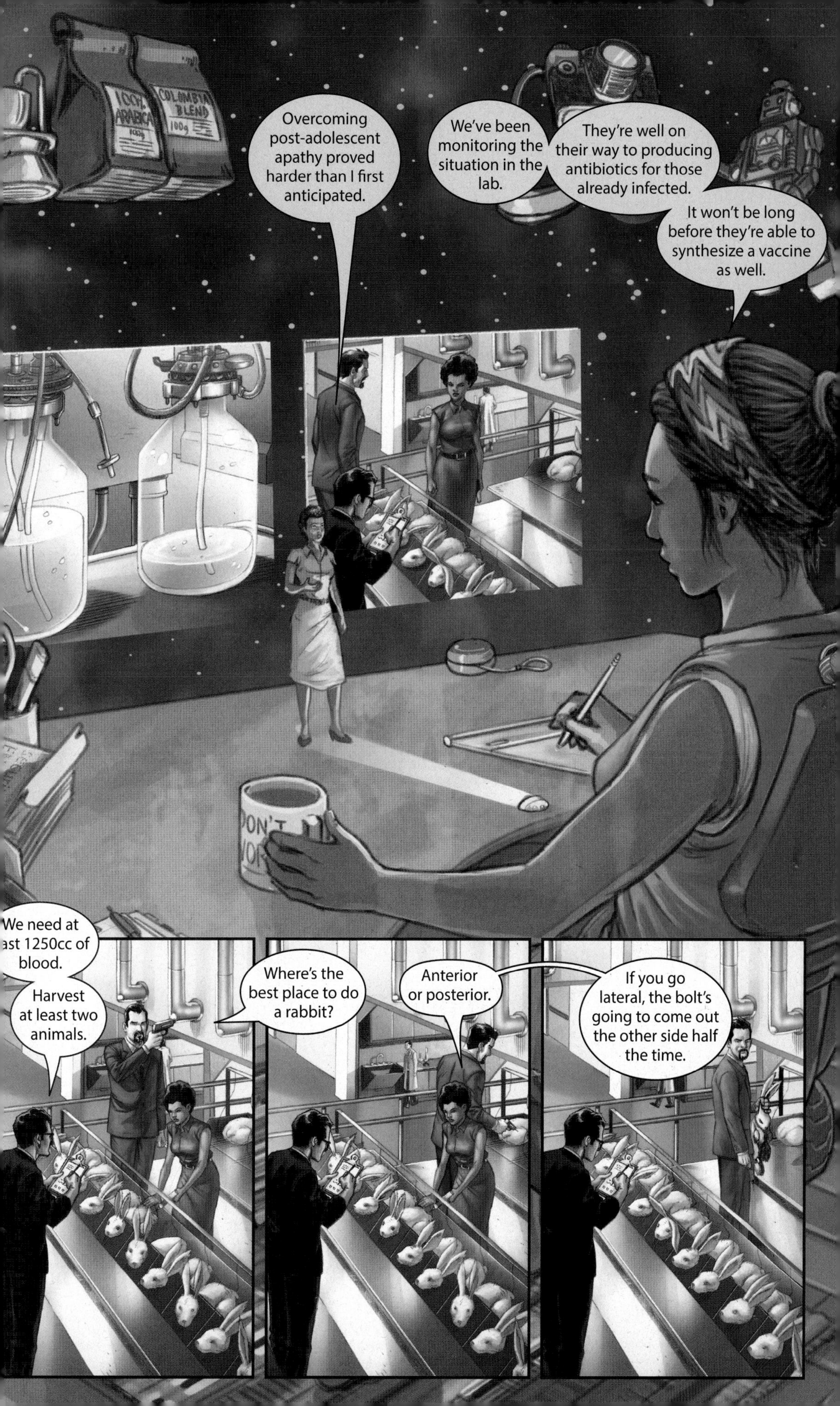
Overcoming post-adolescent apathy proved harder than I first anticipated.
We've been monitoring the situation in the lab.
They're well on their way to producing antibiotics for those already infected.
It won't be long before they're able to synthesize a vaccine as well.
We need at
ast 1250cc of blood.
Harvest at least two animals.
Where's the best place to do a rabbit?
Anterior or posterior.
If you go lateral, the bolt's going to come out the other side half the time.

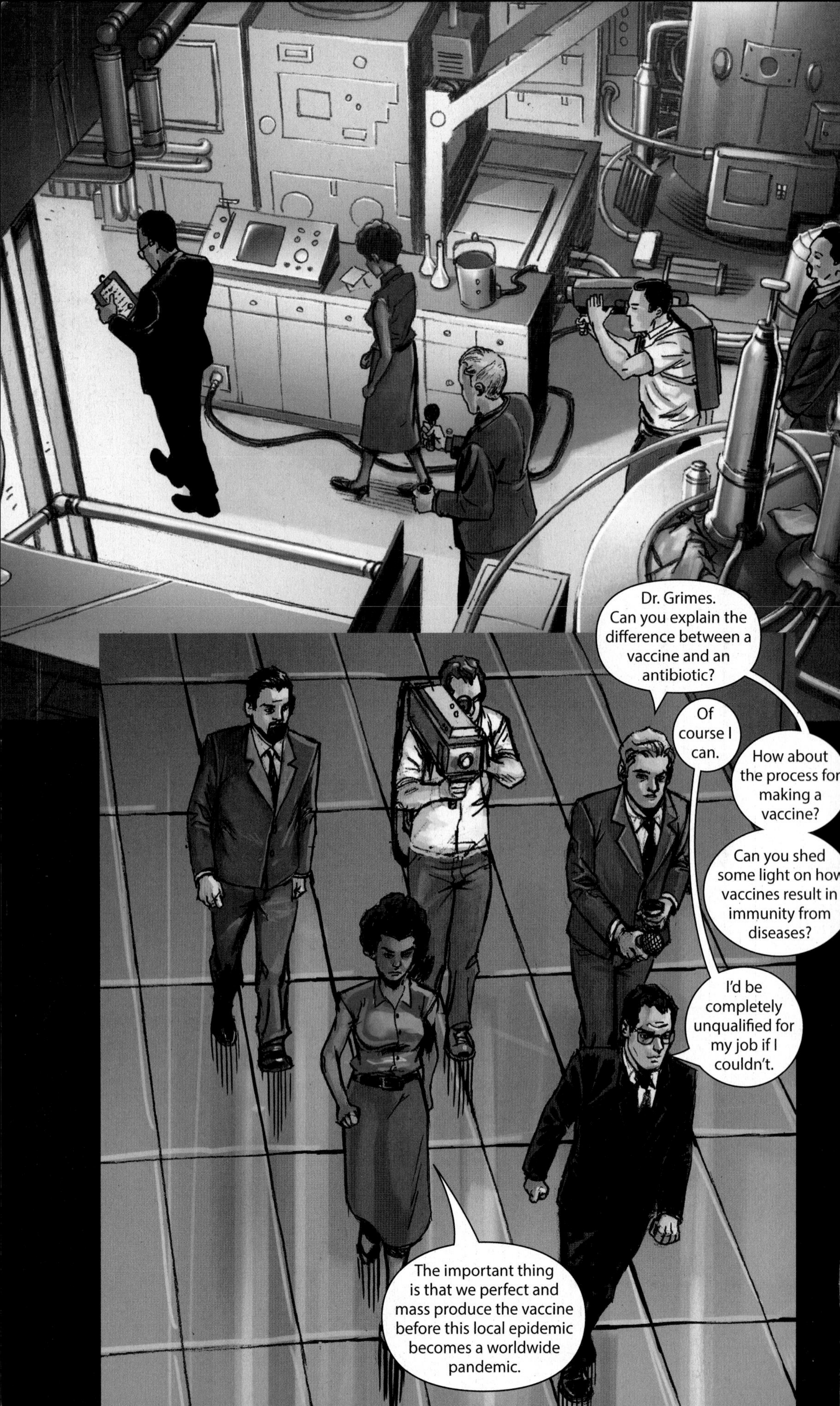
Dr. Grimes. Can you explain the difference between a vaccine and an antibiotic?
Of course I can.
How about the process for making a vaccine?
Can you shed some light on how vaccines result in immunity from diseases?
I'd be completely unqualified for my job if I couldn't.
The important thing is that we perfect and mass produce the vaccine before this local epidemic becomes a worldwide pandemic.

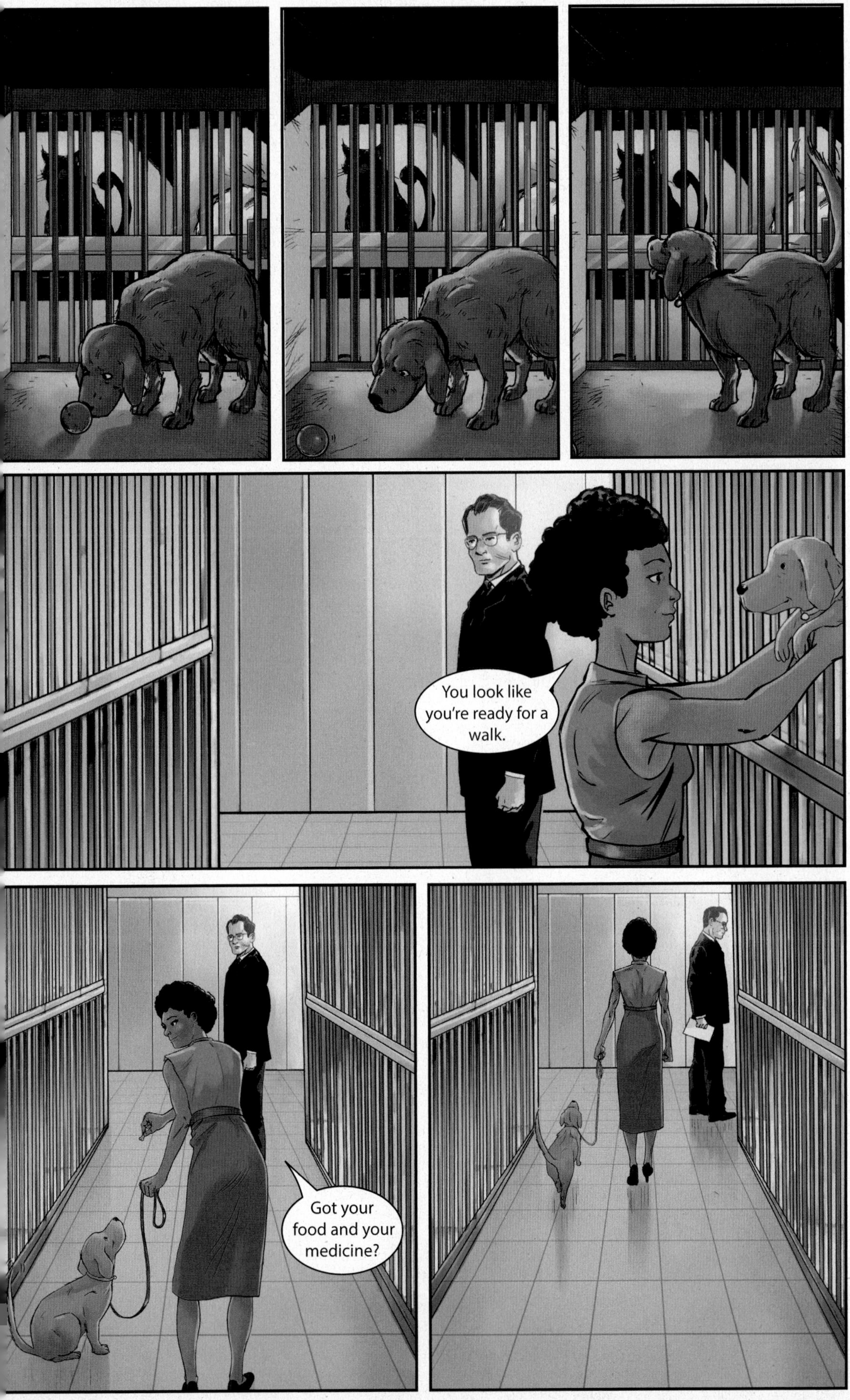
You look like you're ready for a walk.
Got your food and your medicine?

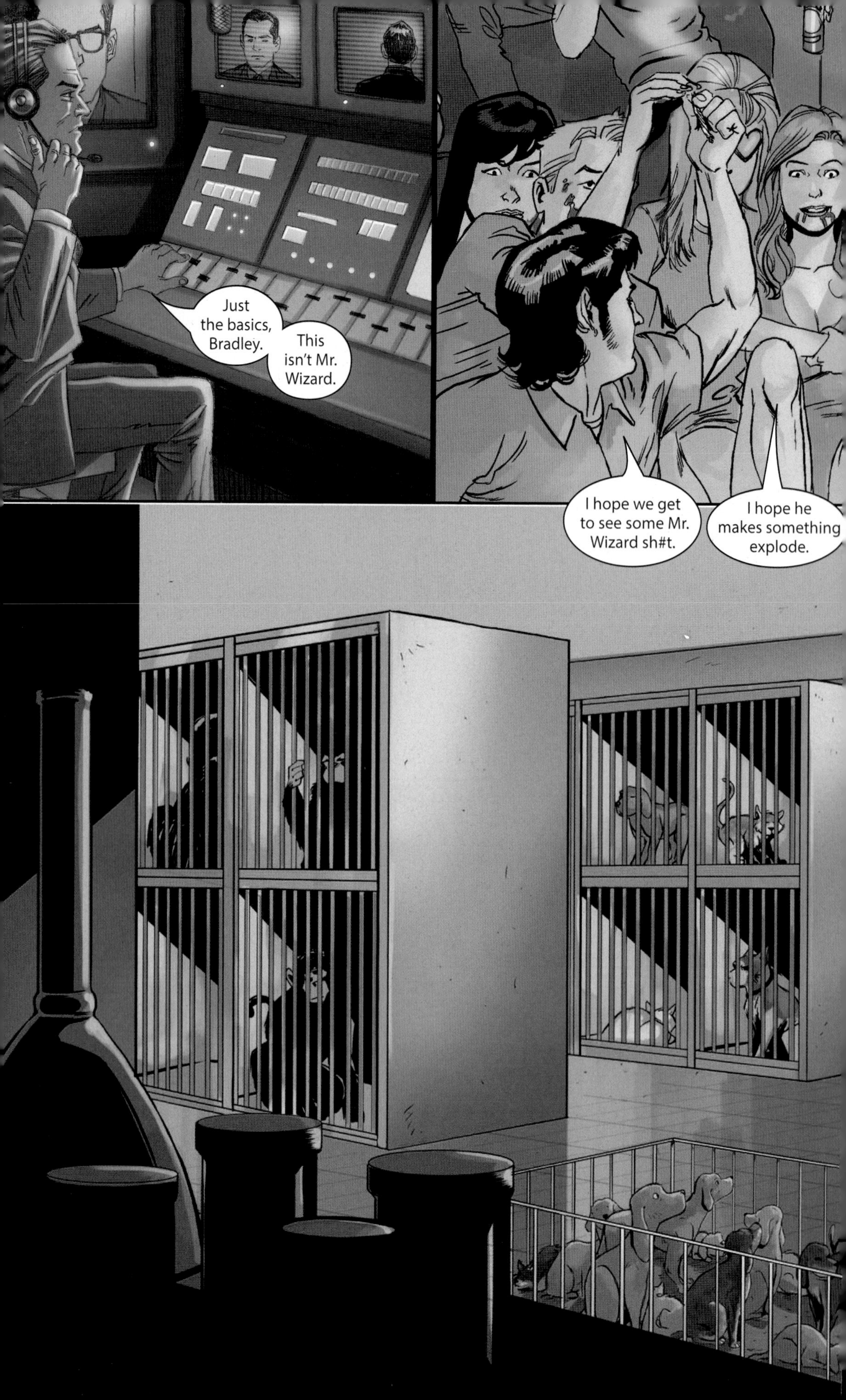
Just the basics, Bradley.
This isn't Mr. Wizard.
I hope we get to see some Mr. Wizard sh#t.
I hope he makes something explode.

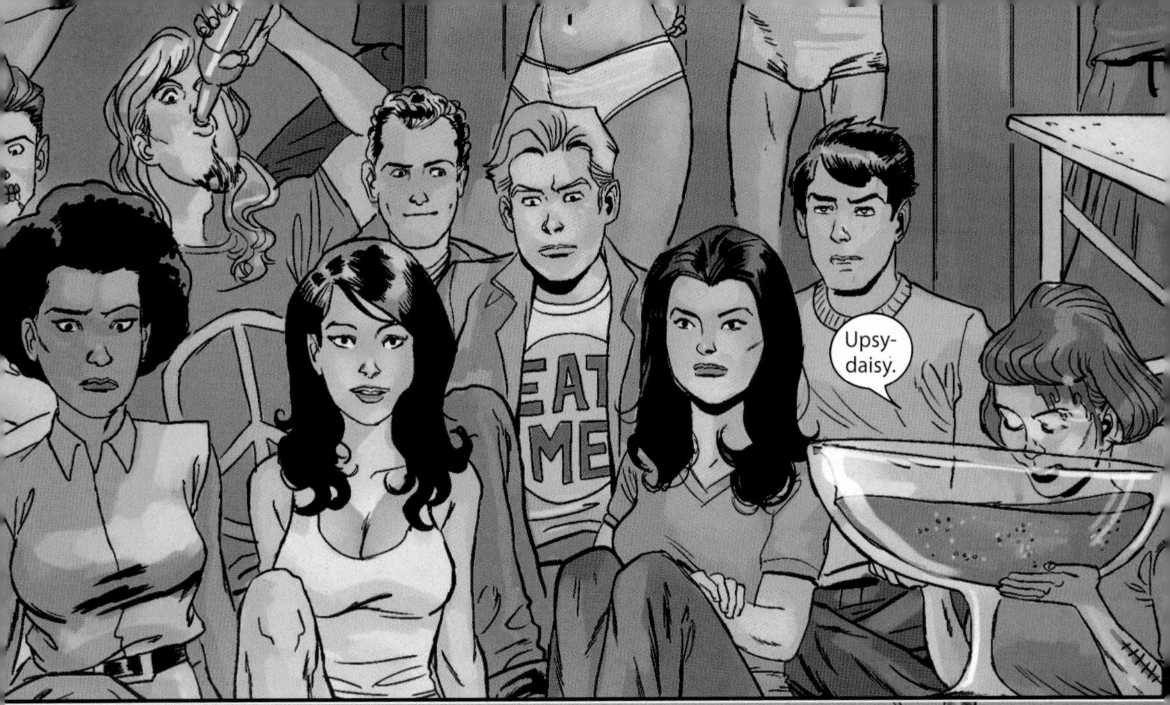
Upsy-daisy.

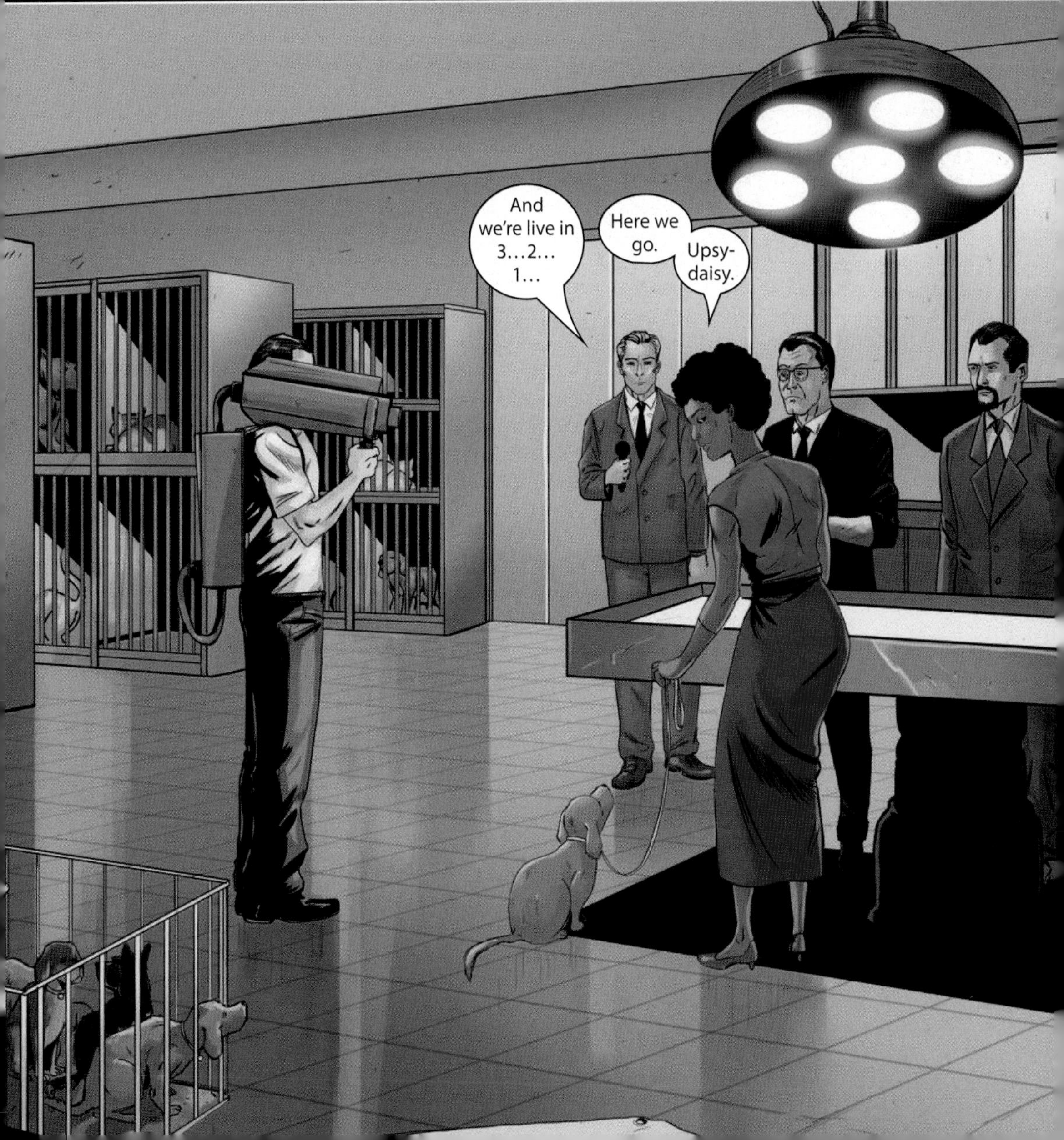
And we're live in 3…2… 1…
Here we go.
Upsy-daisy.

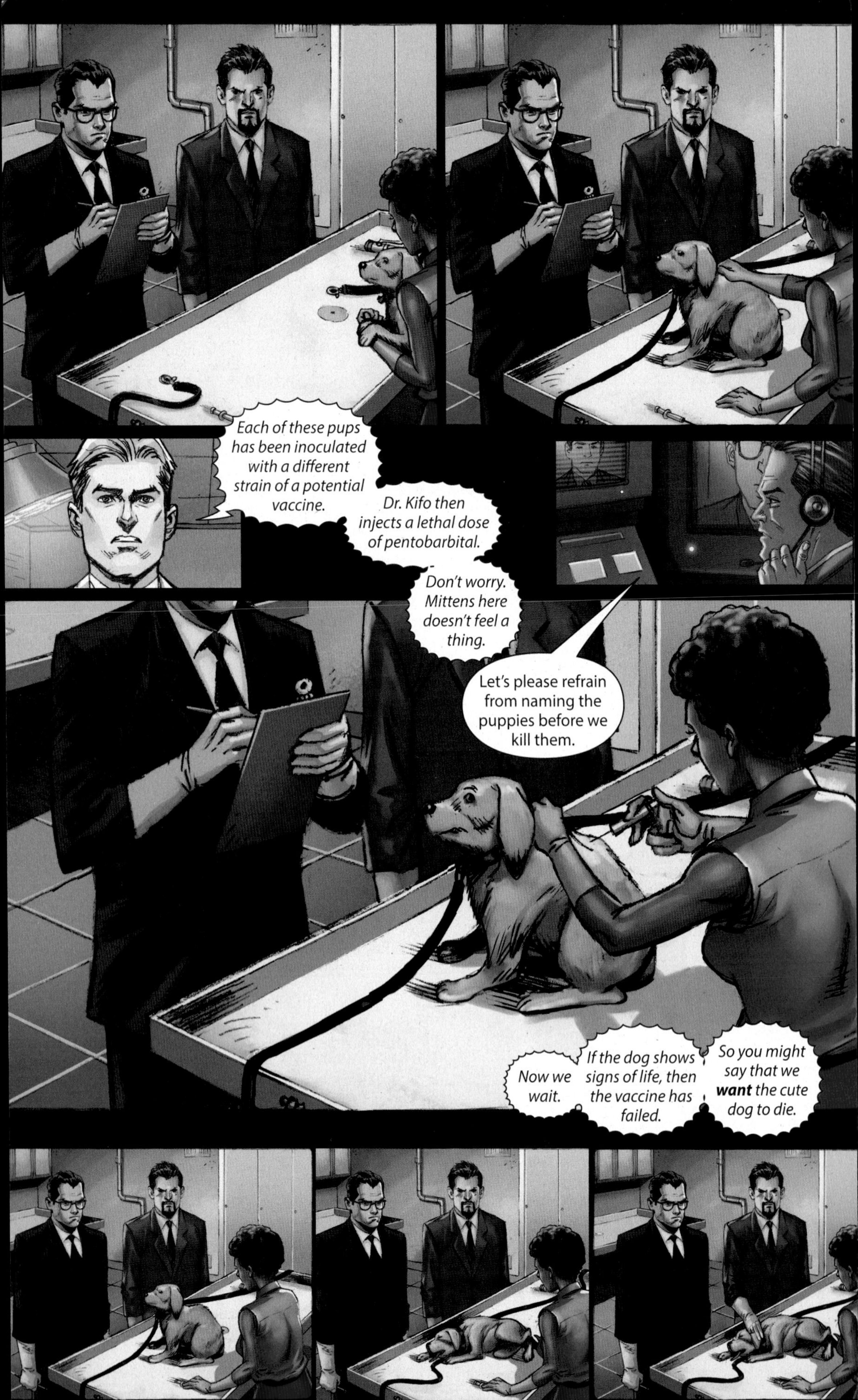
Each of these pups has been inoculated with a different strain of a potential vaccine.
Dr. Kifo then injects a lethal dose of pentobarbital.
Don't worry. Mittens here doesn't feel a thing.
Let's please refrain from naming the puppies before we kill them.
Now we wait.
If the dog shows signs of life, then the vaccine has failed.
So you might say that we **want** the cute dog to die.

DOUBLE TAKE RECORD HOUSE

SUMMER SELECTION

inally you'll be able to understand
ll those album cover parodies!

STEREO
BEACH BOYS
CONCERT

Sunburn for the soul!

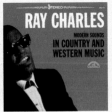

JOHNNY CASH AT SAN QUENTIN

erfectly captures the
eeling of being in
rison!

STEREO
RAY CHARLES
MODERN SOUNDS
IN COUNTRY AND
WESTERN MUSIC

Maybe it will remind you how much you like Jamie Foxx!

Consider it an Eric Clapton prequel!

OBBIE GENTRY
DE TO BILLIE JOE

eally close to being
Billy Joel!'

MIKE NICHOLS–LAWRENCE TURMAN
THE GRADUATE
PAUL SIMON
SIMON & GARFUNKEL

Why bother seeing the movie? Use this musical Cliff Notes!

MY SON, THE NUT
allan SHERMAN

Like Weird Al without the fun!

Led Zeppelin
II

n case your local
lassic rock station isn't
lready playing Zeppelin
wice an hour!

MORE OF THE

12 tracks, 19 credited songwriters - Now that's value!

the doors
WAITING FOR THE SUN

Even the worst poets can find success in this world!

ANY 3 RECORDS FOR ONLY $5.95

A LIFETIME PURCHASE! You may have any three of the best-selling records shown here—for ONLY $5.95! That's the fantastic bargain the Double Take Record House is offering new members who join and commit to purchasing as few as four additional records from our Buying Guide in the next year.

FREE SUBSCRIPTION TO THE RECORD BUYING GUIDE! You'll have no problem selecting four more records with our quarterly Buying Guide, which you'll get for free. With all the movie and musical soundtracks your heart desires, you'll only struggle with your choices!

YOUR OWN CHARGE ACCOUNT! Upon enrollment, the Double Take Record House will open a charge account in your name (or your husband's name, ladies). You pay for your records only after you've received them. They will be mailed and billed to you at the regular service price of $66.95.*

YOU GET FREE RECORDS! Once you've signed on, you'll groove on with a FREE record of your choice for every two records purchased! That's a 33 1/3% discount for your lifetime and post-mortem membership!

Please note under no circumstances will Double Take Record House send you any records.

SEND NO MONEY NOW!

Just fill in and mail the coupon to:

DOUBLE TAKE RECORD HOUSE
38 W. 39th Street, 2nd Floor
New York, New York 10018

Please enroll me as a member of the Double Take Record House. I've indicated here the 3 records I wish to receive for $5.95, plus postage and handling, etc. I agree to purchase four more selections in the next 12 months at the regular service price of $66.95,* and I may try to cancel my membership any time thereafter.** If I continue, I am to receive a FREE record of my choice for every two additional records purchased.

SELECT THREE RECORDS ☐ ☐ ☐

NAME ____________________
Please do not actually

ADDRESS ____________________
fill this out and send it in.

CITY ________ POSTAL ZONE No. ________ STATE ________

*Additional charges include a penalizing upcharge for buying British albums, plus postage, handling, and other charges Double Take Record House will tack on your charge account. **Good luck. Even death won't cancel your membership.

1960s Premieres

	TV SHOWS	HIT MOVIES	TOP SINGLES
1960	The Flintstones The Andy Griffith Show My Three Sons	Spartacus Psycho Exodus	Theme from A Summer Place He'll Have to Go
1961	The Dick Van Dyke Show ABC's Wide World of Sports The Avengers	The Gun of Navarone West Side Story El Cid	Tossin' and Turnin I Fall to Pieces Michael
1962	The Jetsons The Beverly Hillbillies Tonight Show: Johnny Carson	Lawrence of Arabia The Longest Day In Search of the Castaways	Stranger on the Shore I Can't Stop Loving You Mashed Potato Time
1963	Doctor Who General Hospital Let's Make a Deal	Cleopatra How the West Was Won It's a Mad, Mad, Mad, Mad, World	Sugar Shack Surfin' U.S.A. The End of the World
1964	The Addams Family Gilligan's Island Jeopardy!	Mary Poppins Goldfinger My Fair Lady	I Want to Hold Your Hand She Loves You Hello, Dolly!
1965	I Dream of Jeannie Get Smart Hogan's Heroes	The Sound of Music Thunderball Dr. Zhivago	Wooly Bully I Can't Help Myself Satisfaction
1966	Batman Mission: Impossible Star Trek	The Bible: In the Beginning Hawaii Who's Afraid of Virginia Woolf?	Ballad of the Green Berets Cherish Soul and Inspiration
1967	The Smothers Brothers The Newlywed Game The Prisoner	The Graduate The Jungle Book Doctor Dolittle	To Sir With Love The Letter Ode to Billie Joe
1968	Hawaii Five-O The Mod Squad 60 Minutes	Rosemary's Baby 2001: A Space Odyssey Planet of the Apes	Hey Jude Love is Blue Honey
1969	Sesame Street The Brady Bunch Monty Python's Flying Circus	Easy Rider Midnight Cowboy Butch Cassidy and the Sundance Kid	Sugar, Sugar Aquarius I Can't Get Next to You

Oh well. Too bad. The dog lives again. The vaccine is ineffective.

Zoom in on our canine friend.

THUNKT

Zoom out! Zoom out!

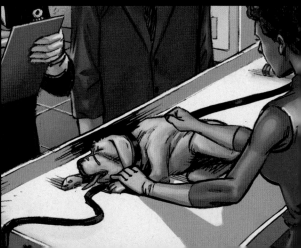

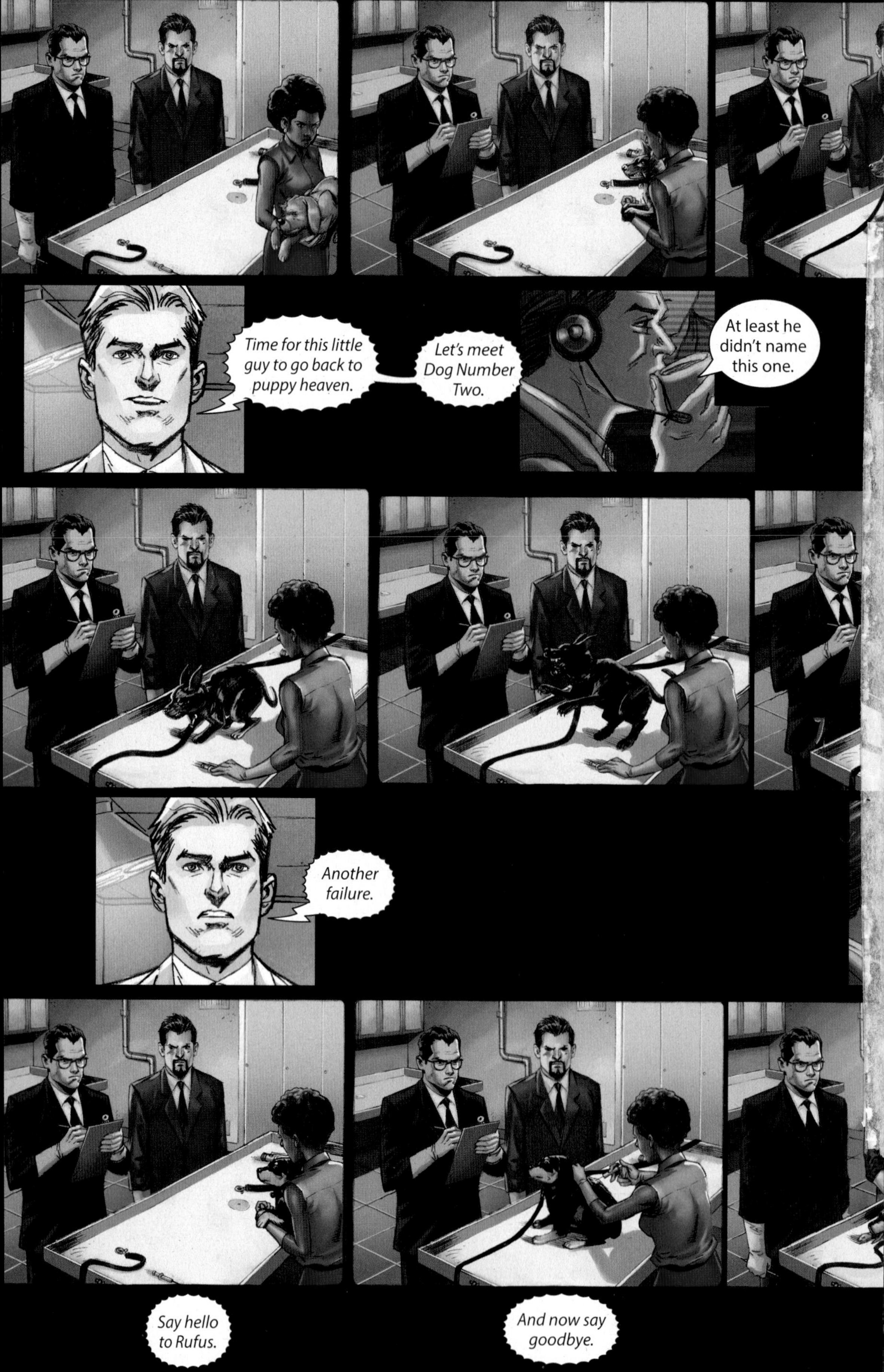

Time for this little guy to go back to puppy heaven.
Let's meet Dog Number Two.
At least he didn't name this one.
Another failure.
Say hello to Rufus.
And now say goodbye.

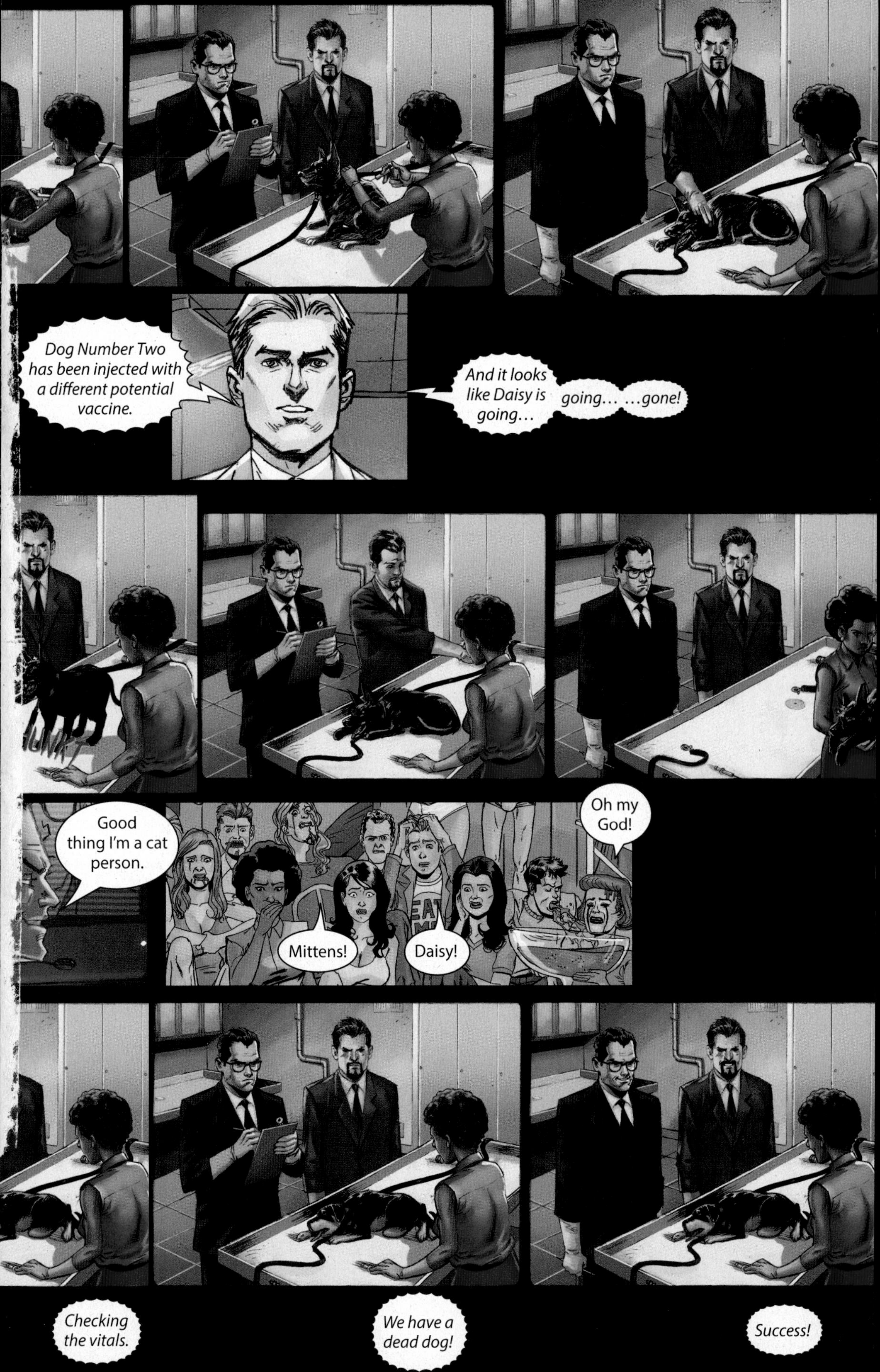
Dog Number Two has been injected with a different potential vaccine.
And it looks like Daisy is going…
going… …gone!
Good thing I'm a cat person.
Oh my God!
Mittens!
Daisy!
Checking the vitals.
We have a dead dog!
Success!

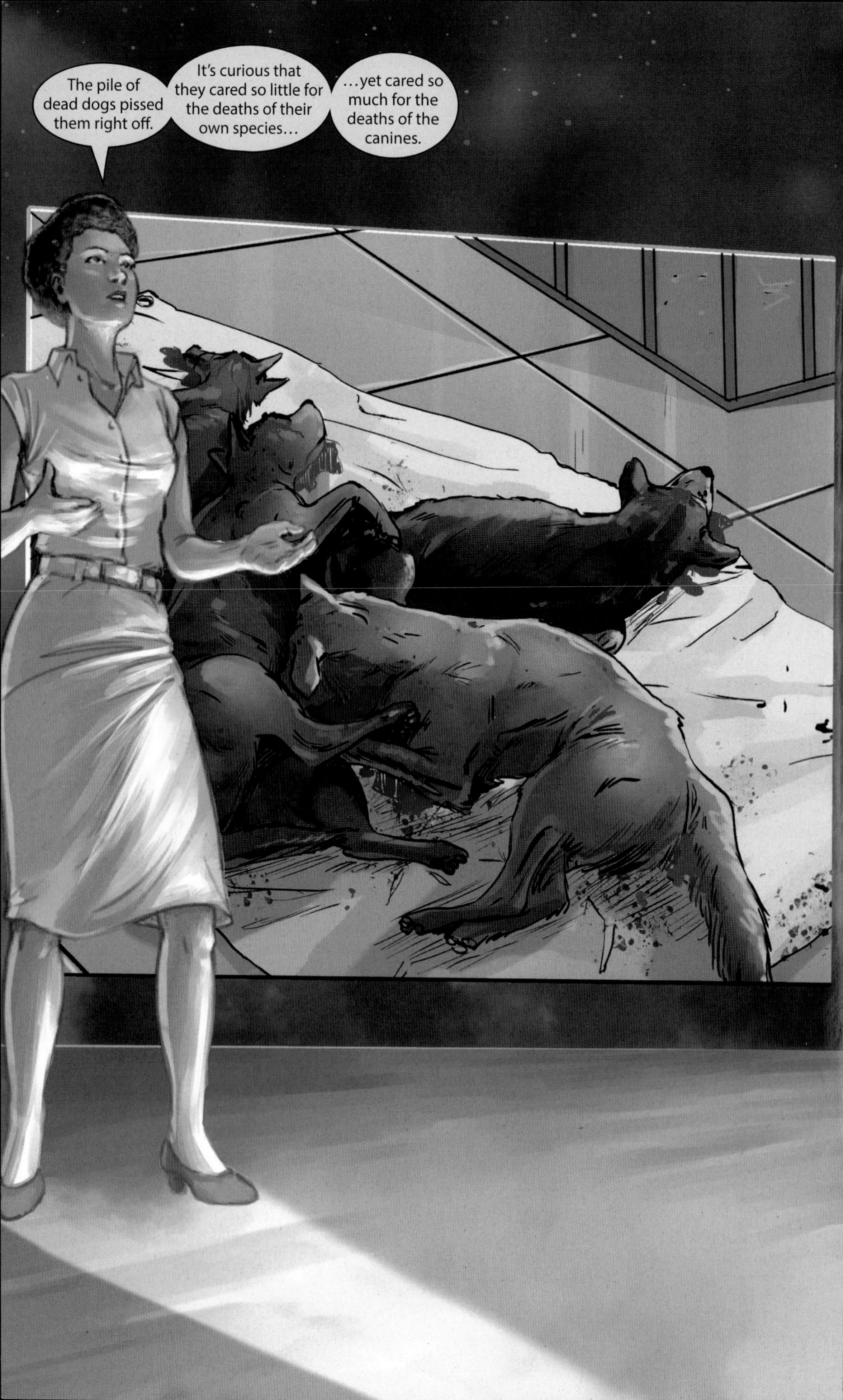
The pile of dead dogs pissed them right off.
It's curious that they cared so little for the deaths of their own species…
…yet cared so much for the deaths of the canines.

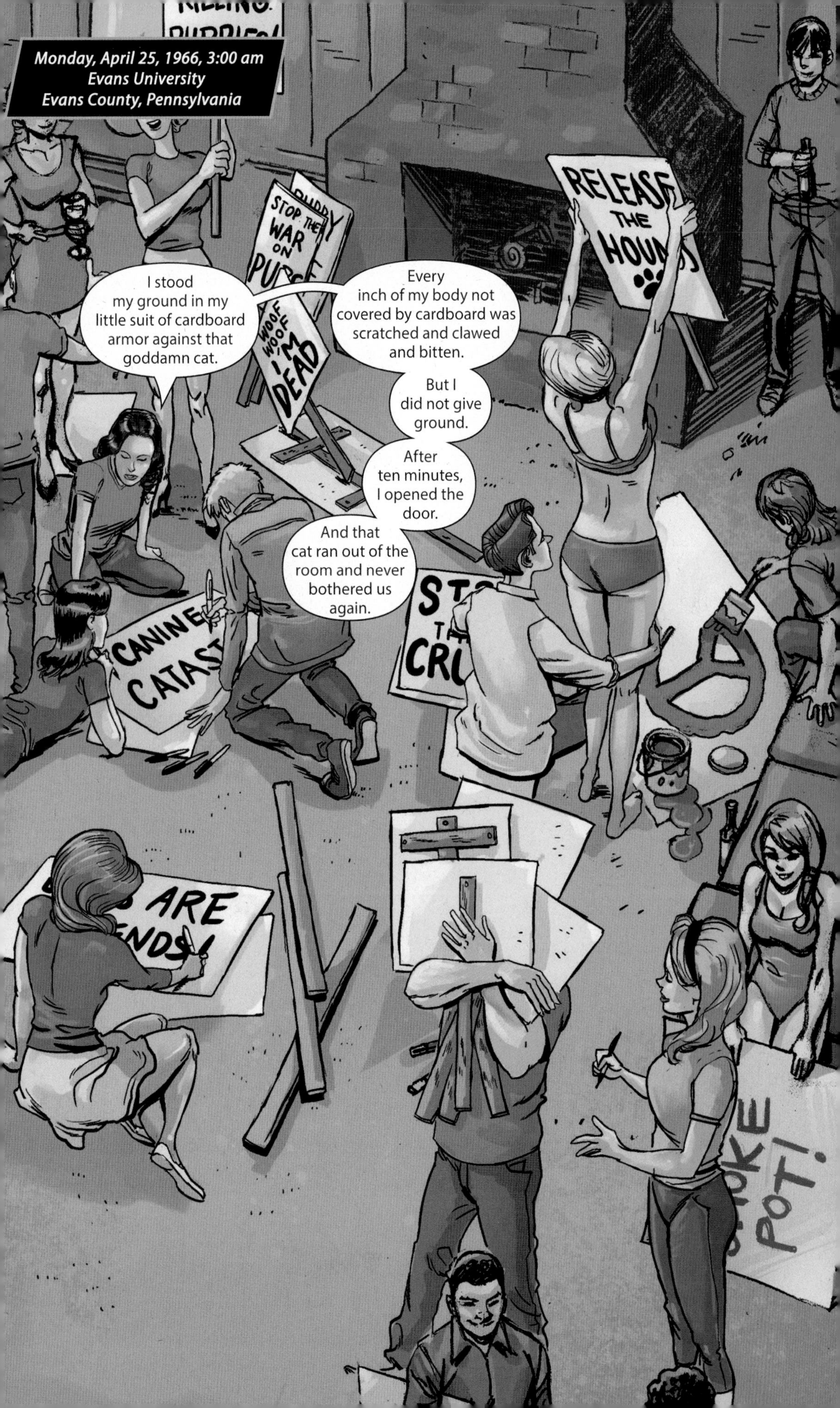

Monday, April 25, 1966, 3:00 am
Evans University
Evans County, Pennsylvania
I stood my ground in my little suit of cardboard armor against that goddamn cat.
Every inch of my body not covered by cardboard was scratched and clawed and bitten.
But I did not give ground.
After ten minutes, I opened the door.
And that cat ran out of the room and never bothered us again.
STOP THE WAR ON
WOOF WOOF I'M DEAD
THE
CANINE
ARE
POT!

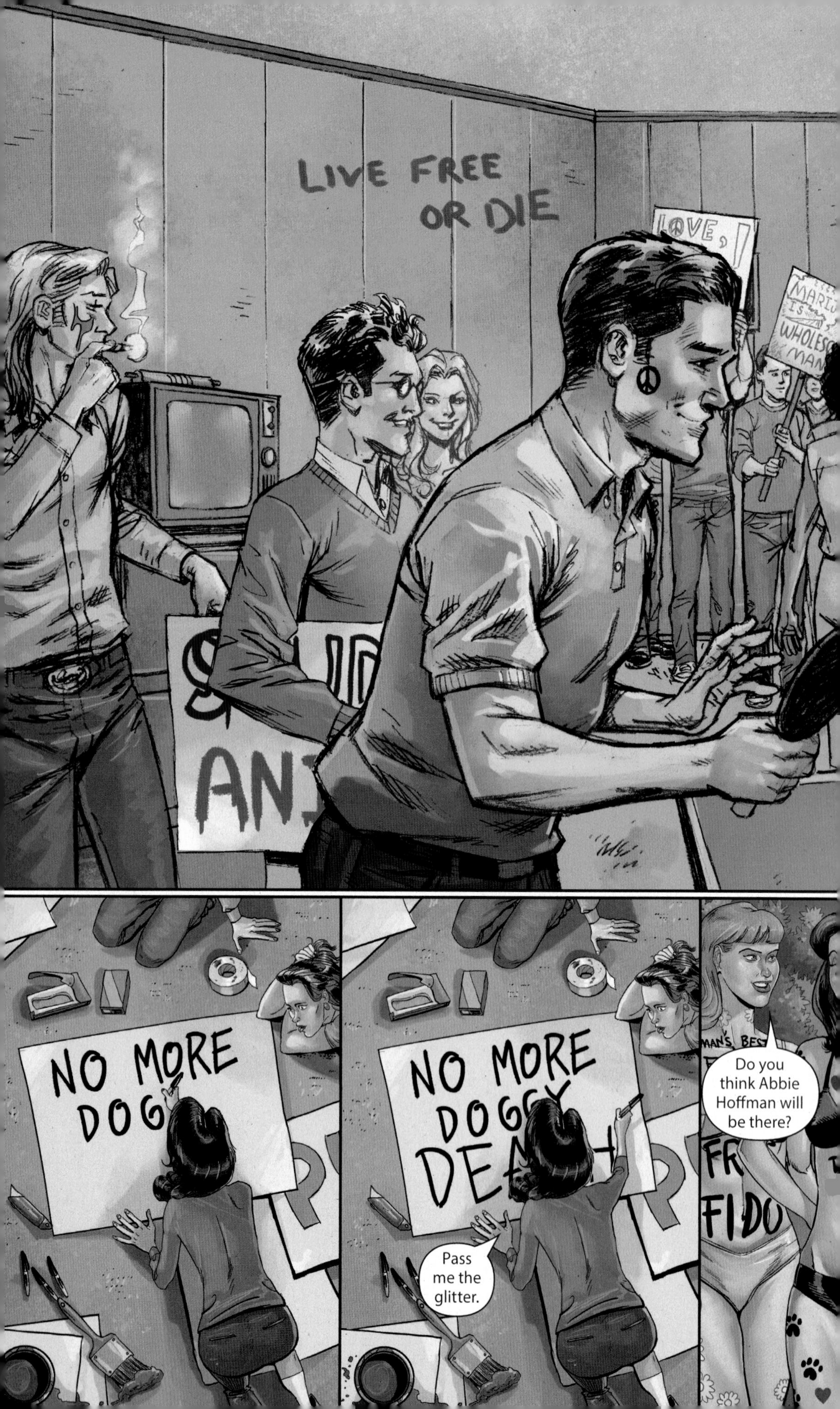

LIVE FREE OR DIE
NO MORE DOG
NO MORE DOGGY
Pass me the glitter.
Do you think Abbie Hoffman will be there?
FIDO

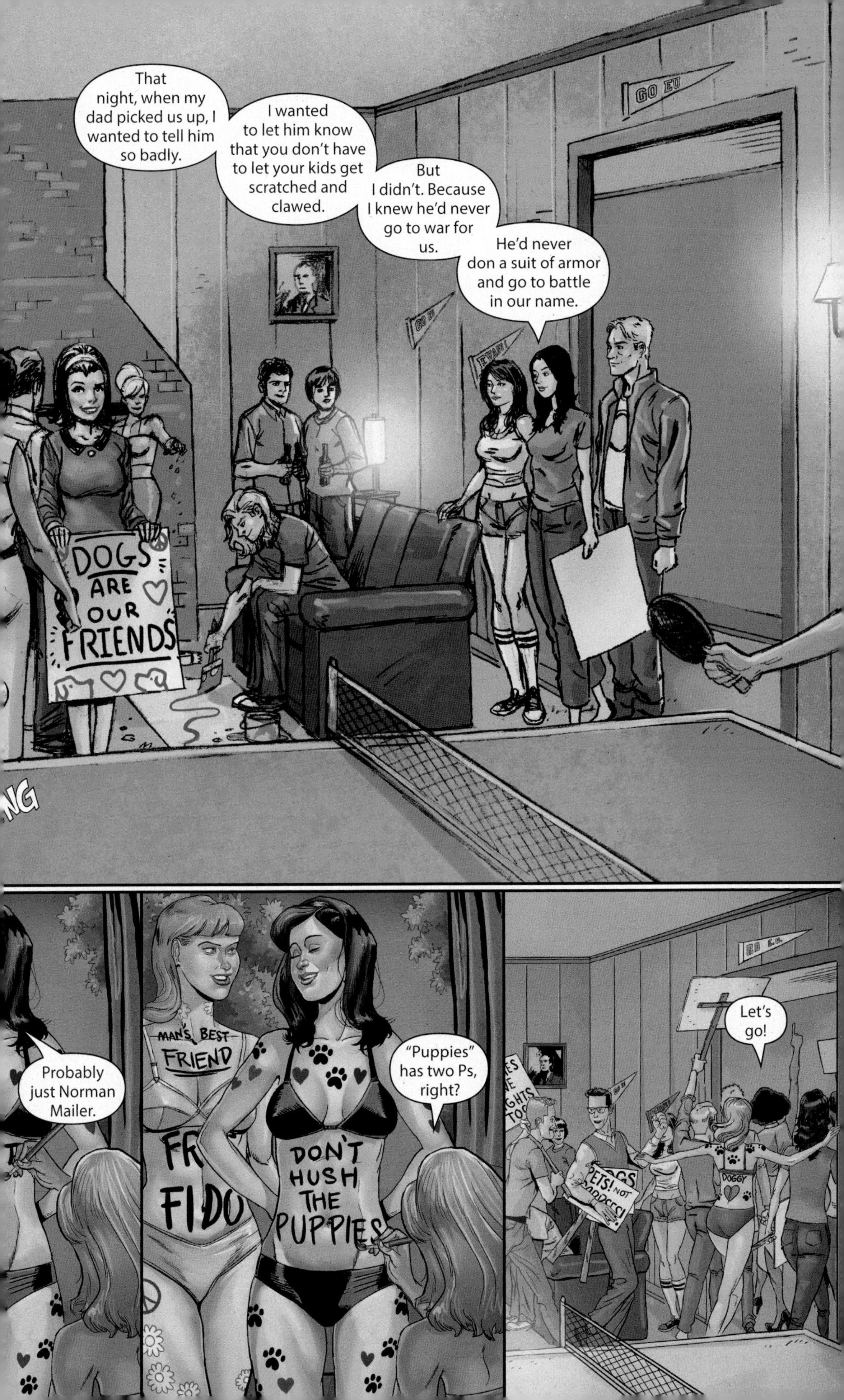
That night, when my dad picked us up, I wanted to tell him so badly.
I wanted to let him know that you don't have to let your kids get scratched and clawed.
But I didn't. Because I knew he'd never go to war for us.
He'd never don a suit of armor and go to battle in our name.
GO EU
DOGS ARE OUR FRIENDS
Probably just Norman Mailer.
MAN'S BEST FRIEND
FIDO
DON'T HUSH THE PUPPIES
"Puppies" has two Ps, right?
Let's go!
DOGGY

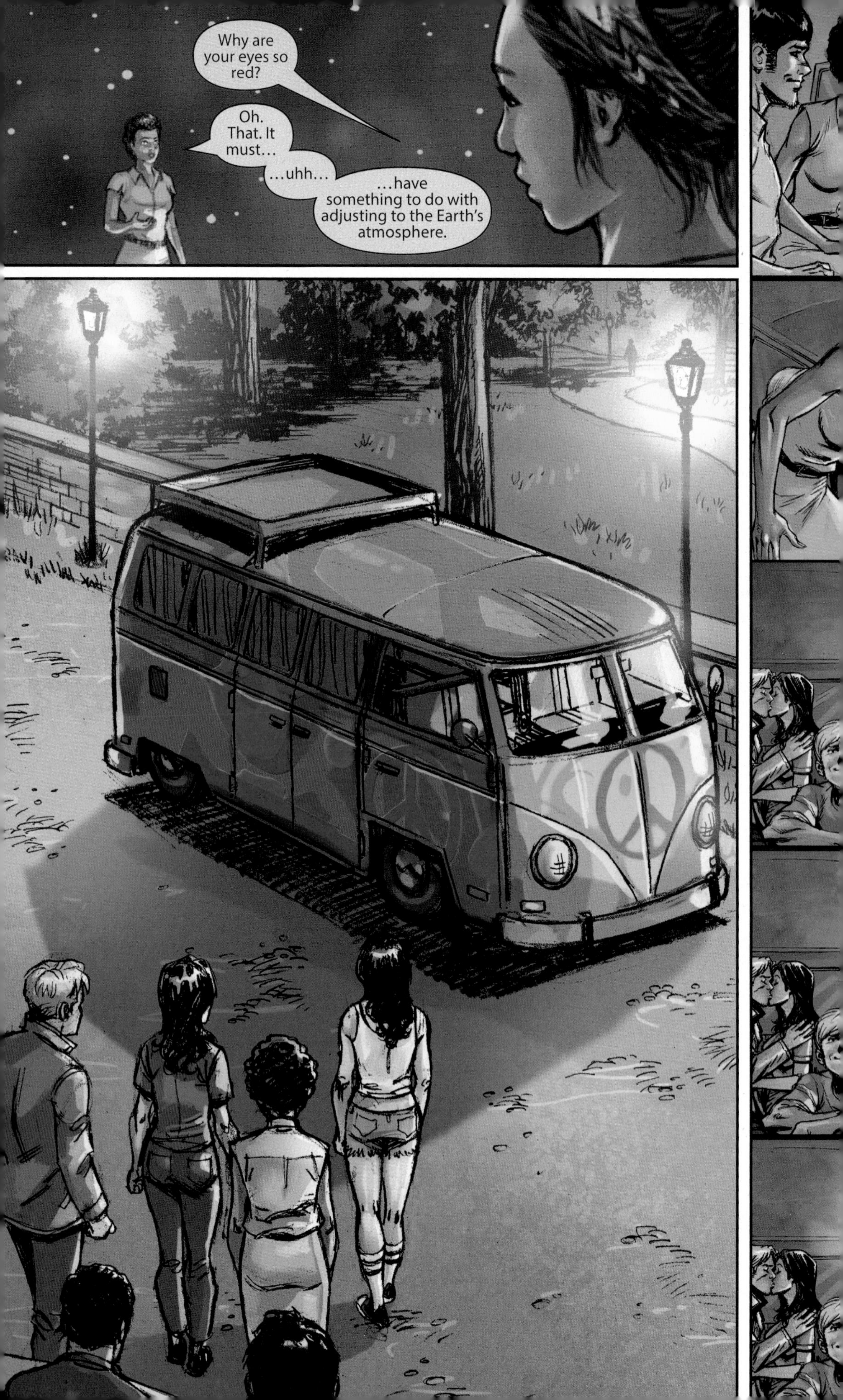
Why are your eyes so red?
Oh. That. It must…
…uhh…
…have something to do with adjusting to the Earth's atmosphere.

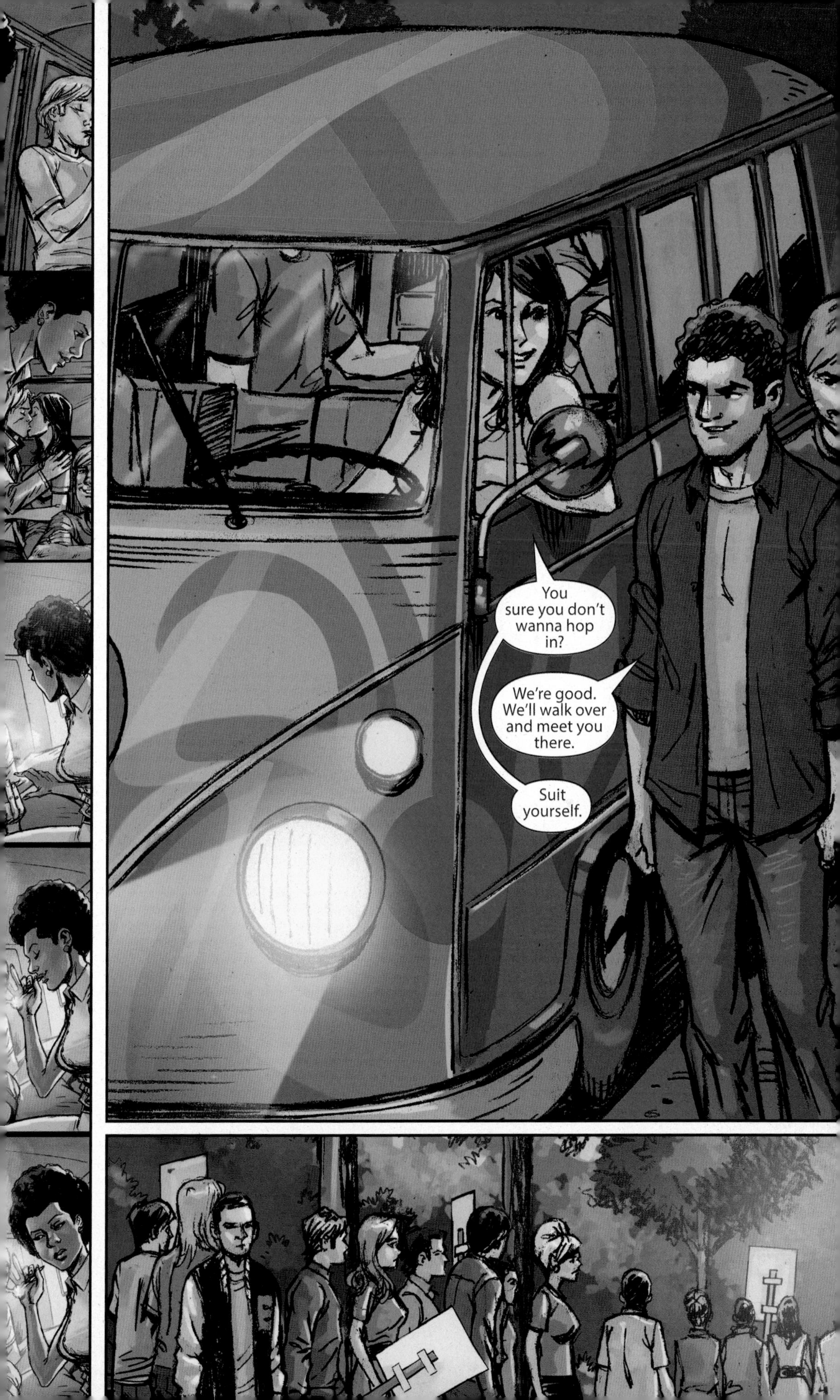
You sure you don't wanna hop in?
We're good. We'll walk over and meet you there.
Suit yourself.

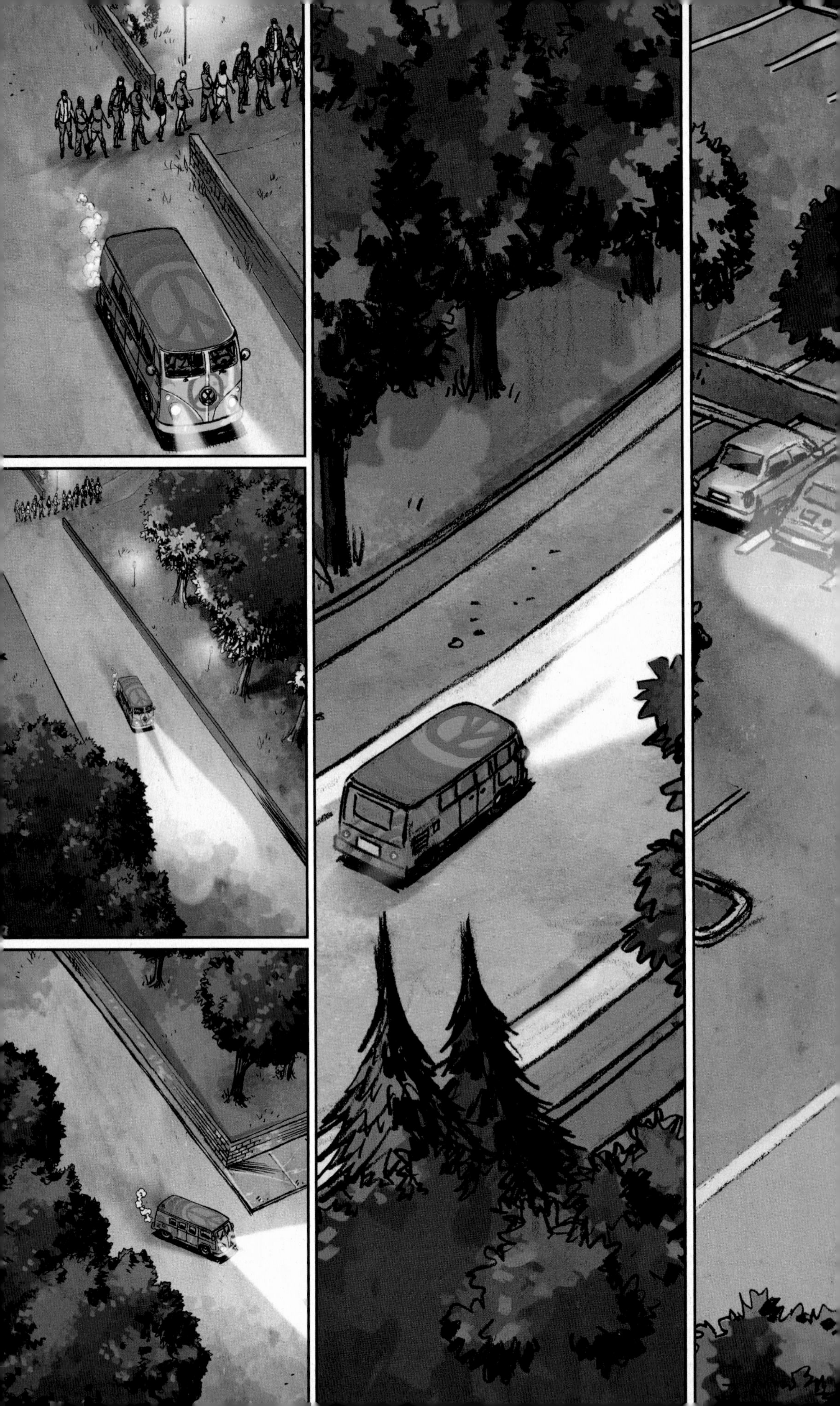

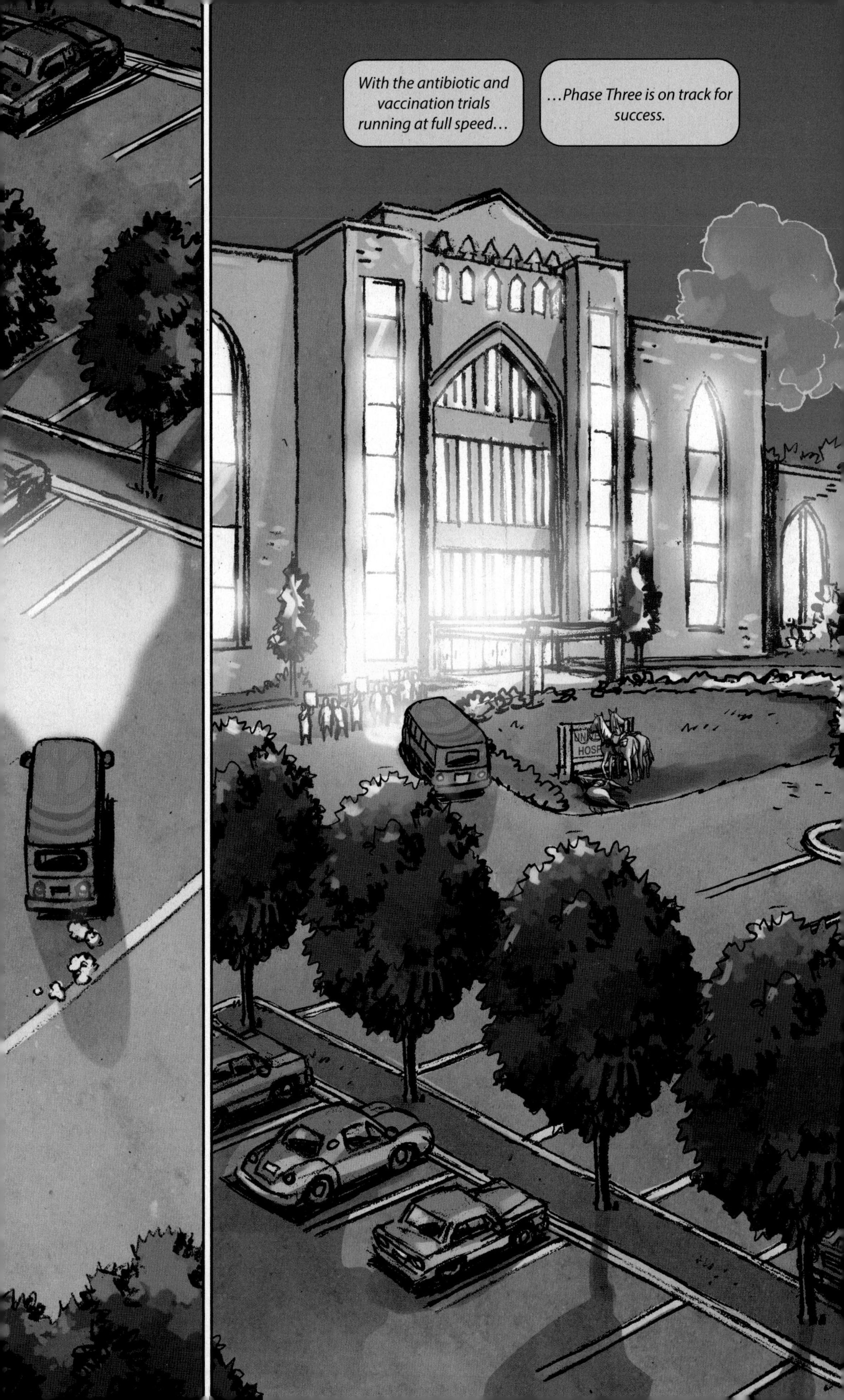
With the antibiotic and vaccination trials running at full speed…
…Phase Three is on track for success.

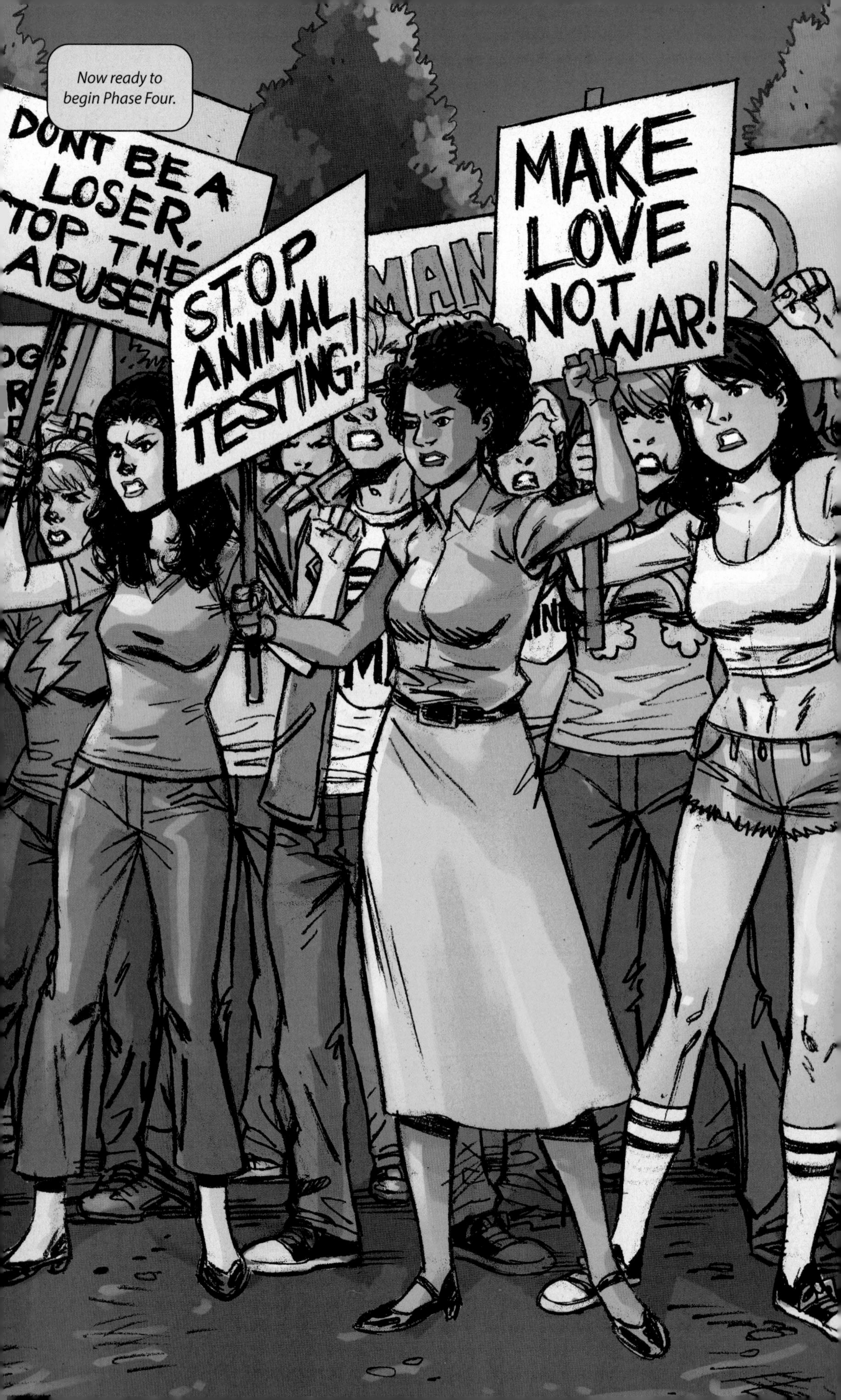

Now ready to begin Phase Four.
DONT BE A LOSER, STOP THE ABUSER
STOP ANIMAL TESTING!
MAKE LOVE NOT WAR!

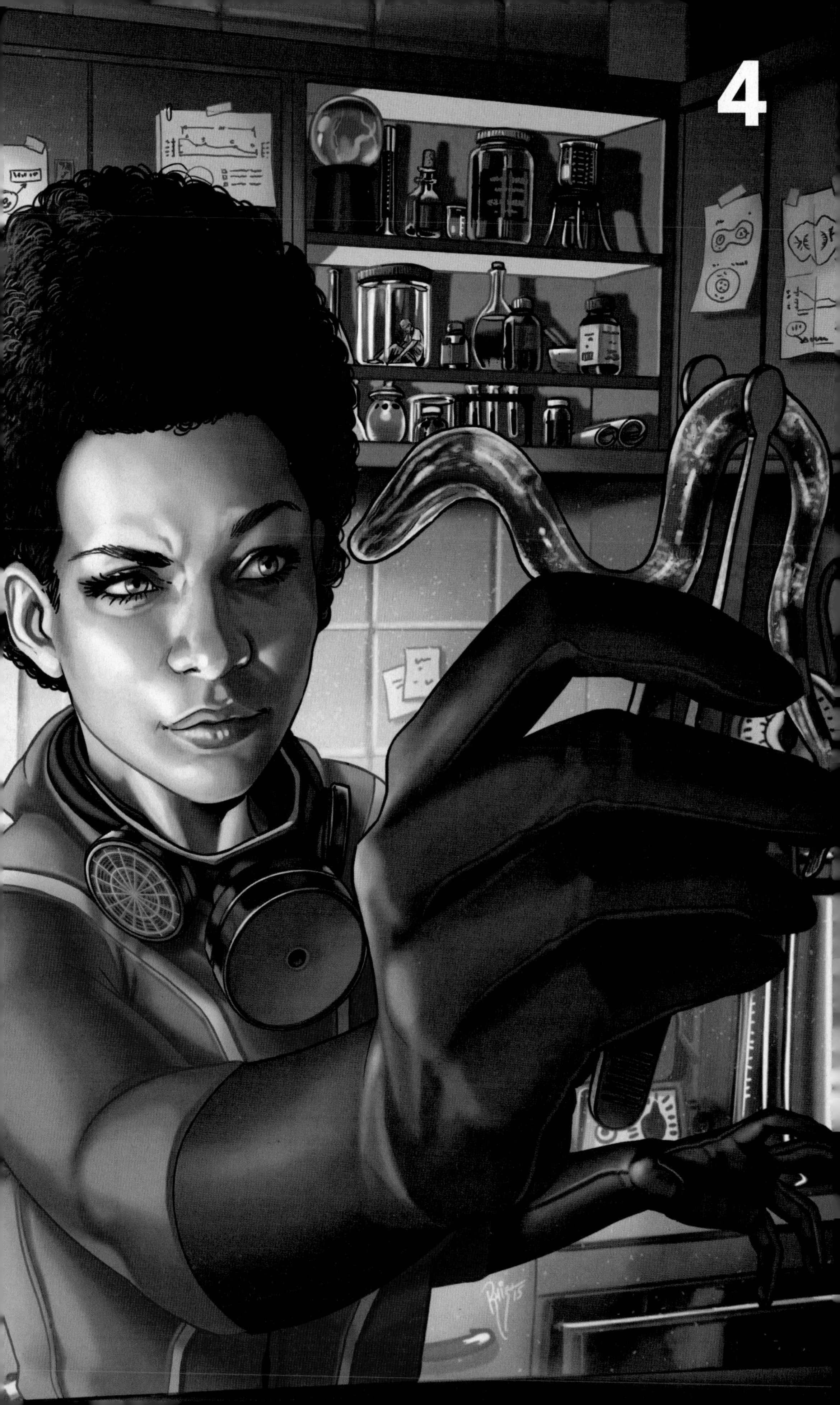
4

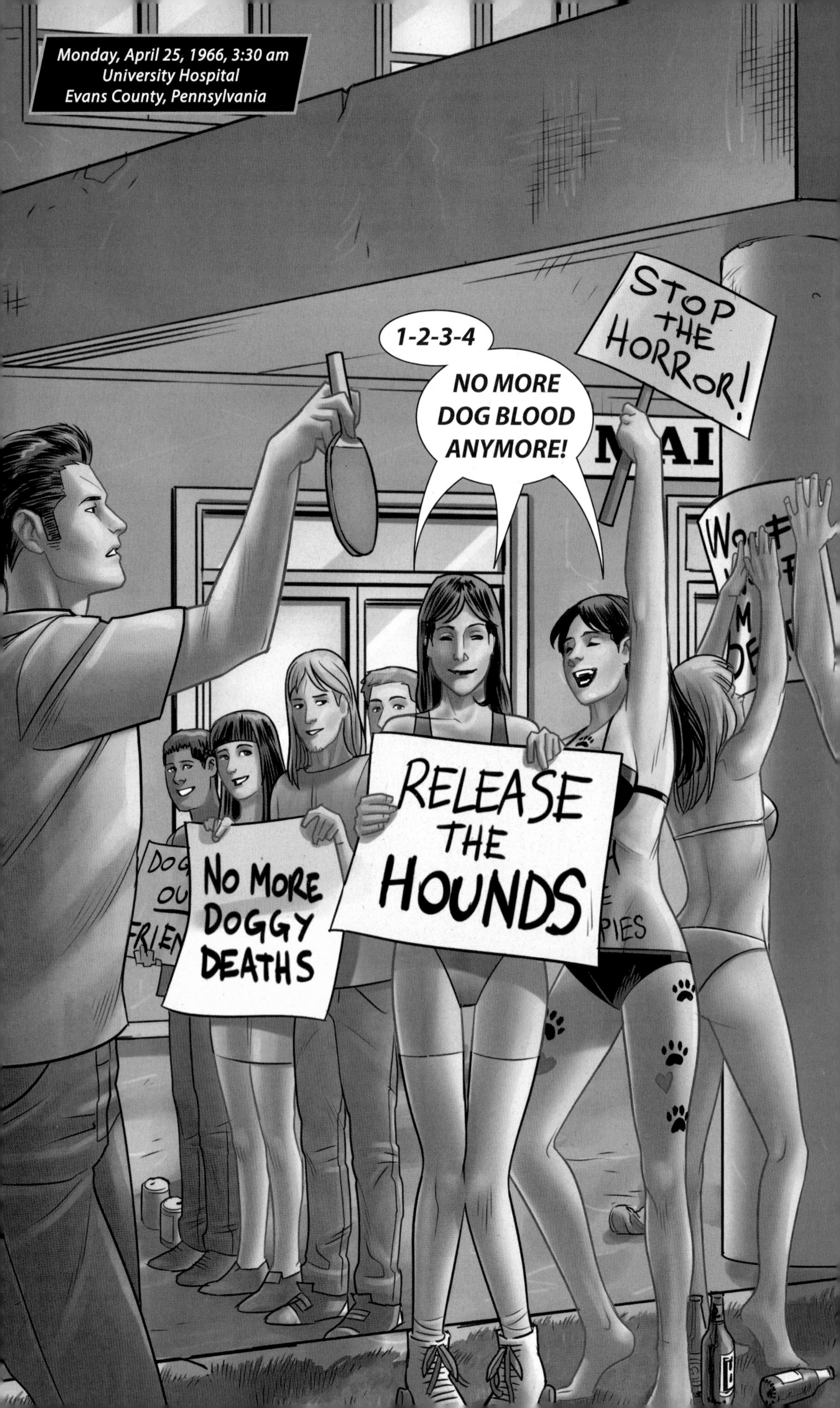

Monday, April 25, 1966, 3:30 am
University Hospital
Evans County, Pennsylvania
1-2-3-4
NO MORE DOG BLOOD ANYMORE!
STOP THE HORROR!
RELEASE THE HOUNDS
No More Doggy Deaths

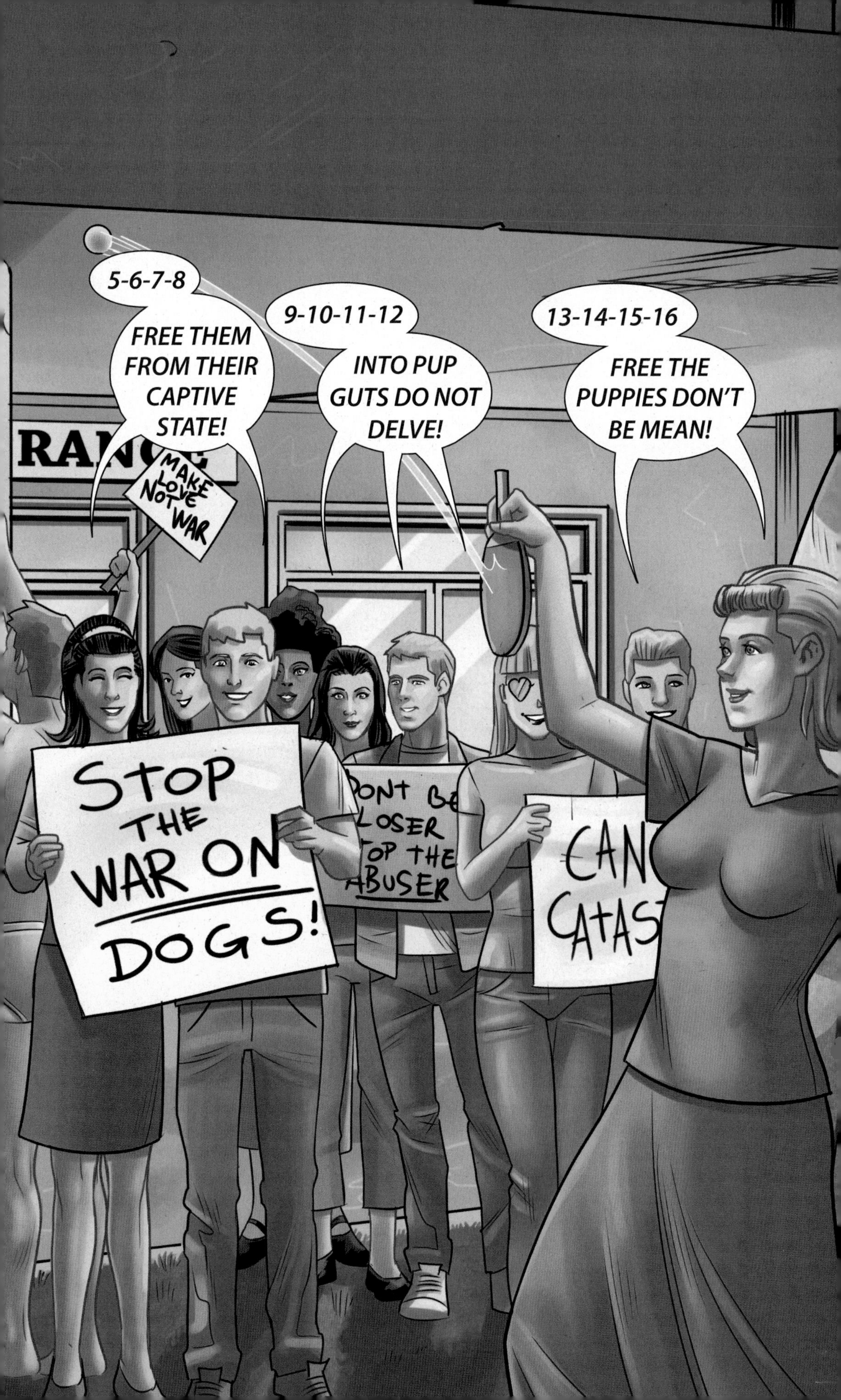
5-6-7-8
FREE THEM FROM THEIR CAPTIVE STATE!
9-10-11-12
INTO PUP GUTS DO NOT DELVE!
13-14-15-16
FREE THE PUPPIES DON'T BE MEAN!
MAKE LOVE NOT WAR
STOP THE WAR ON DOGS!

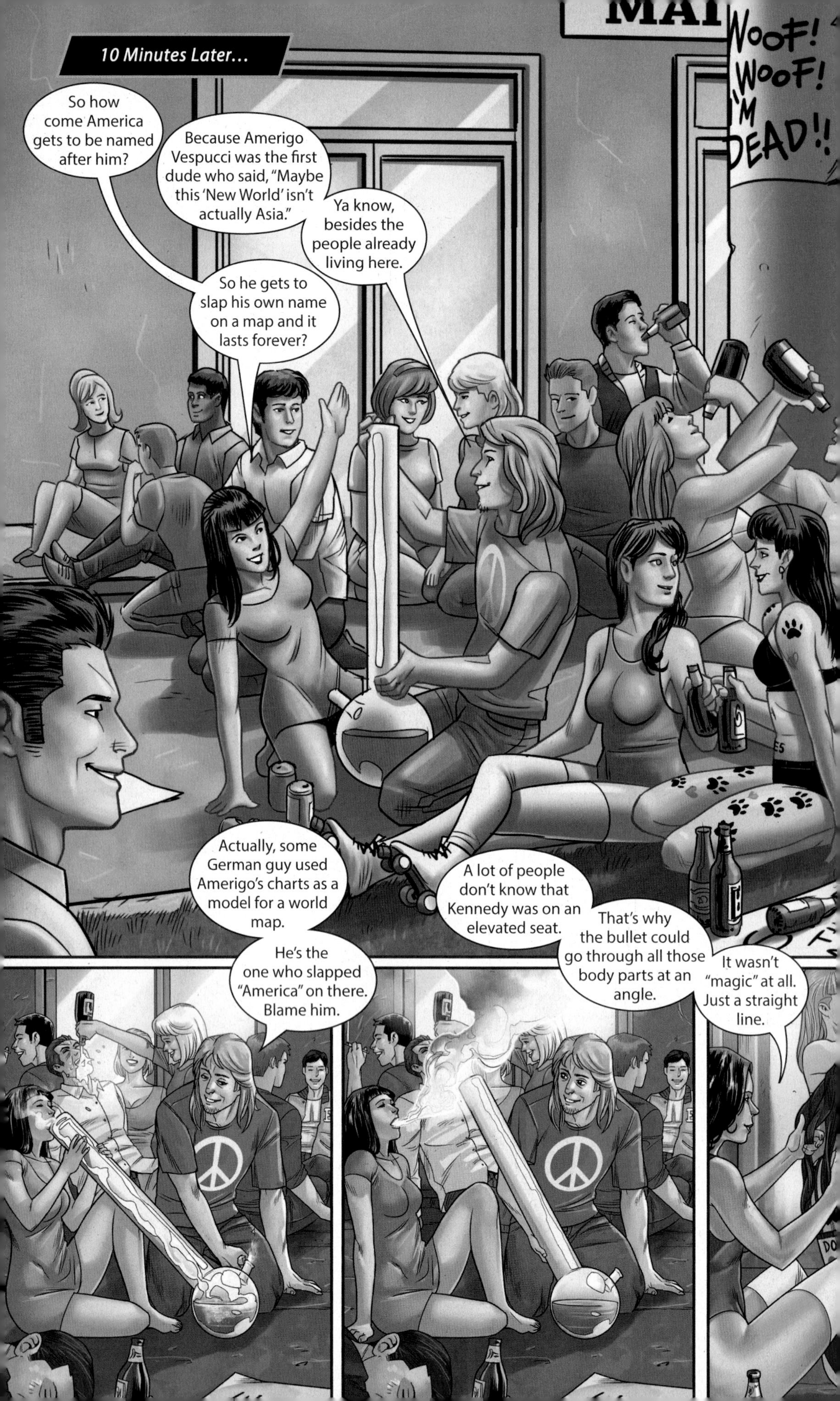

MA
WOOF! WOOF! I'M DEAD!!
10 Minutes Later...
So how come America gets to be named after him?
Because Amerigo Vespucci was the first dude who said, "Maybe this 'New World' isn't actually Asia."
Ya know, besides the people already living here.
So he gets to slap his own name on a map and it lasts forever?
Actually, some German guy used Amerigo's charts as a model for a world map.
He's the one who slapped "America" on there. Blame him.
A lot of people don't know that Kennedy was on an elevated seat.
That's why the bullet could go through all those body parts at an angle.
It wasn't "magic" at all. Just a straight line.

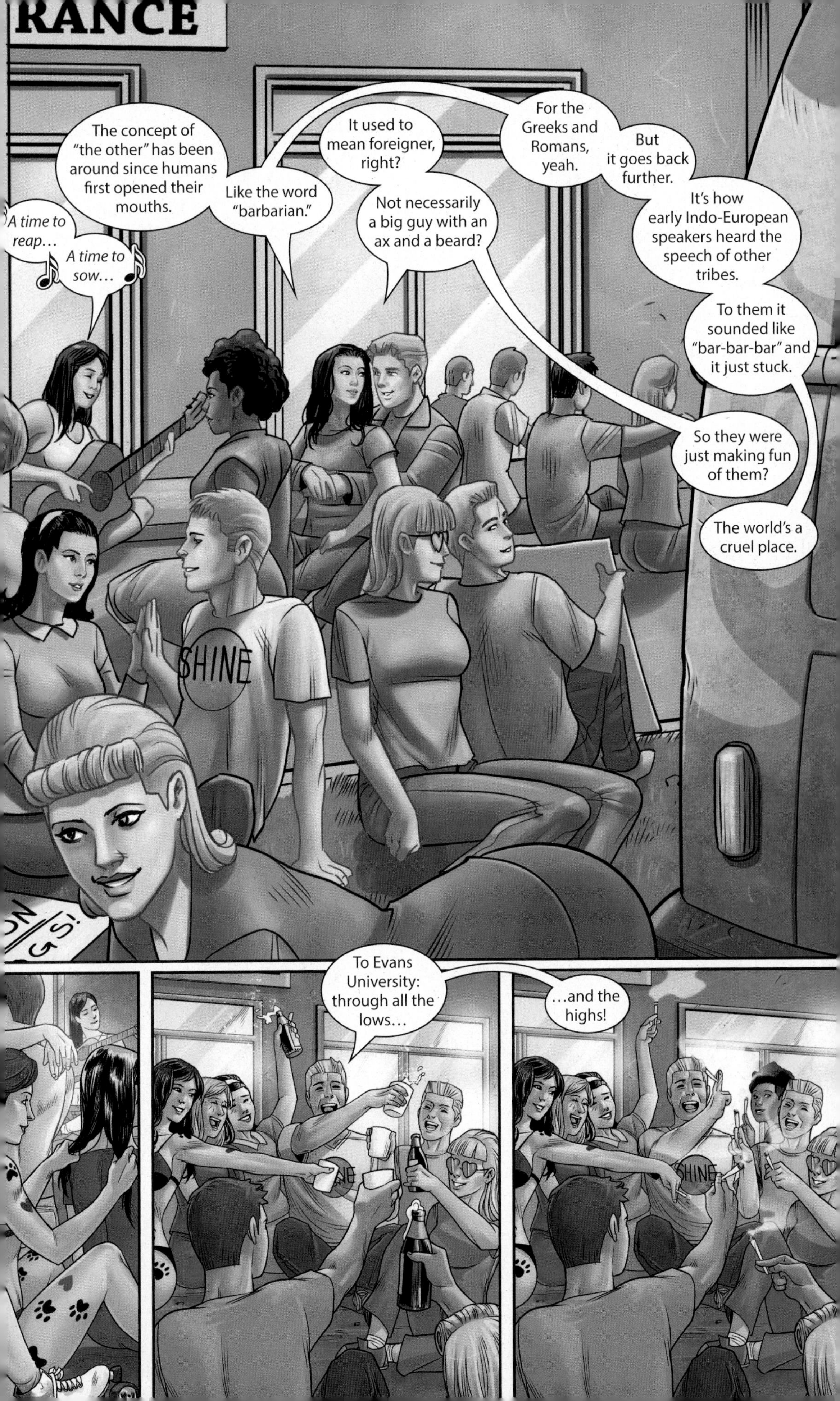
RANCE
The concept of "the other" has been around since humans first opened their mouths.
A time to reap…
A time to sow…
Like the word "barbarian."
It used to mean foreigner, right?
For the Greeks and Romans, yeah.
But it goes back further.
Not necessarily a big guy with an ax and a beard?
It's how early Indo-European speakers heard the speech of other tribes.
To them it sounded like "bar-bar-bar" and it just stuck.
So they were just making fun of them?
The world's a cruel place.
SHINE
To Evans University: through all the lows…
…and the highs!
SHINE

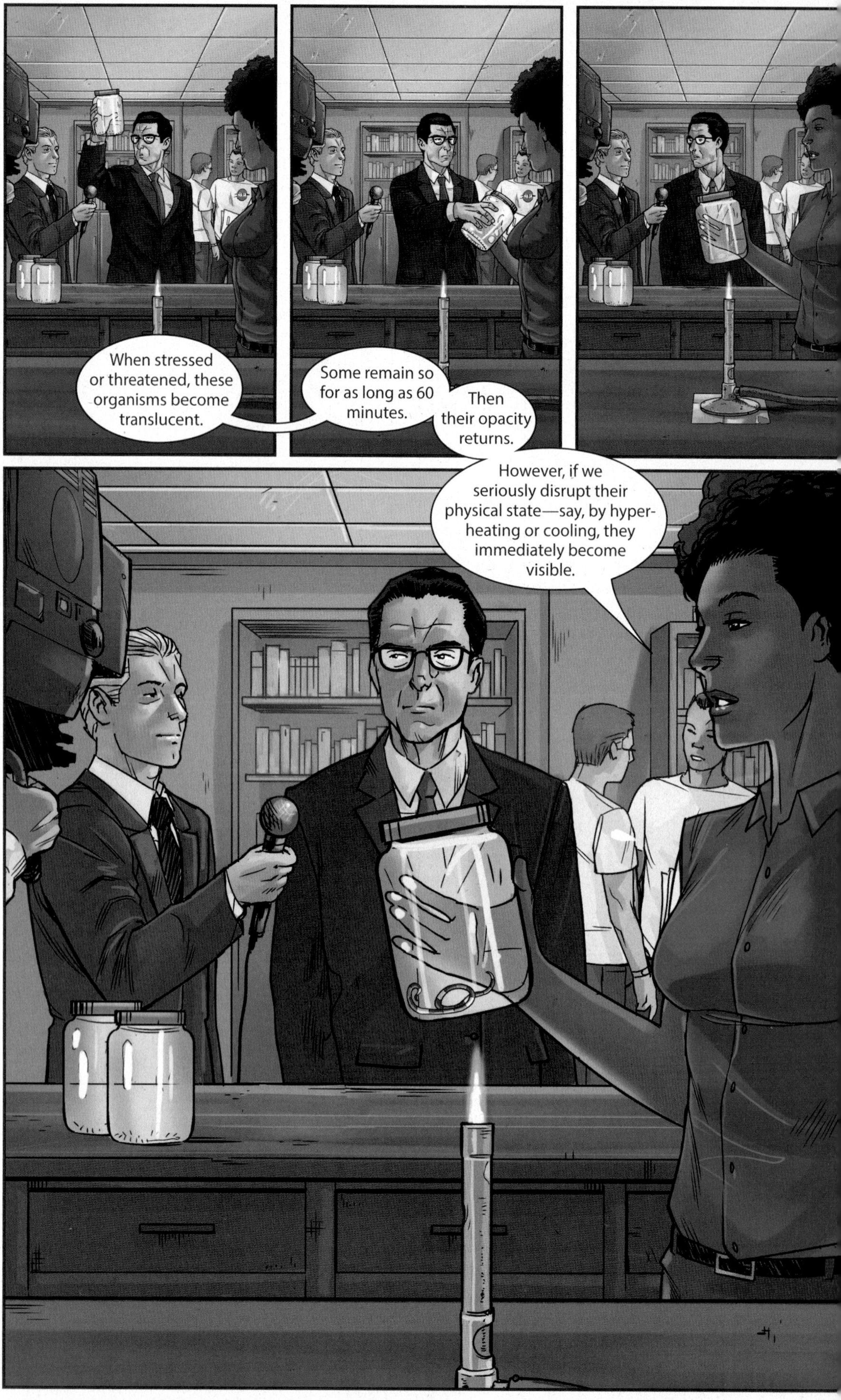
When stressed or threatened, these organisms become translucent.
Some remain so for as long as 60 minutes.
Then their opacity returns.
However, if we seriously disrupt their physical state—say, by hyper-heating or cooling, they immediately become visible.

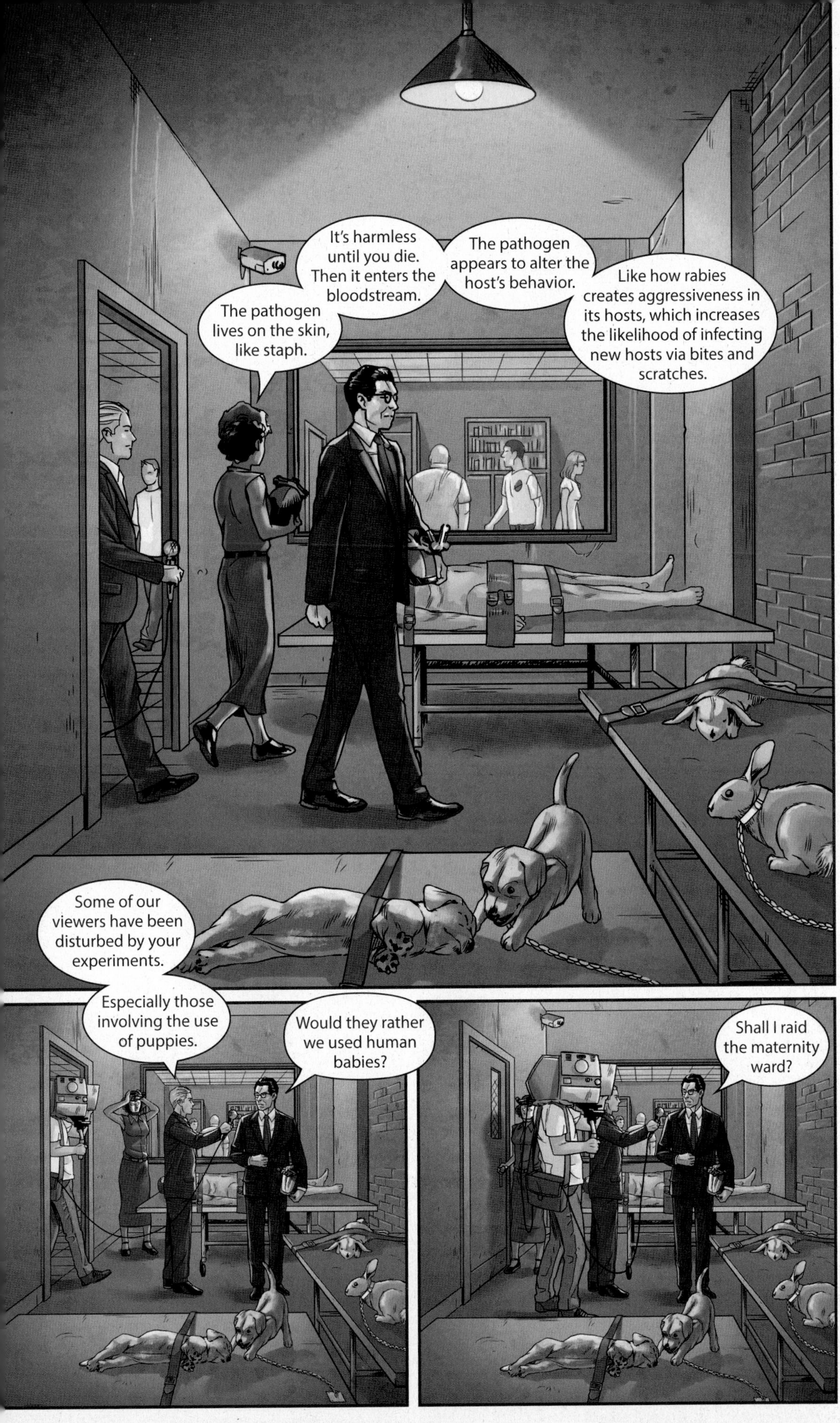
The pathogen lives on the skin, like staph.
It's harmless until you die. Then it enters the bloodstream.
The pathogen appears to alter the host's behavior.
Like how rabies creates aggressiveness in its hosts, which increases the likelihood of infecting new hosts via bites and scratches.
Some of our viewers have been disturbed by your experiments.
Especially those involving the use of puppies.
Would they rather we used human babies?
Shall I raid the maternity ward?

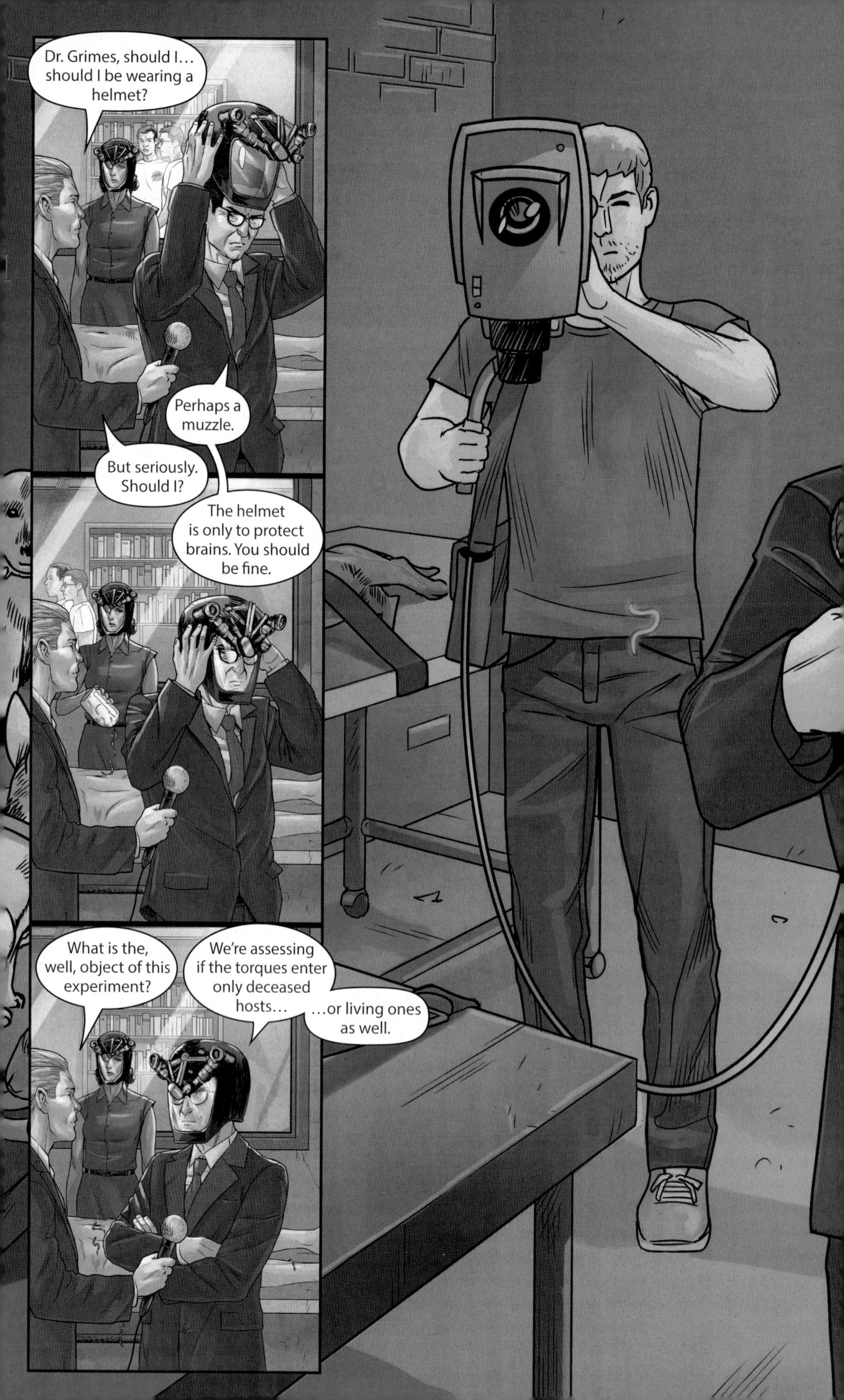
Dr. Grimes, should I… should I be wearing a helmet?
Perhaps a muzzle.
But seriously. Should I?
The helmet is only to protect brains. You should be fine.
What is the, well, object of this experiment?
We're assessing if the torques enter only deceased hosts…
…or living ones as well.

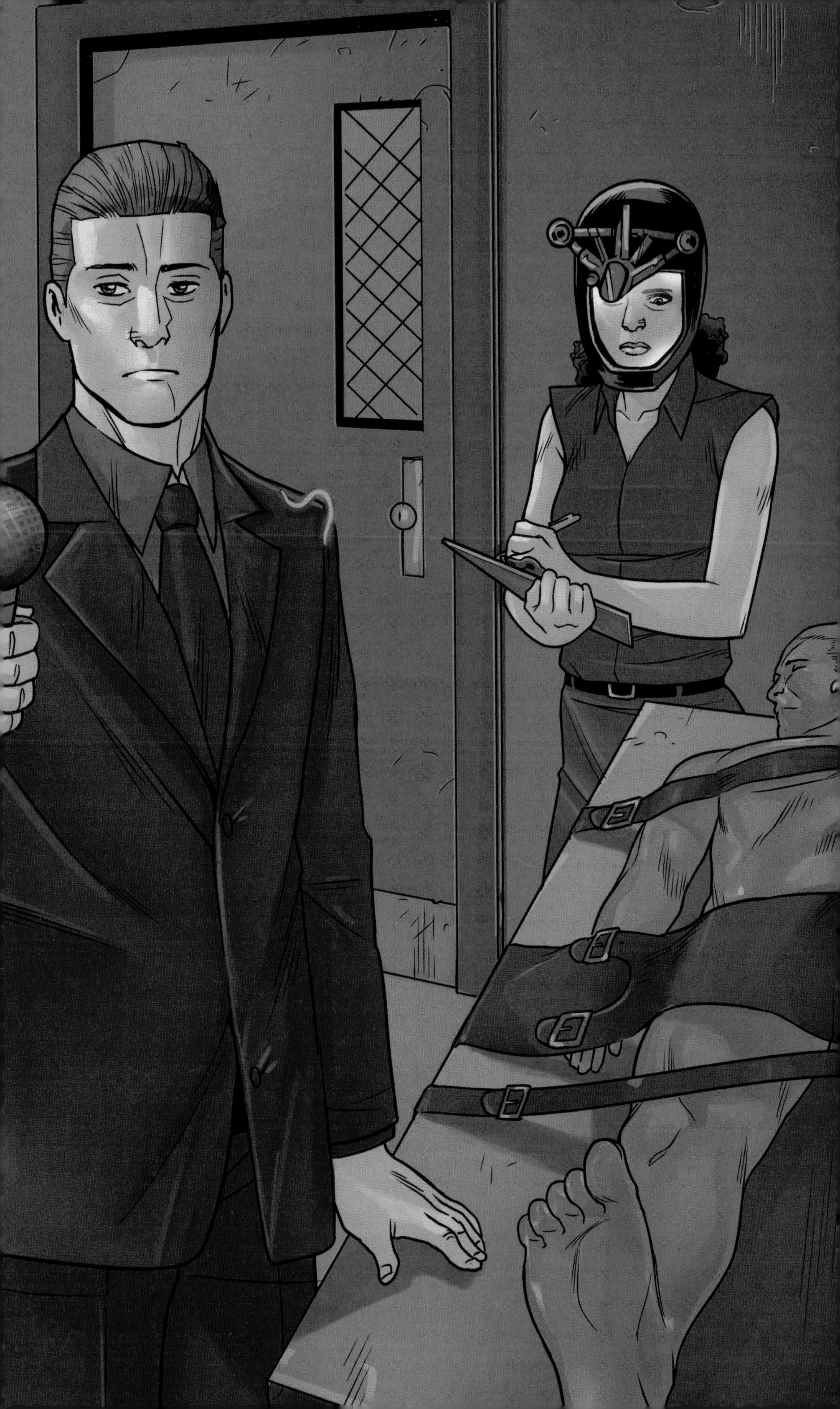

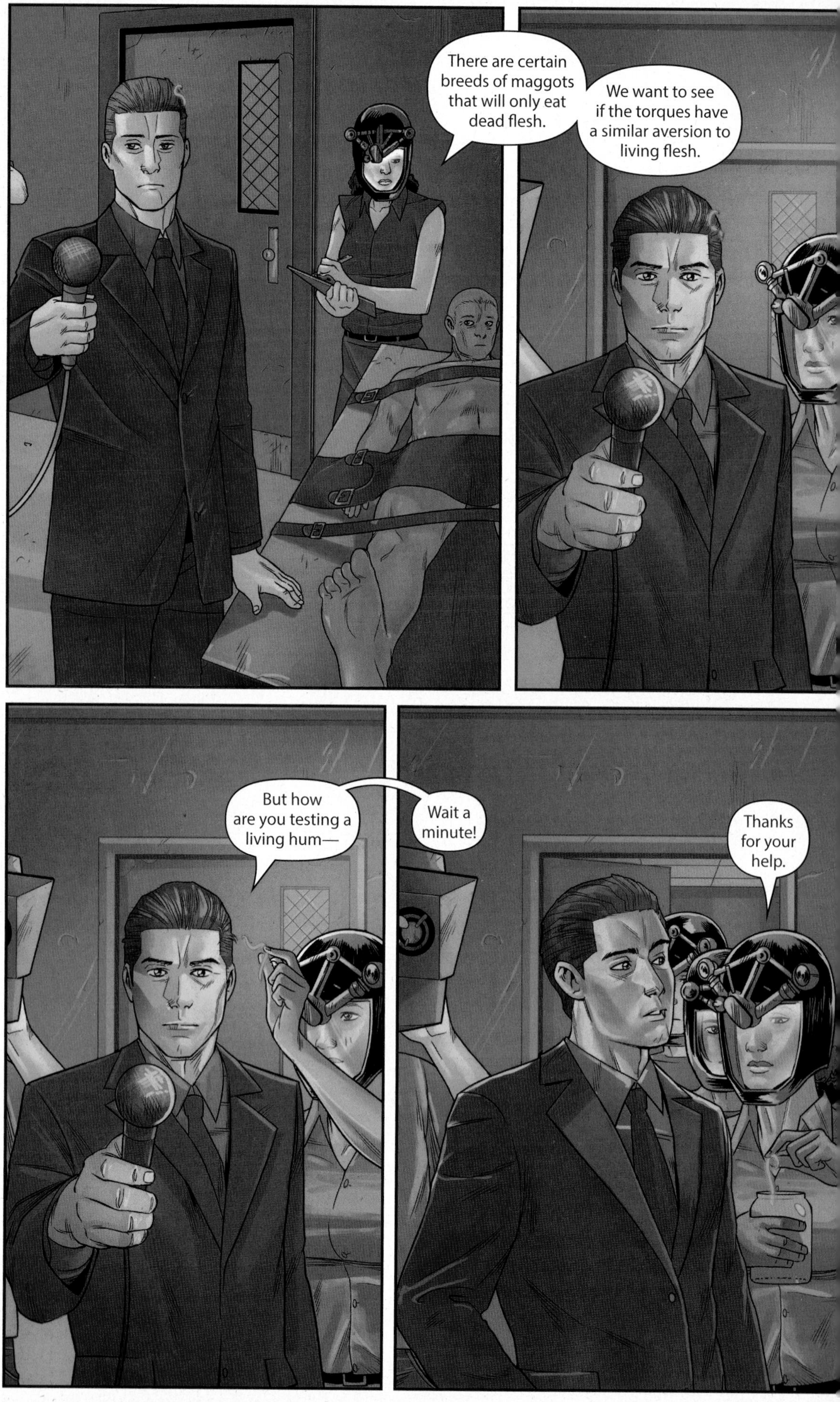
There are certain breeds of maggots that will only eat dead flesh.
We want to see if the torques have a similar aversion to living flesh.
But how are you testing a living hum—
Wait a minute!
Thanks for your help.

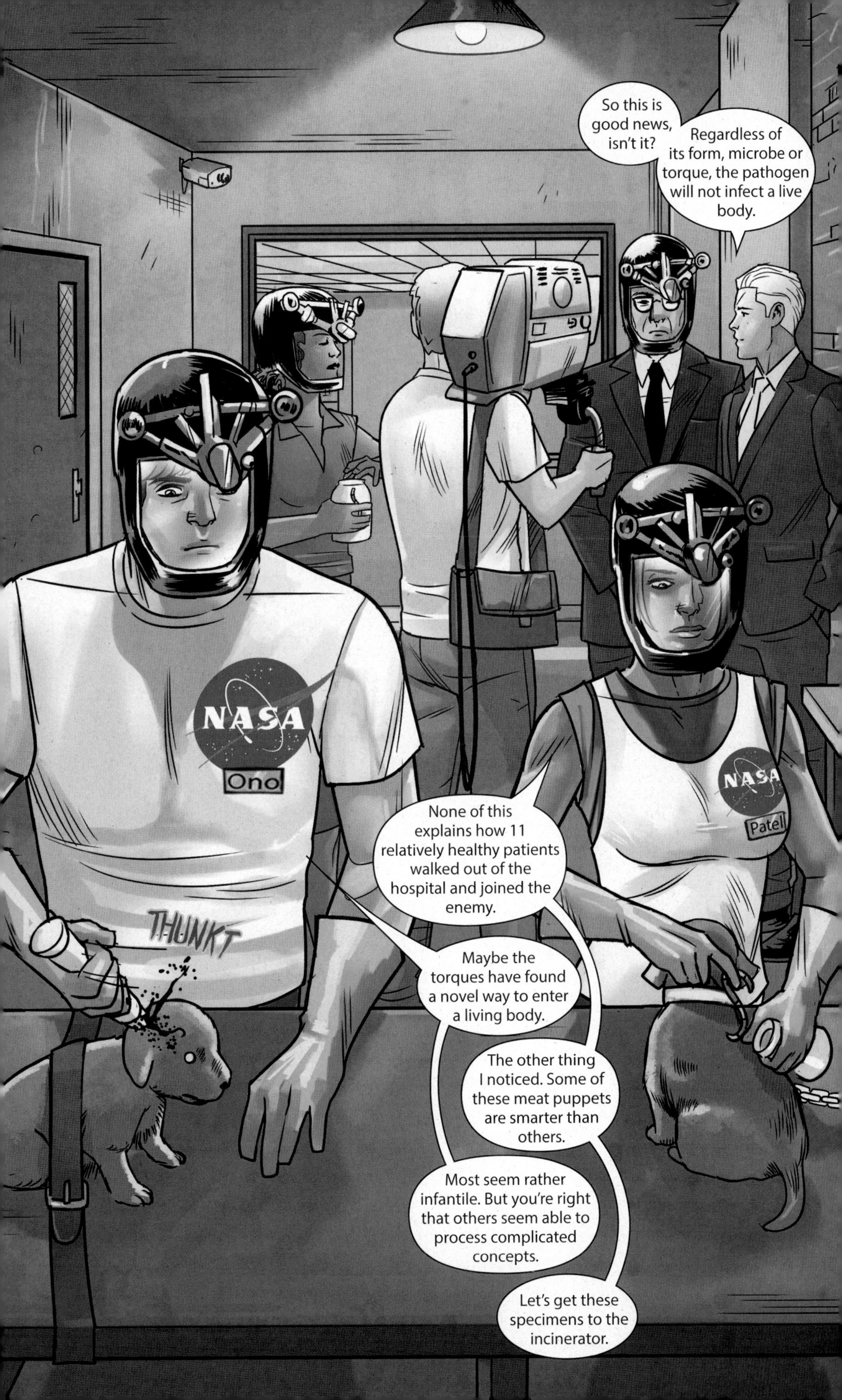
So this is good news, isn't it?
Regardless of its form, microbe or torque, the pathogen will not infect a live body.
Ono
Patel
NASA
NASA
None of this explains how 11 relatively healthy patients walked out of the hospital and joined the enemy.
THUNKT
Maybe the torques have found a novel way to enter a living body.
The other thing I noticed. Some of these meat puppets are smarter than others.
Most seem rather infantile. But you're right that others seem able to process complicated concepts.
Let's get these specimens to the incinerator.

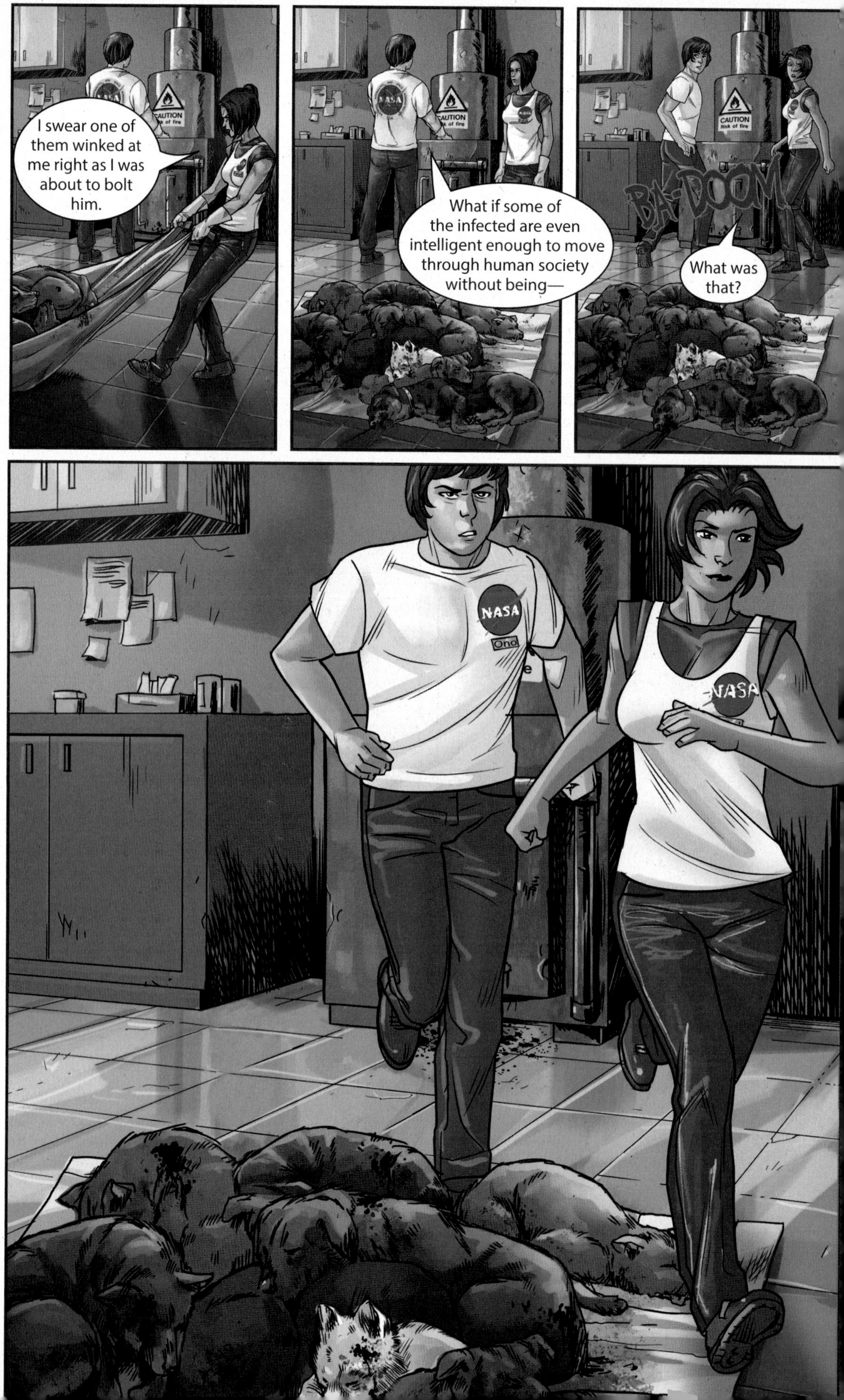
I swear one of them winked at me right as I was about to bolt him.
CAUTION Risk of fire
What if some of the infected are even intelligent enough to move through human society without being—
BA-DOOM
What was that?
NASA
Ono

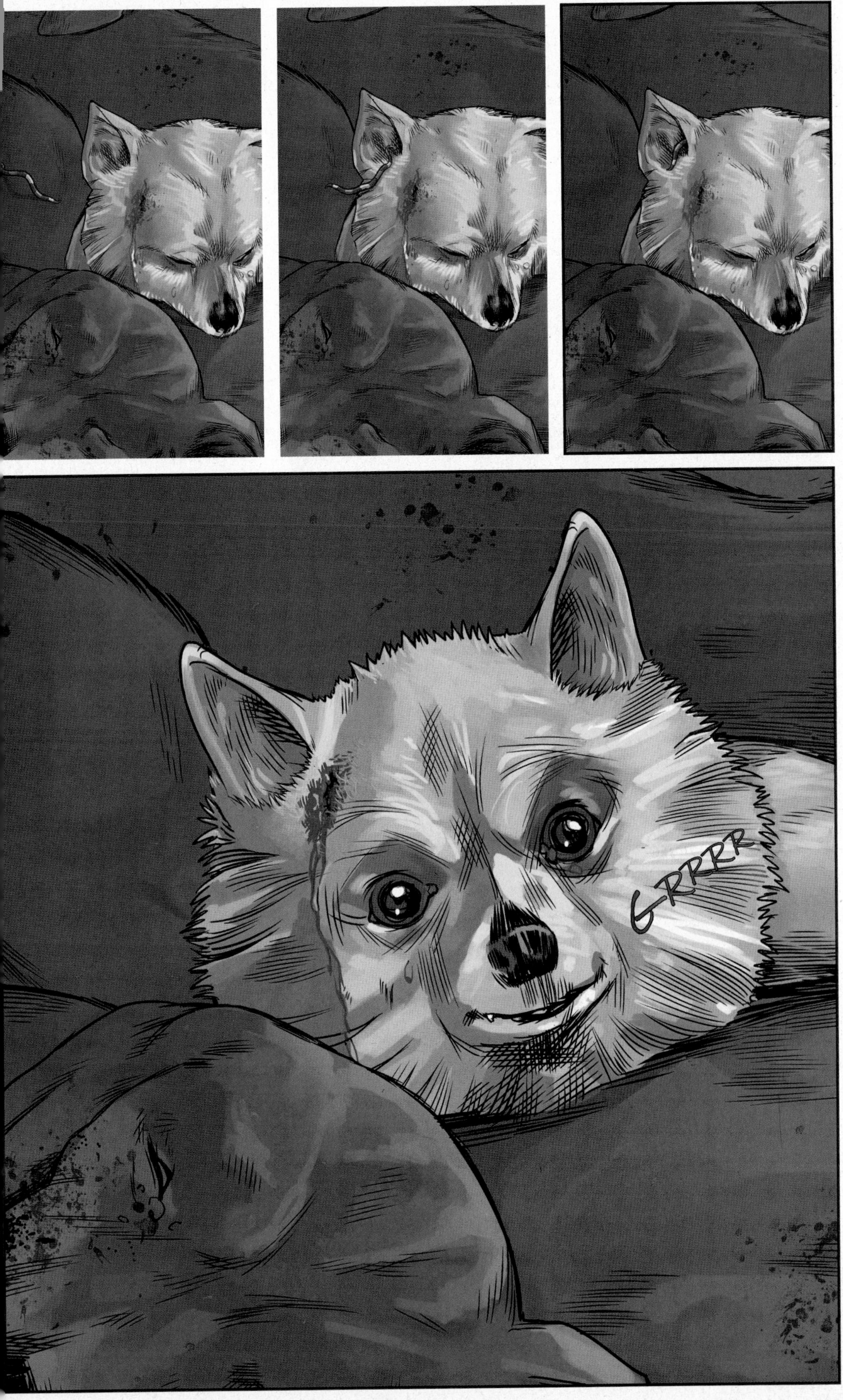
GRRRR

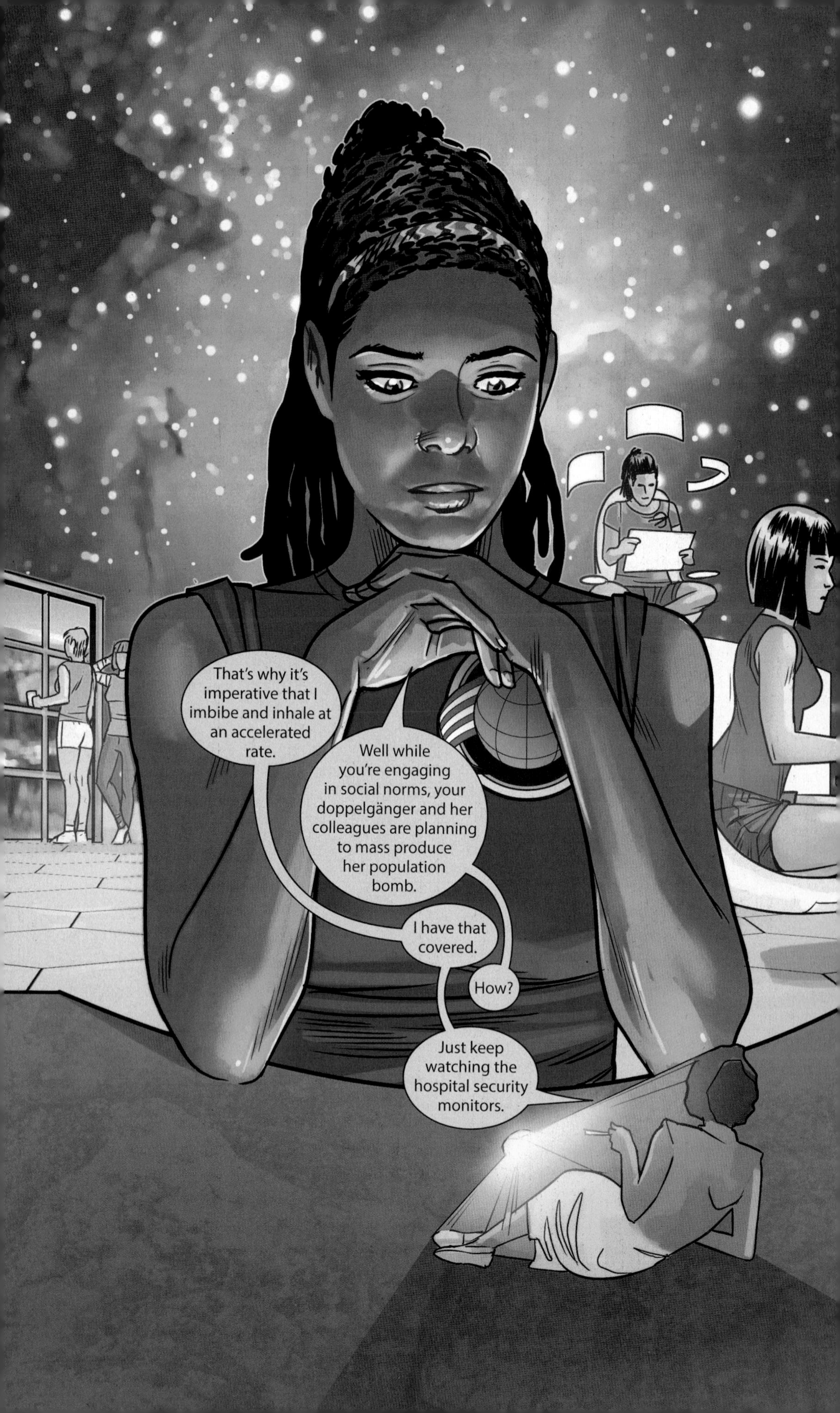
That's why it's imperative that I imbibe and inhale at an accelerated rate.
Well while you're engaging in social norms, your doppelgänger and her colleagues are planning to mass produce her population bomb.
I have that covered.
How?
Just keep watching the hospital security monitors.

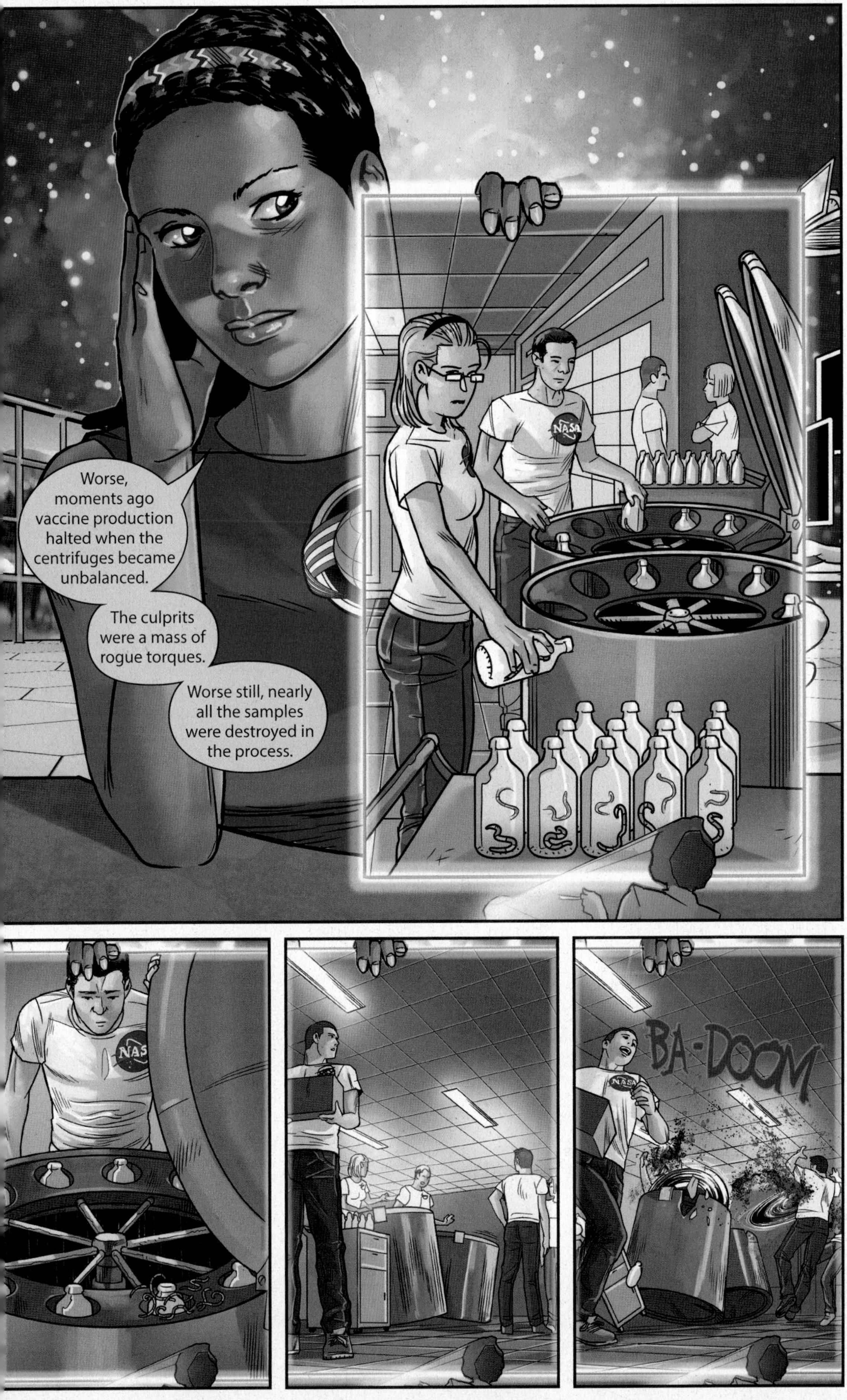
Worse, moments ago vaccine production halted when the centrifuges became unbalanced.
The culprits were a mass of rogue torques.
Worse still, nearly all the samples were destroyed in the process.
NASA
NASA
NASA
BA-DOOM

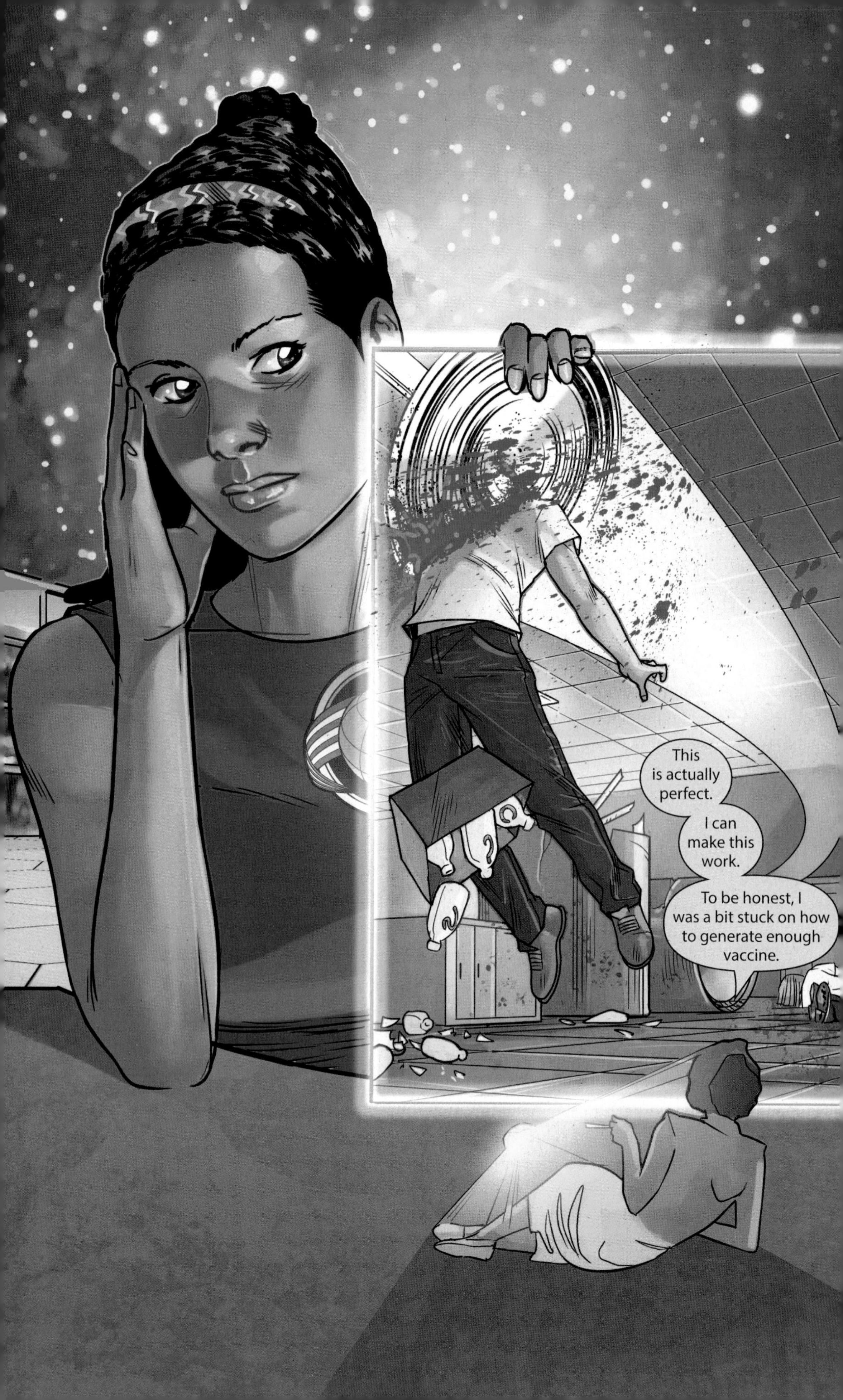
This is actually perfect.
I can make this work.
To be honest, I was a bit stuck on how to generate enough vaccine.

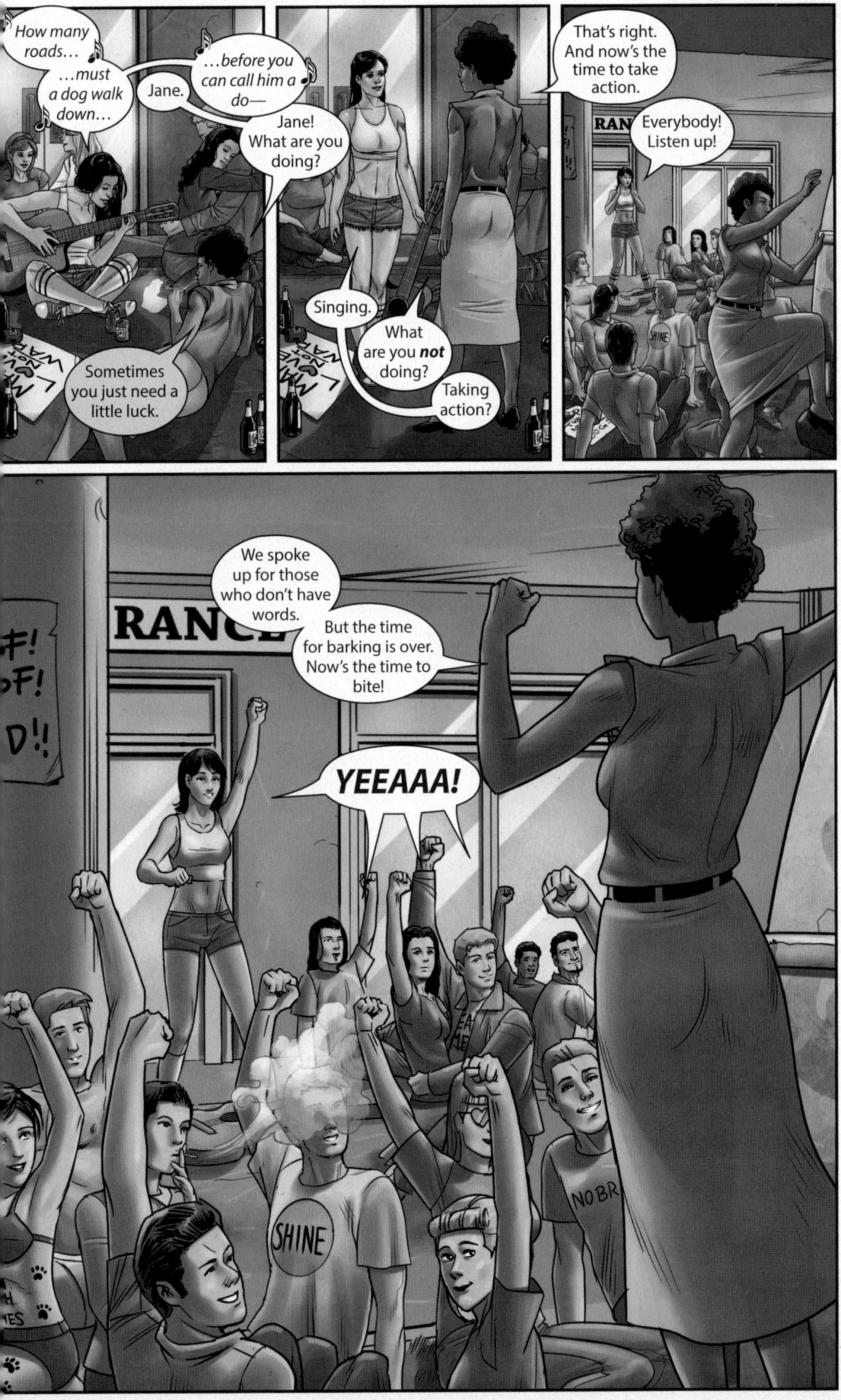
How many roads…
…must a dog walk down…
Jane.
…before you can call him a do—
Jane! What are you doing?
MAKE LOVE NOT WAR
Sometimes you just need a little luck.
Singing.
What are you *not* doing?
Taking action?
That's right. And now's the time to take action.
RAN
Everybody! Listen up!
SHINE
RANCE
We spoke up for those who don't have words.
But the time for barking is over. Now's the time to bite!
YEEAAA!
SHINE
NO BR

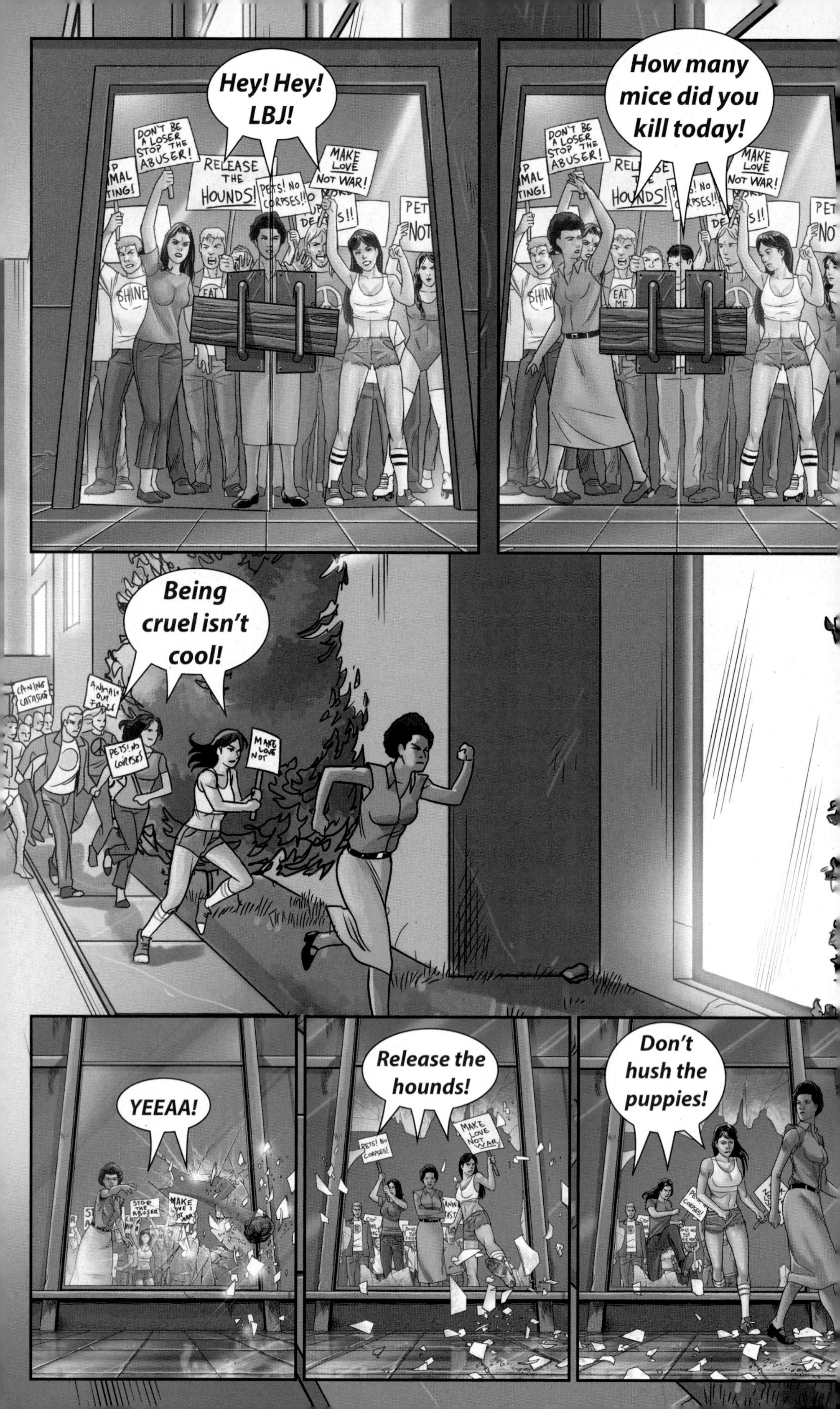
Hey! Hey! LBJ!
DON'T BE A LOSER STOP THE ABUSER!
RELEASE THE HOUNDS!
PETS! NO CORPSES!!
MAKE LOVE NOT WAR!
How many mice did you kill today!
Being cruel isn't cool!
YEEAA!
Release the hounds!
Don't hush the puppies!

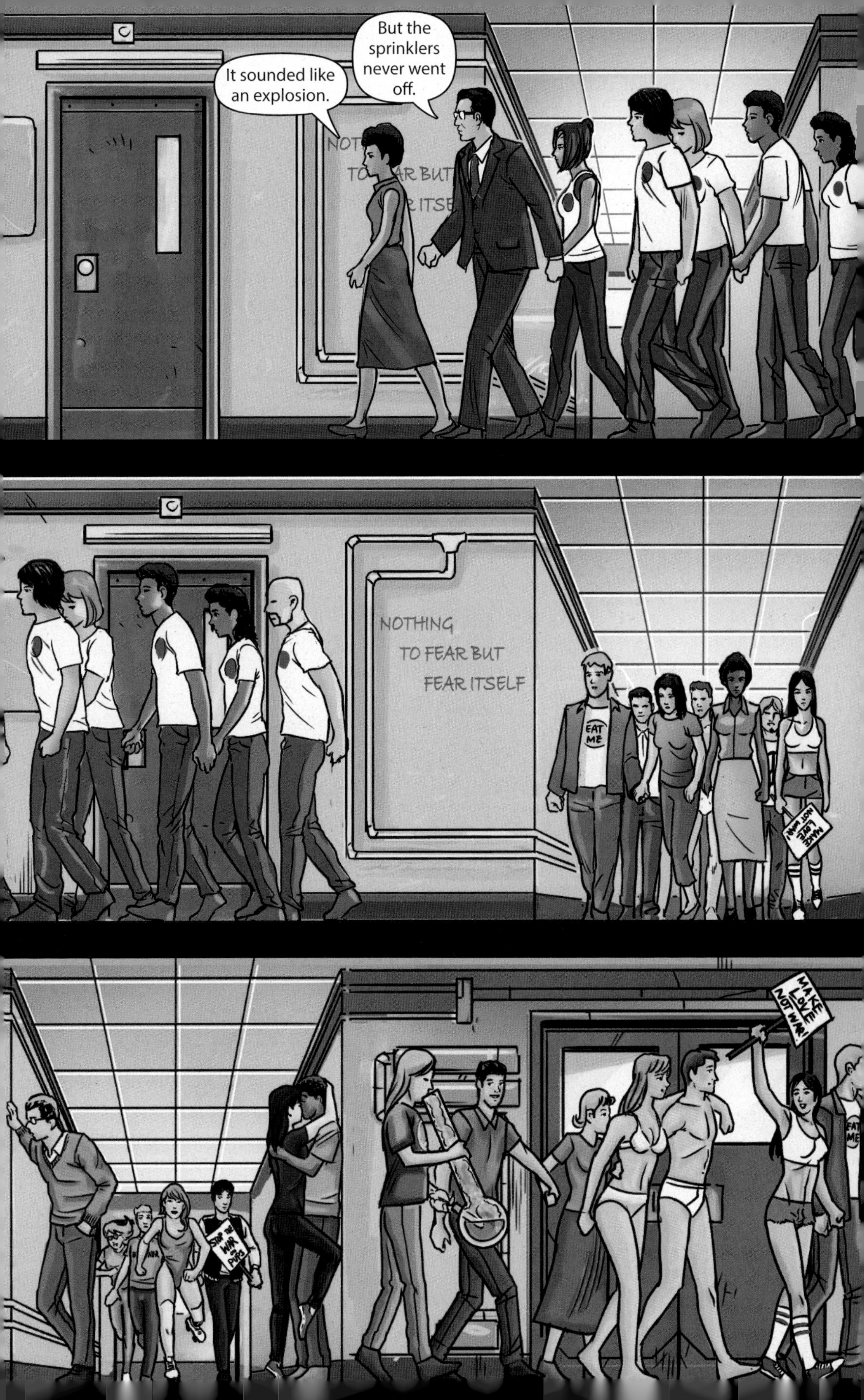
It sounded like an explosion.
But the sprinklers never went off.
NOTHING TO FEAR BUT FEAR ITSELF
EAT ME
MAKE LOVE NOT WAR!
MAKE LOVE NOT WAR!

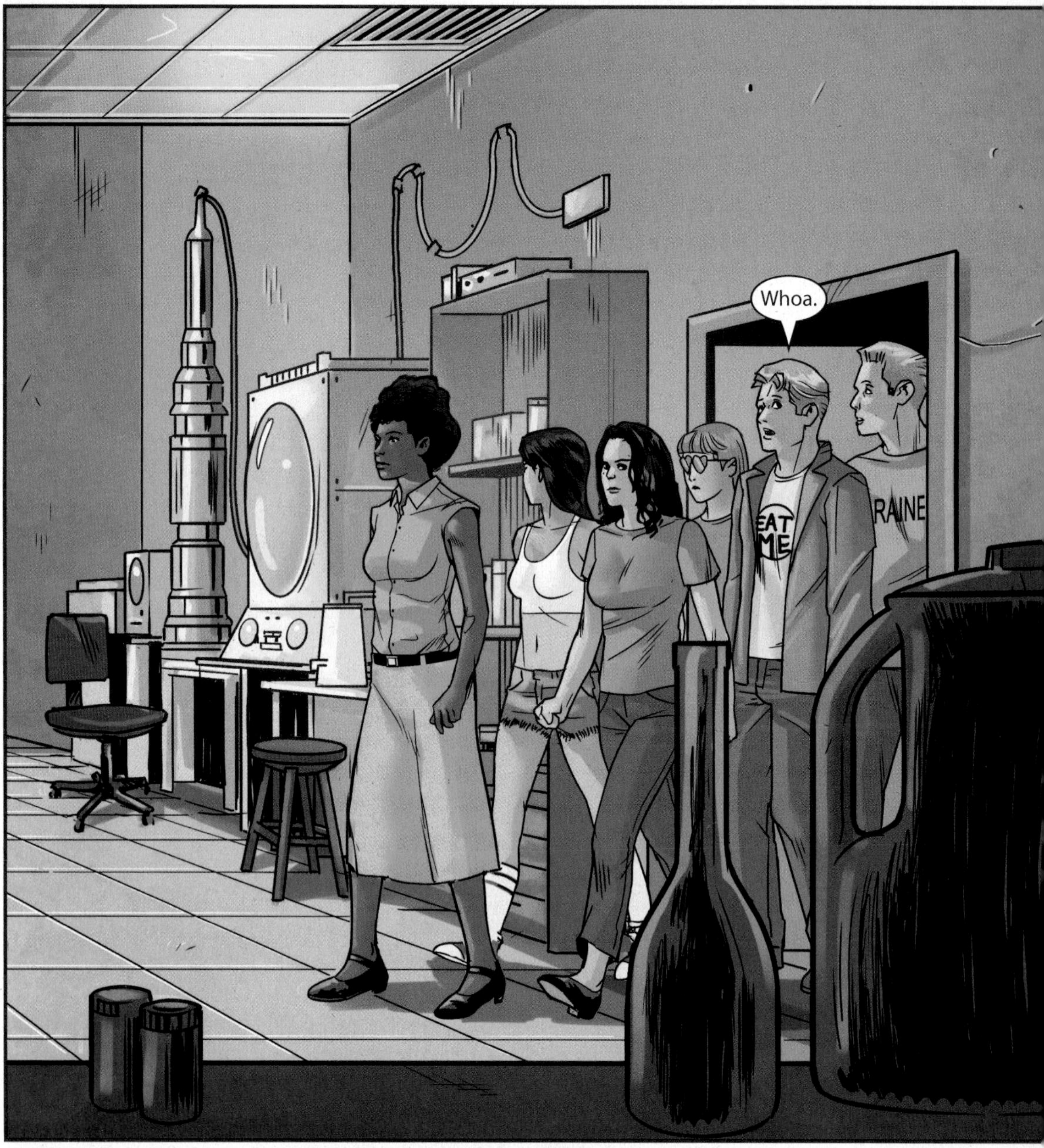
Whoa.
EAT ME
RAINE

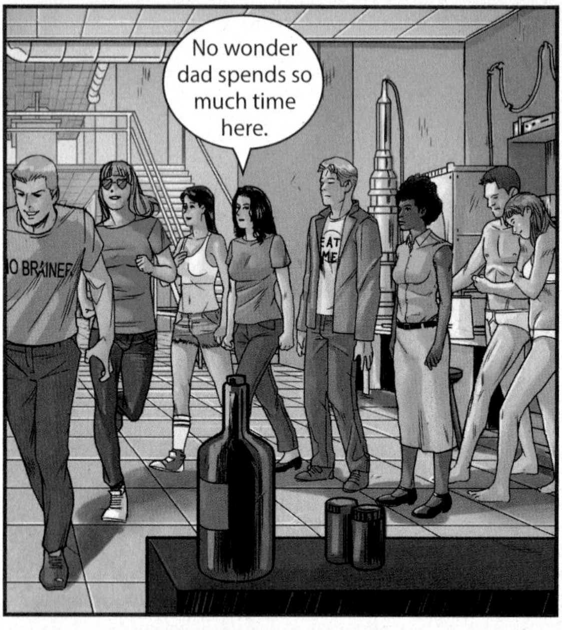
No wonder dad spends so much time here.
NO BRAINER
EAT ME

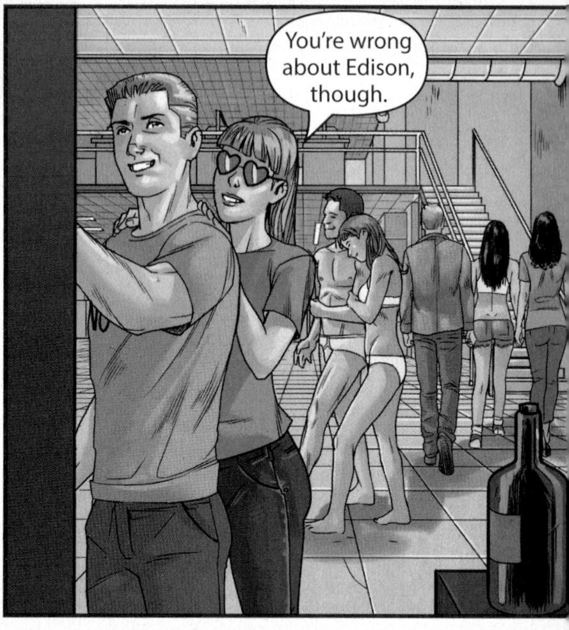
You're wrong about Edison, though.

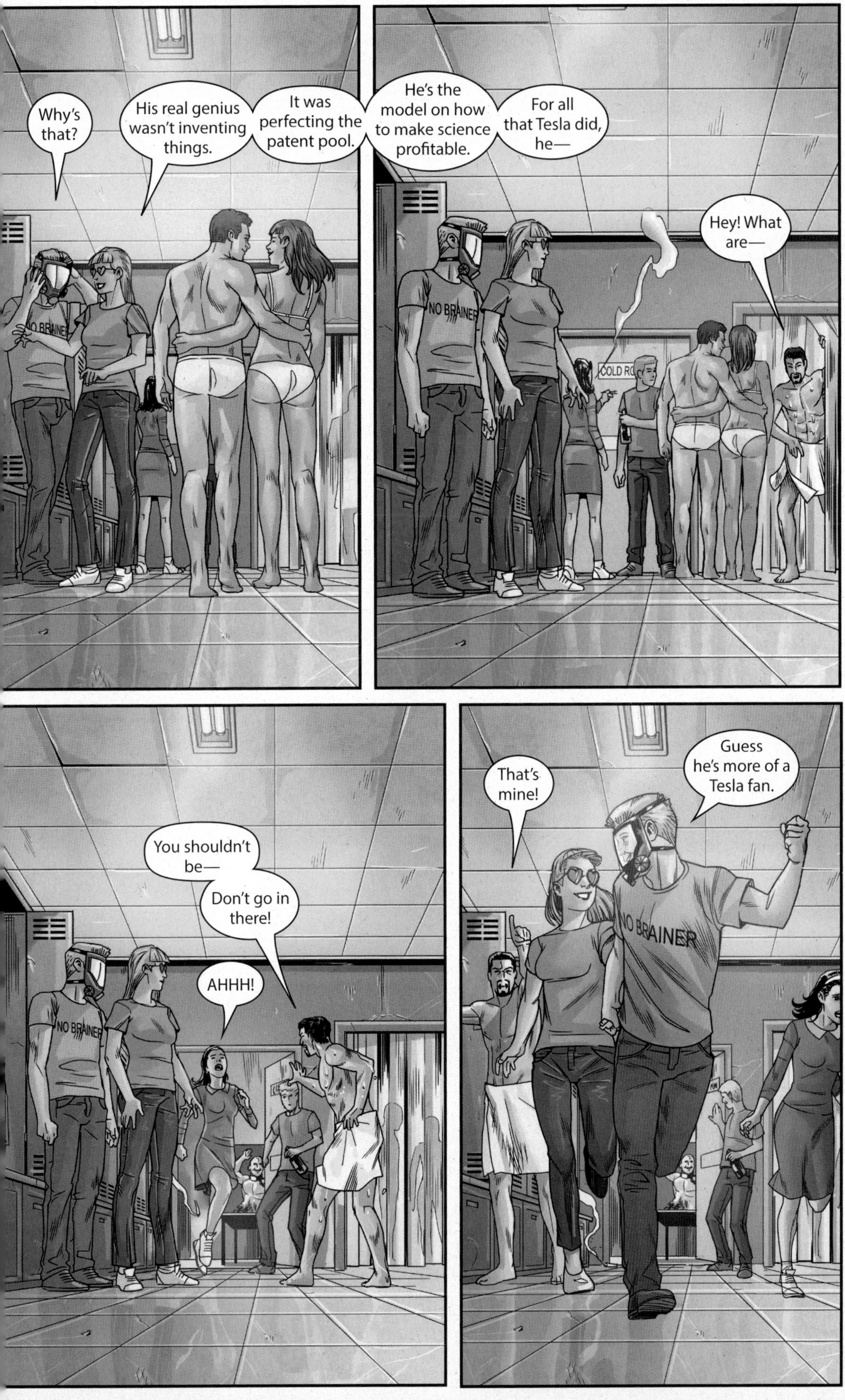
Why's that?
His real genius wasn't inventing things.
It was perfecting the patent pool.
He's the model on how to make science profitable.
For all that Tesla did, he—
Hey! What are—
You shouldn't be—
Don't go in there!
AHHH!
That's mine!
Guess he's more of a Tesla fan.

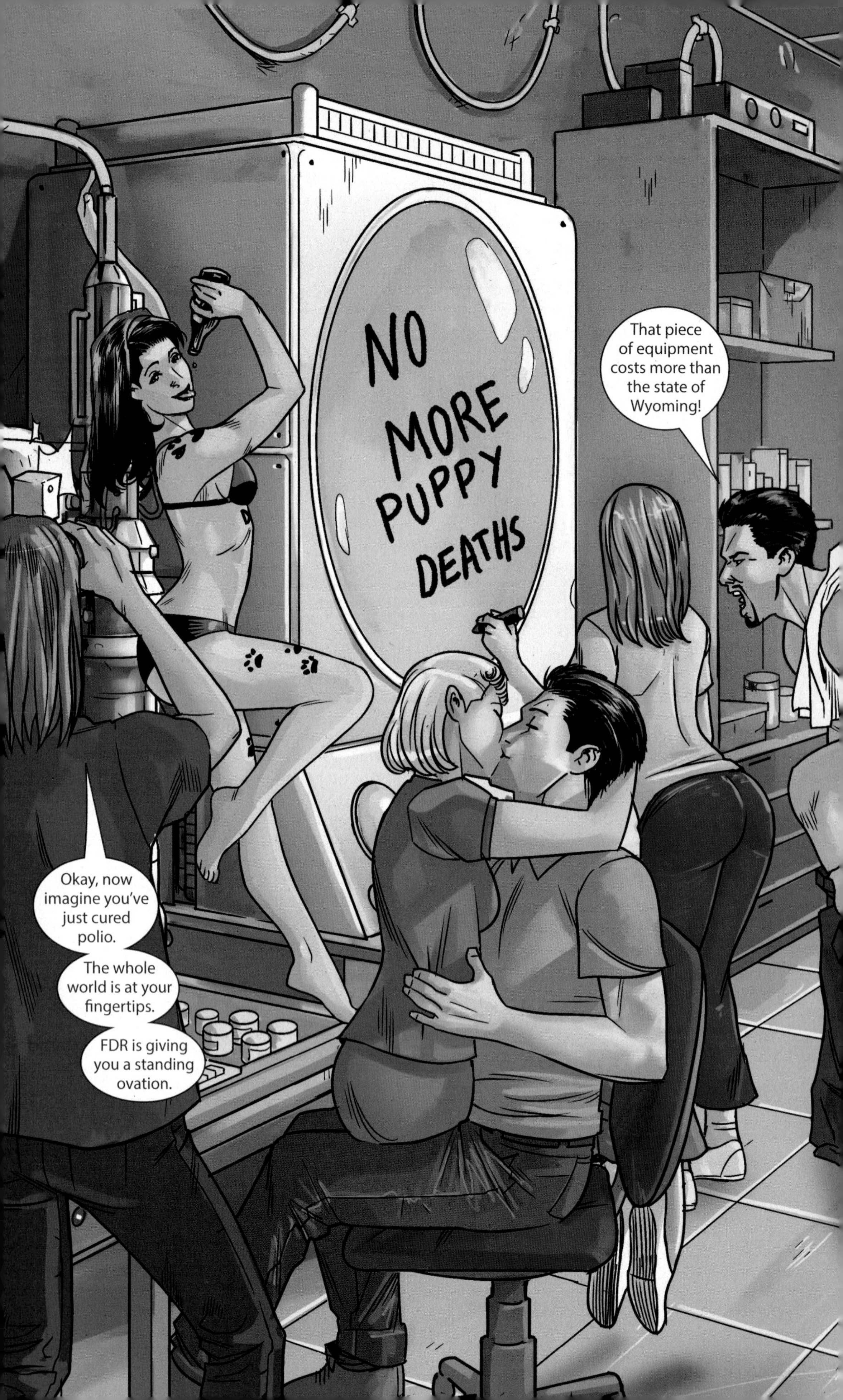
NO MORE PUPPY DEATHS
That piece of equipment costs more than the state of Wyoming!
Okay, now imagine you've just cured polio.
The whole world is at your fingertips.
FDR is giving you a standing ovation.

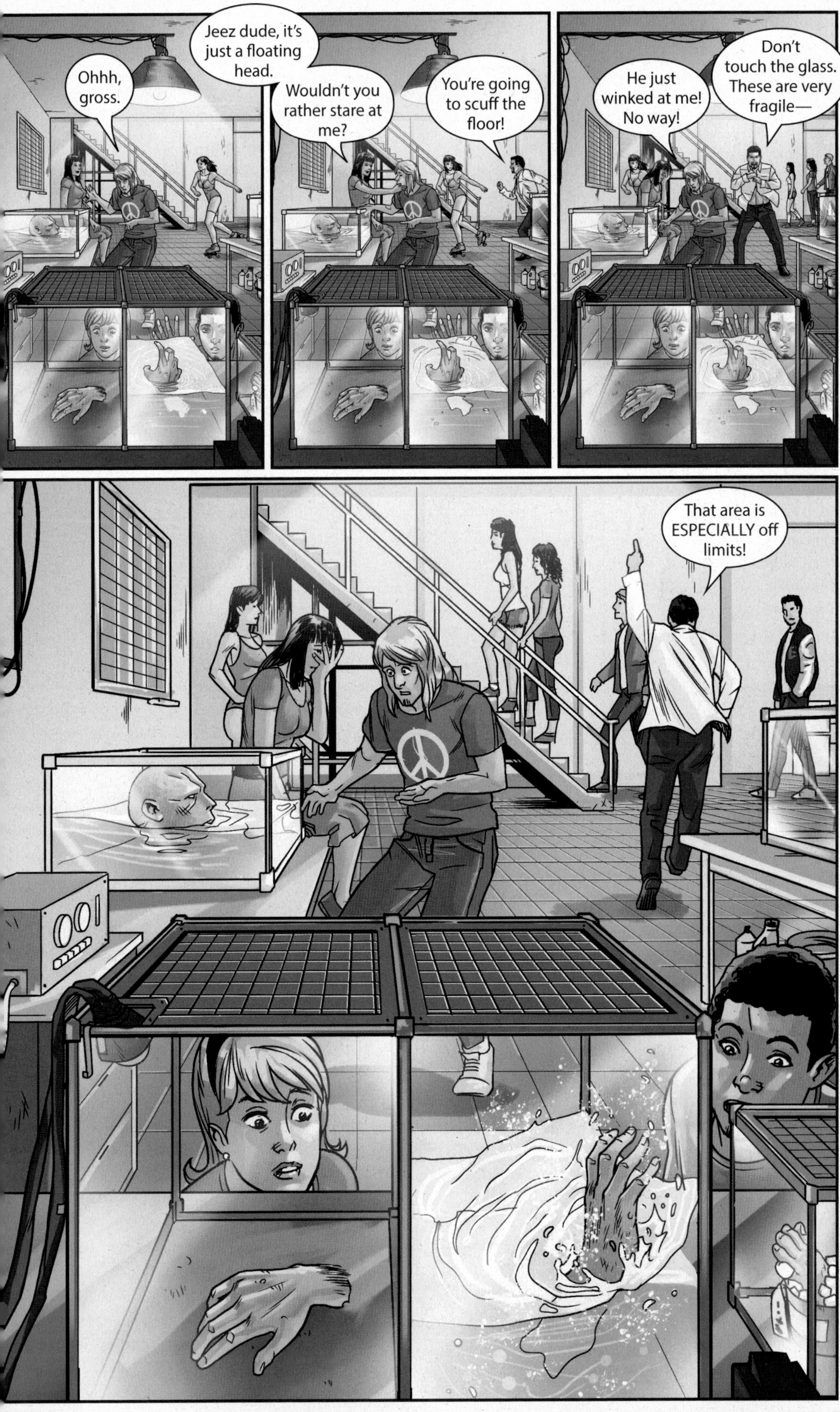

Ohhh, gross.
Jeez dude, it's just a floating head.
Wouldn't you rather stare at me?
You're going to scuff the floor!
He just winked at me! No way!
Don't touch the glass. These are very fragile—
That area is ESPECIALLY off limits!

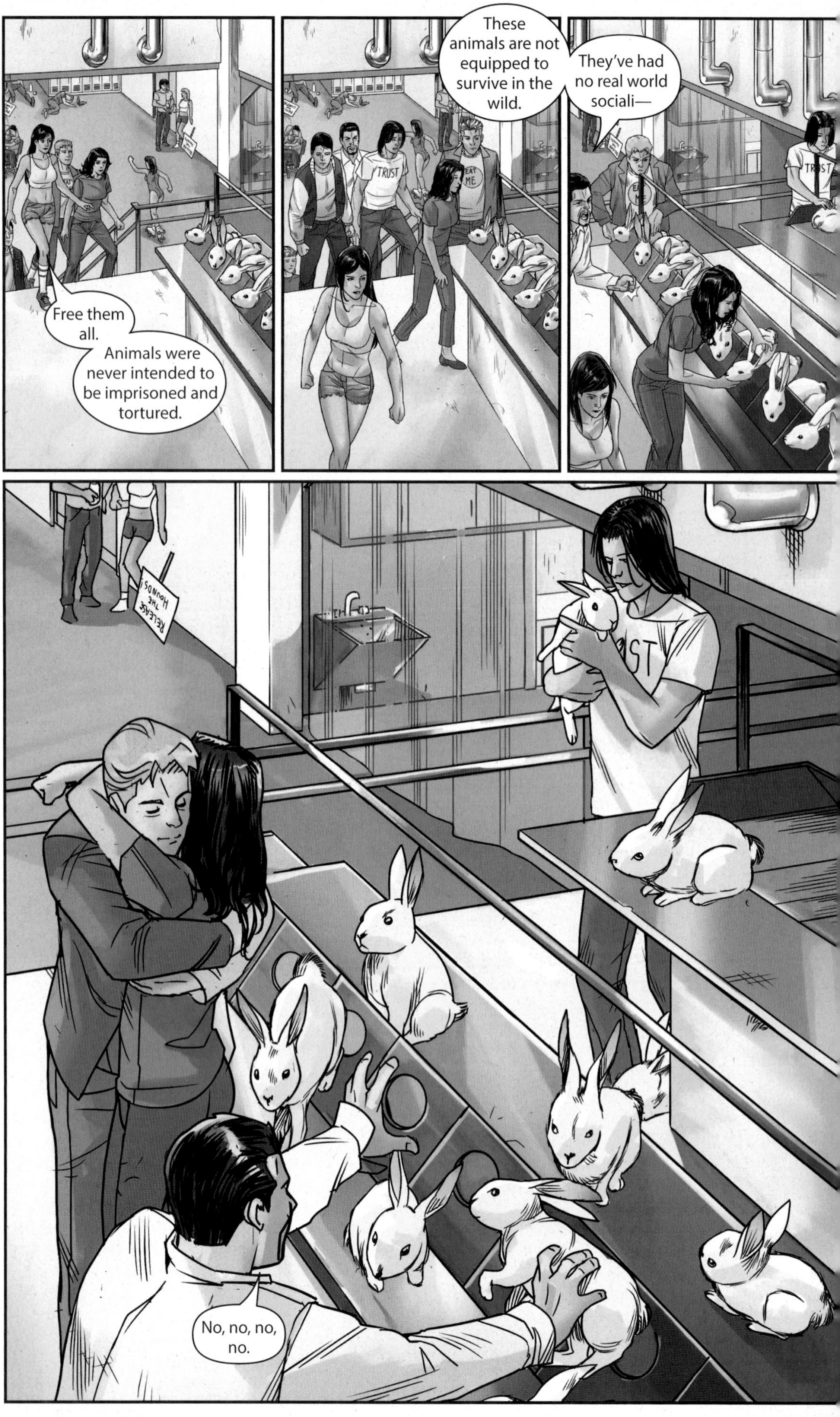
Free them all.
Animals were never intended to be imprisoned and tortured.
These animals are not equipped to survive in the wild.
They've had no real world sociali—
RELEASE THE HOUNDS!
No, no, no, no.

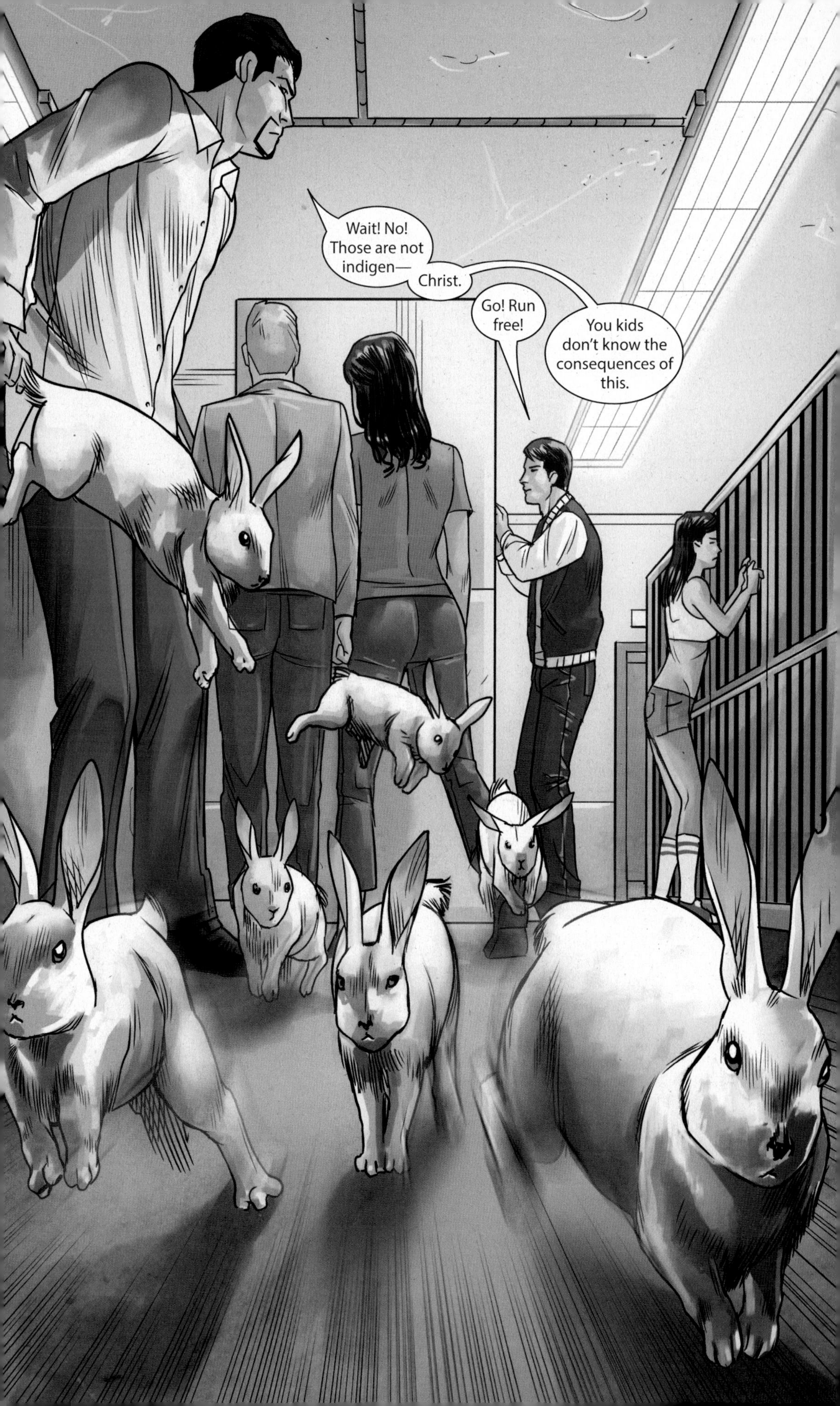
Wait! No! Those are not indigen—
Christ.
Go! Run free!
You kids don't know the consequences of this.

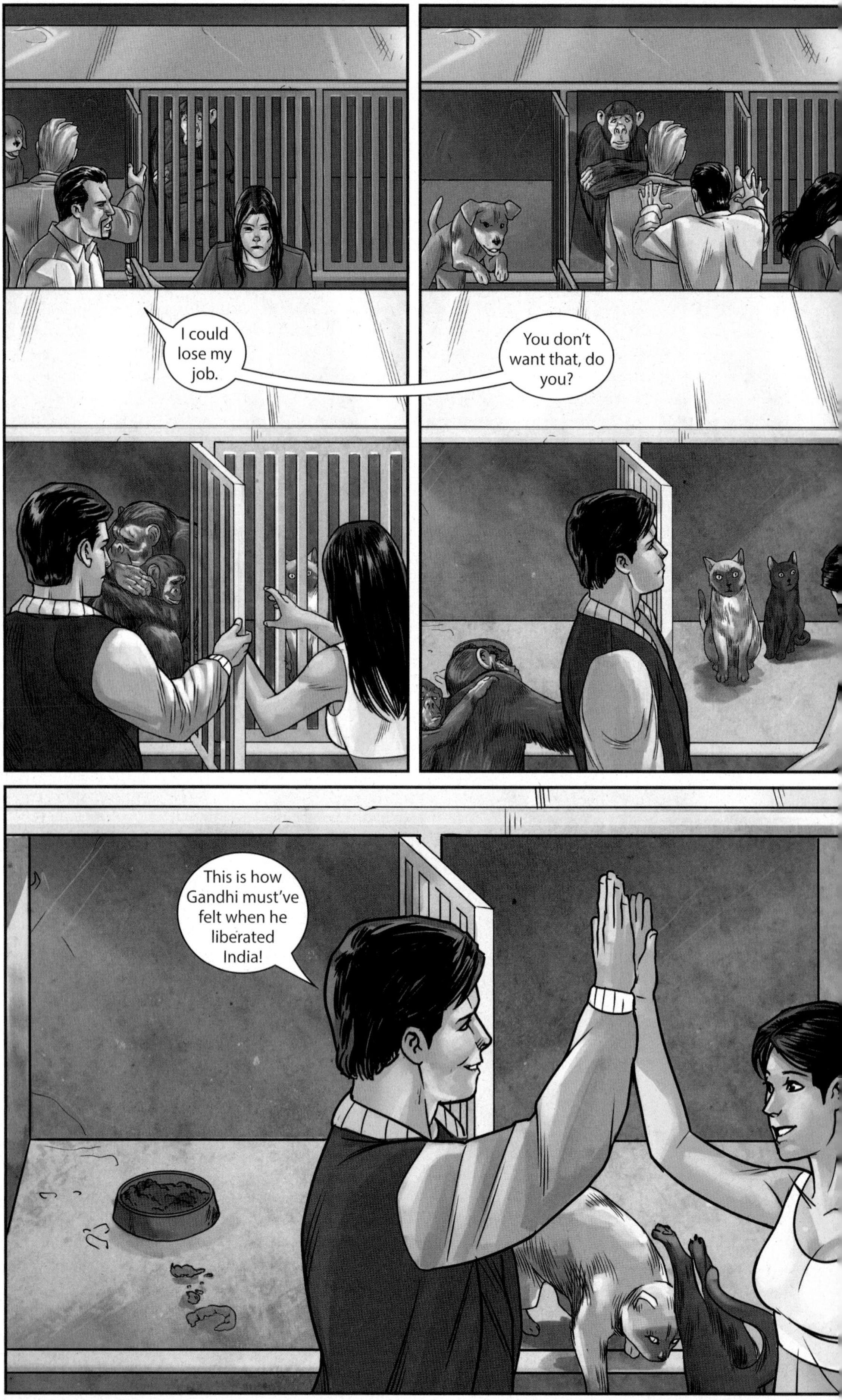
I could lose my job.
You don't want that, do you?
This is how Gandhi must've felt when he liberated India!

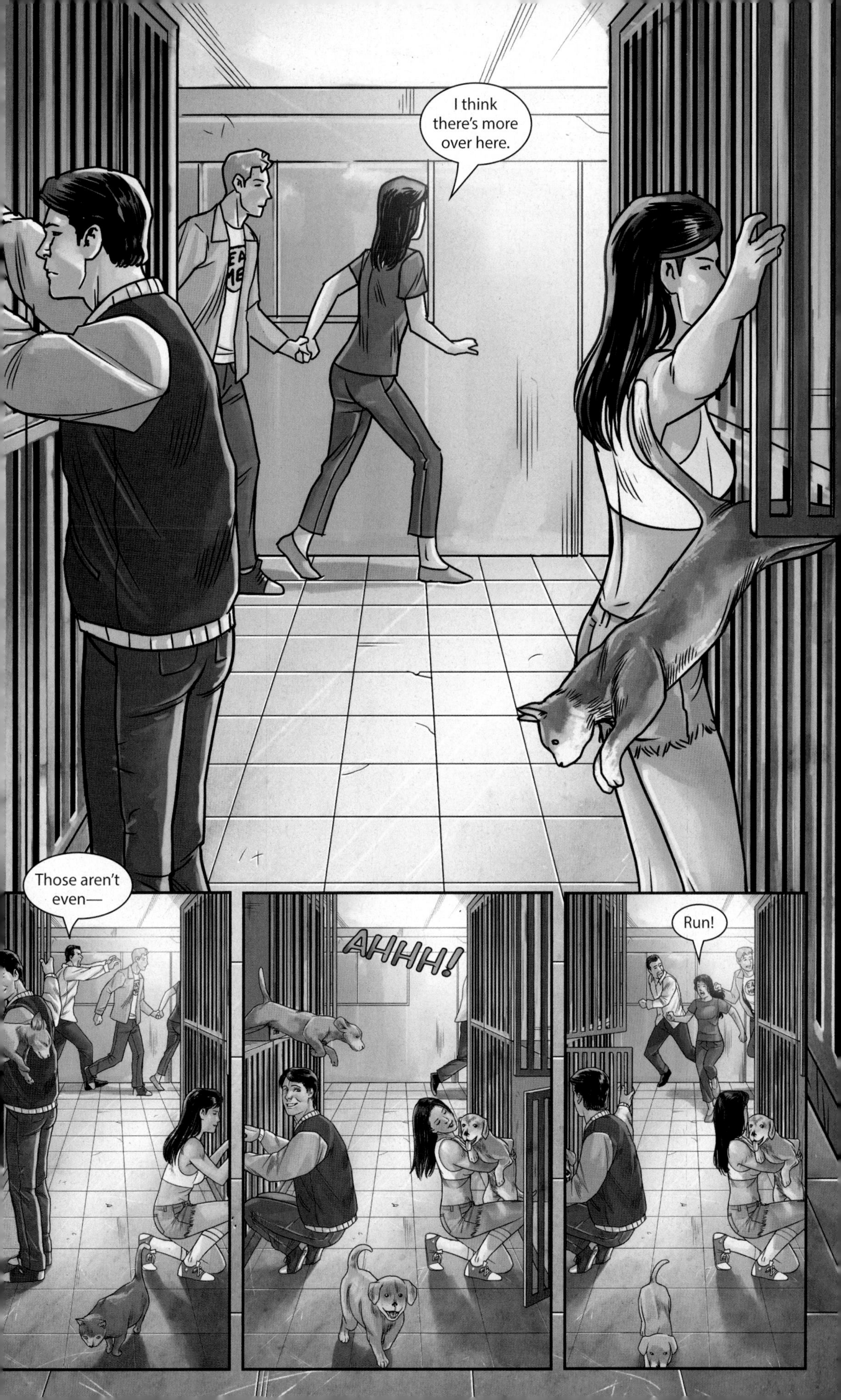
I think there's more over here.
Those aren't even—
AHHH!
Run!

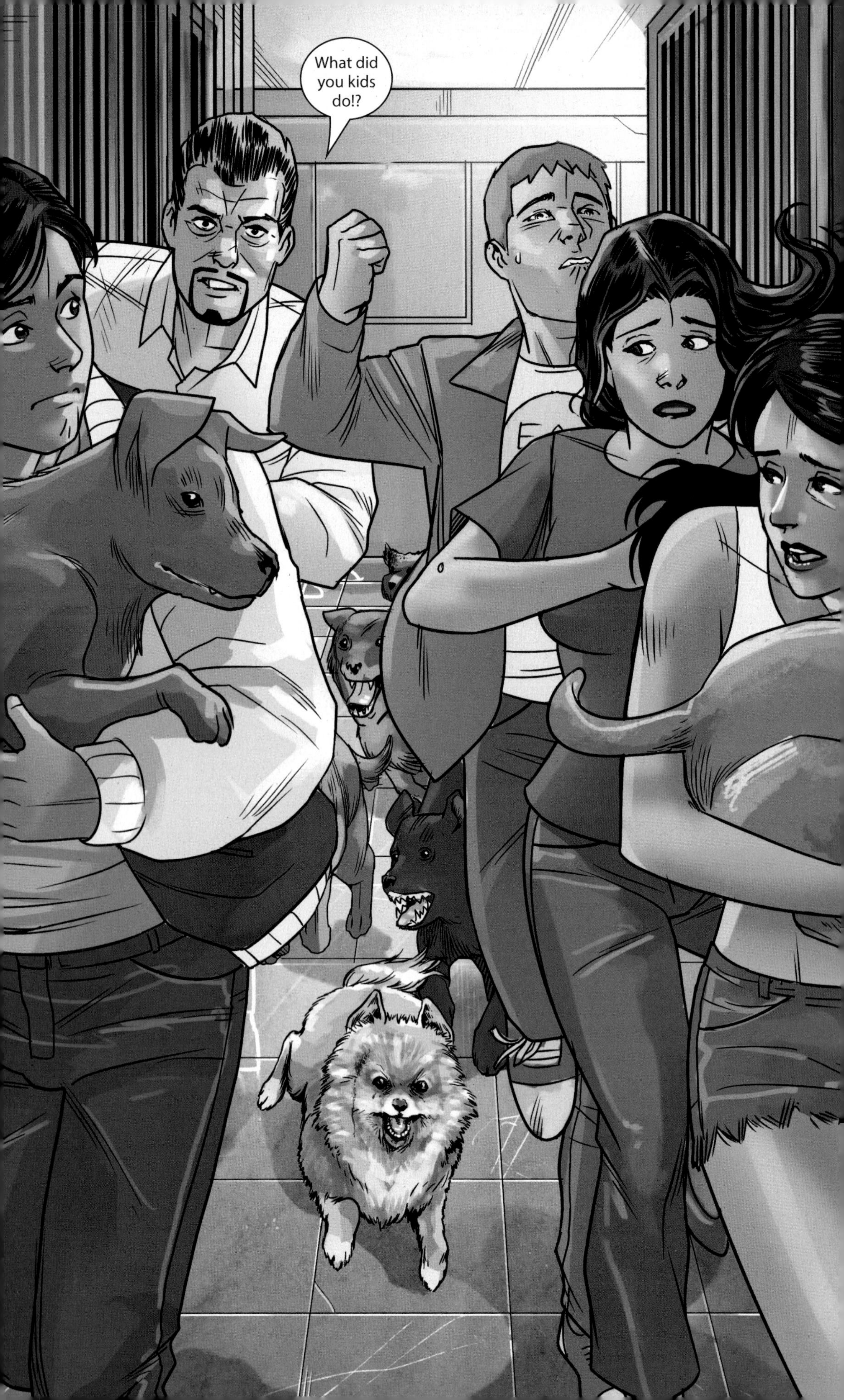
What did you kids do!?

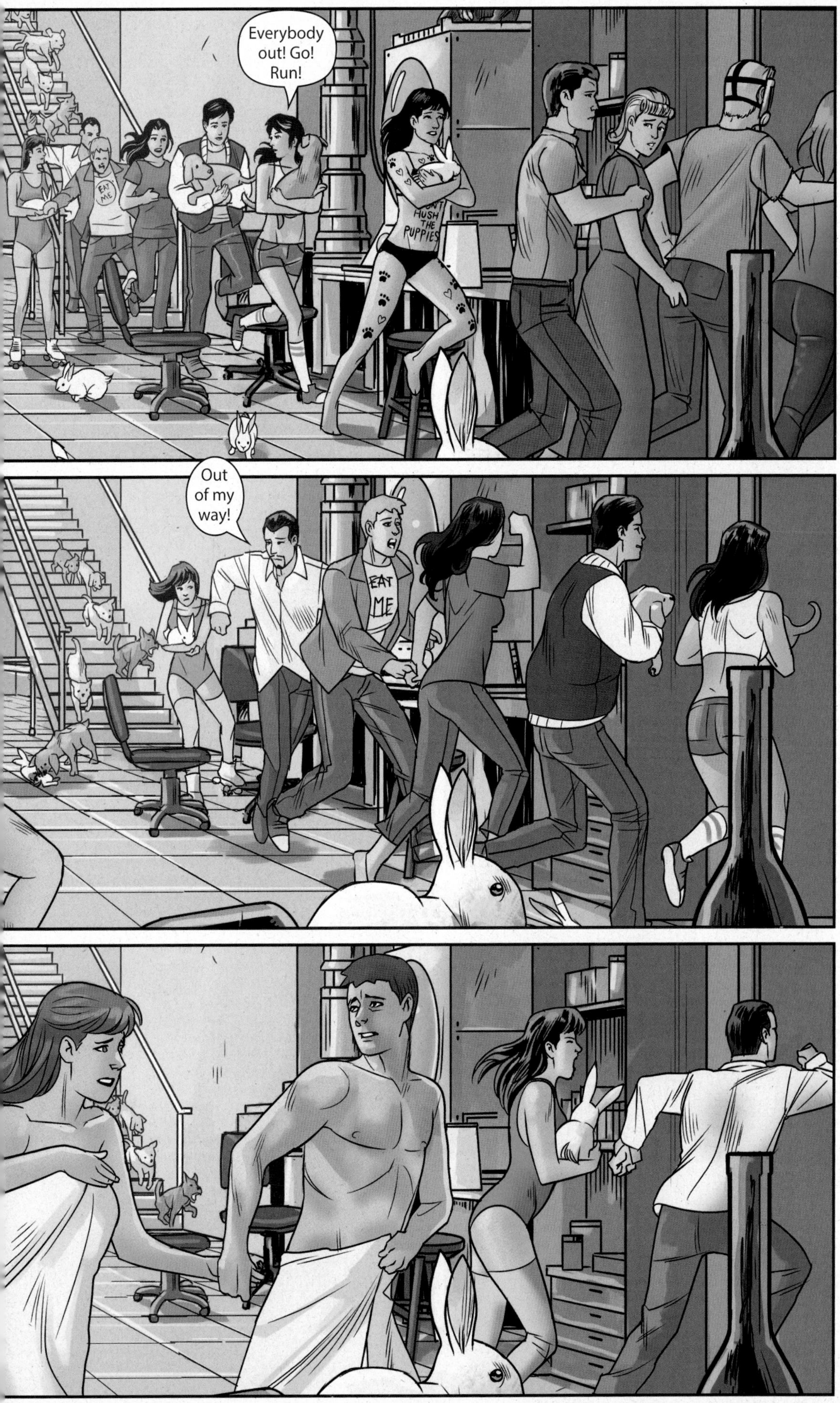
Everybody out! Go! Run!
EAT ME
DON'T HUSH THE PUPPIES
Out of my way!
EAT ME

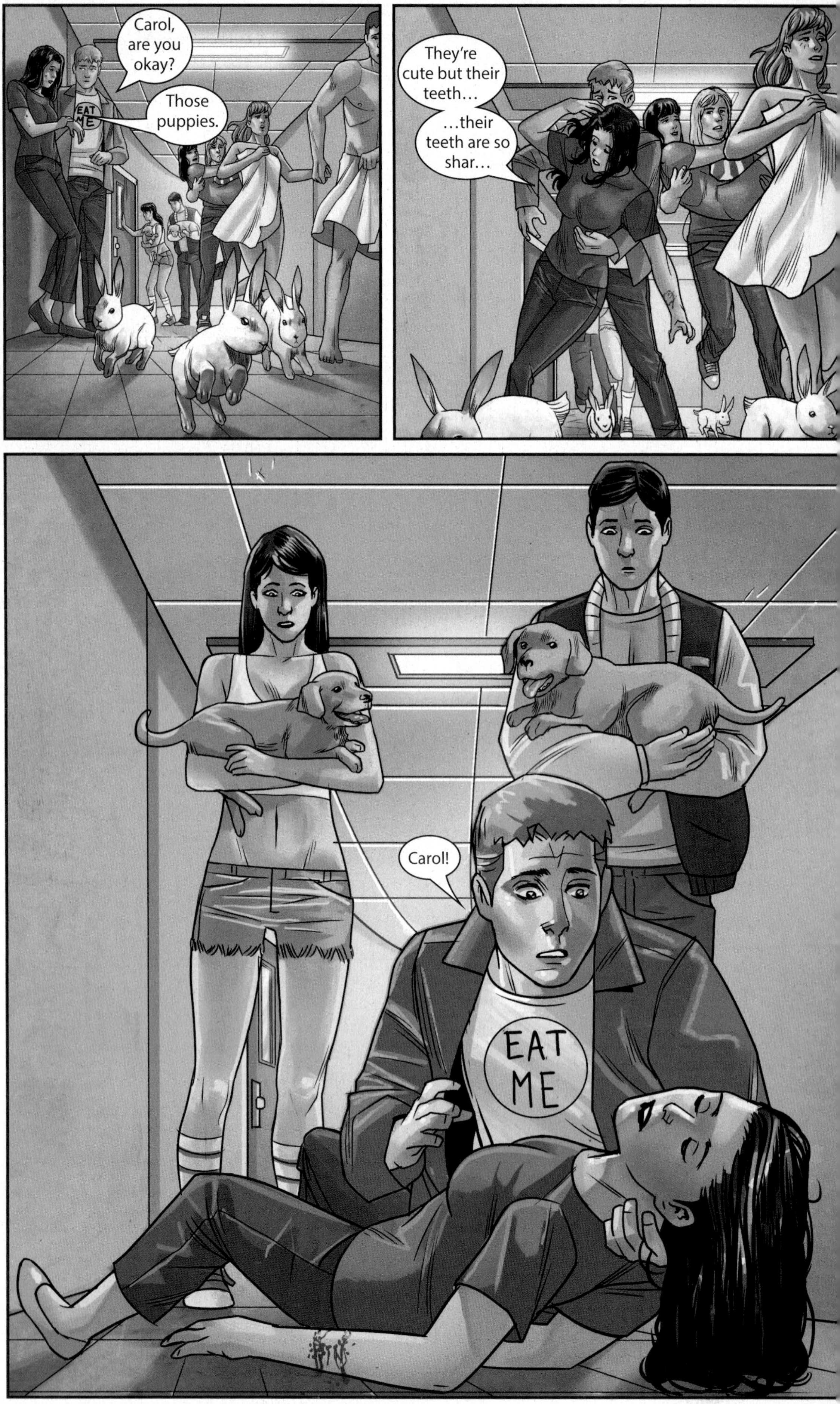
Carol, are you okay?
Those puppies.
They're cute but their teeth…
…their teeth are so shar…
EAT ME
Carol!

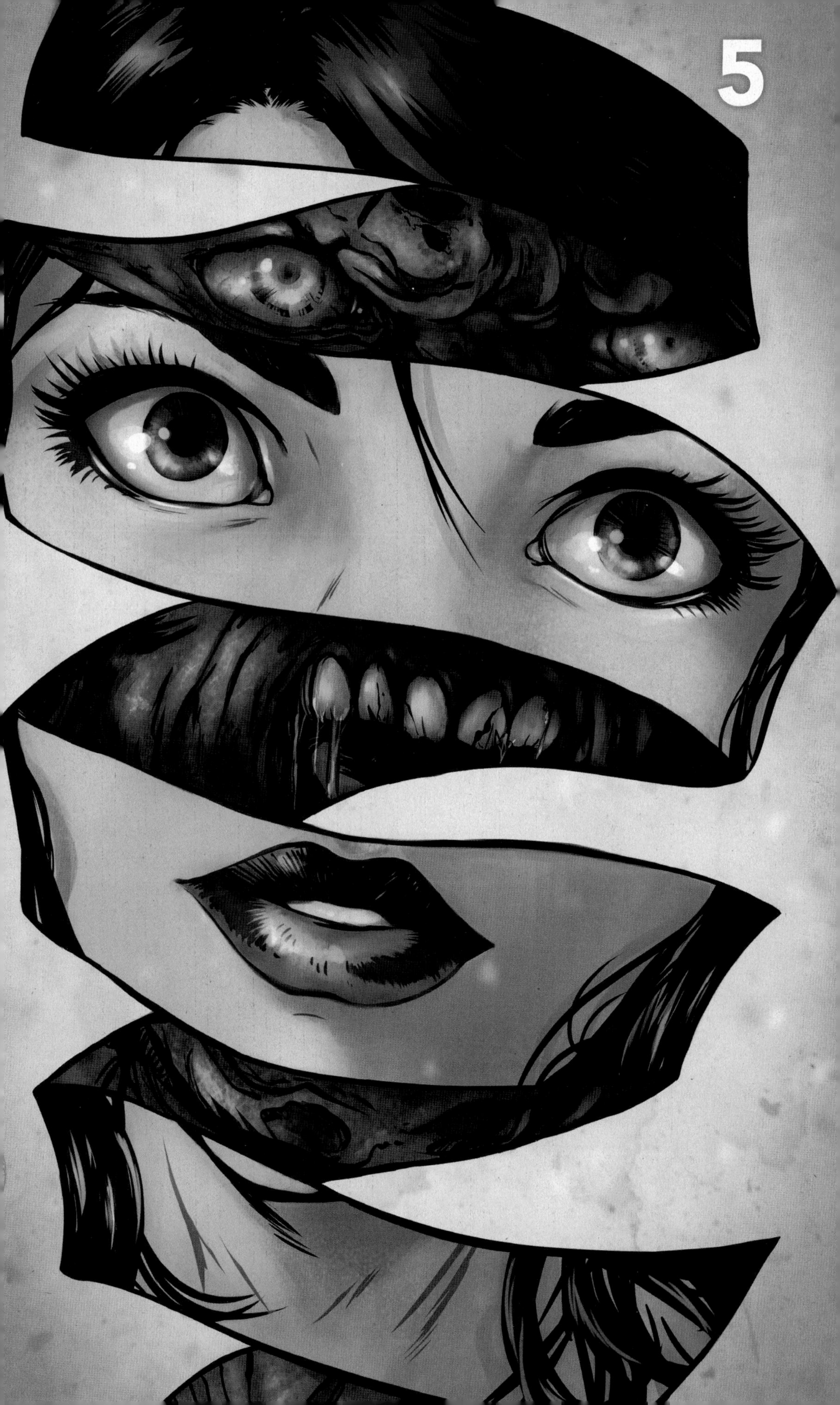
5

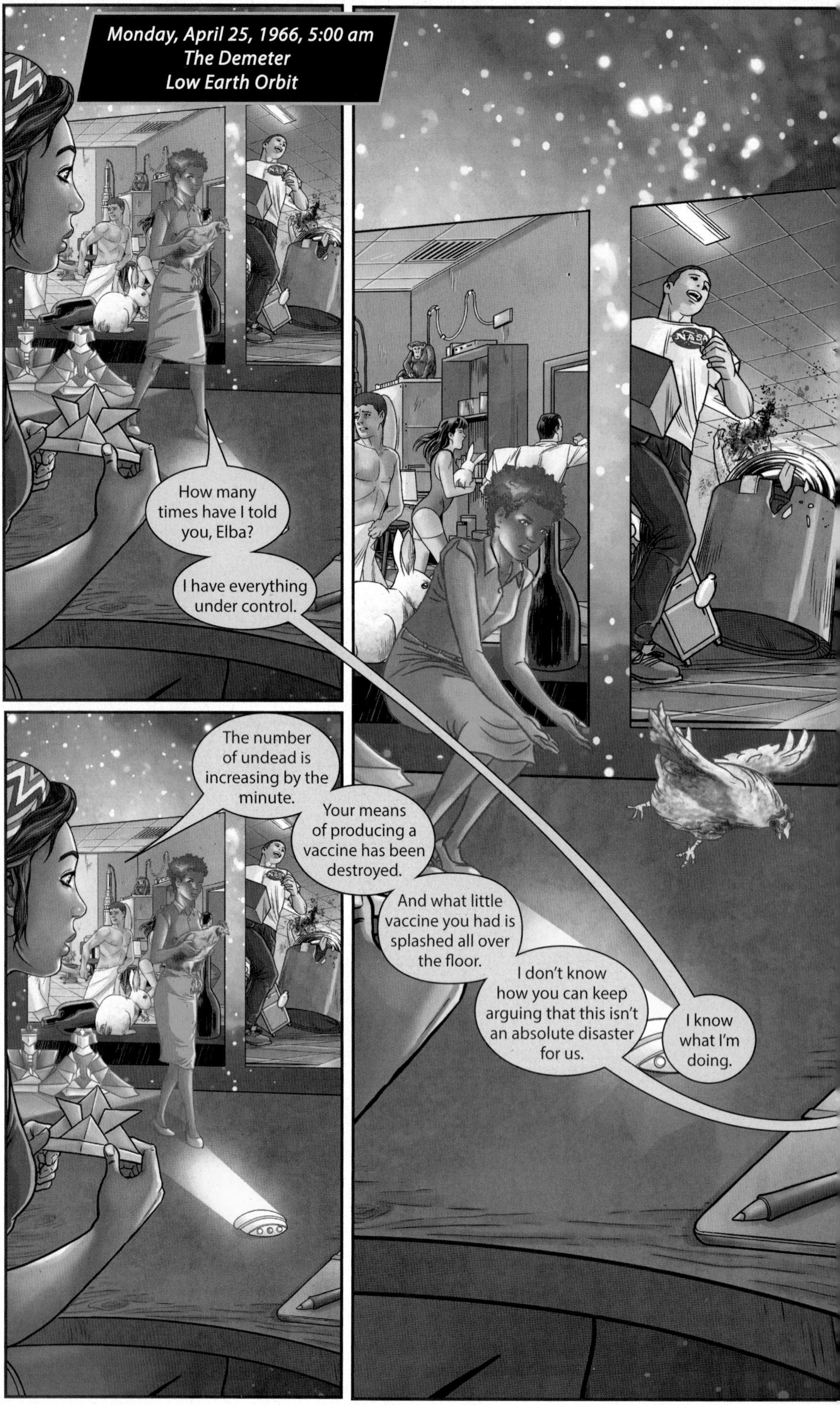

Monday, April 25, 1966, 5:00 am
The Demeter
Low Earth Orbit
How many times have I told you, Elba?
I have everything under control.
The number of undead is increasing by the minute.
Your means of producing a vaccine has been destroyed.
And what little vaccine you had is splashed all over the floor.
I don't know how you can keep arguing that this isn't an absolute disaster for us.
I know what I'm doing.
NASA

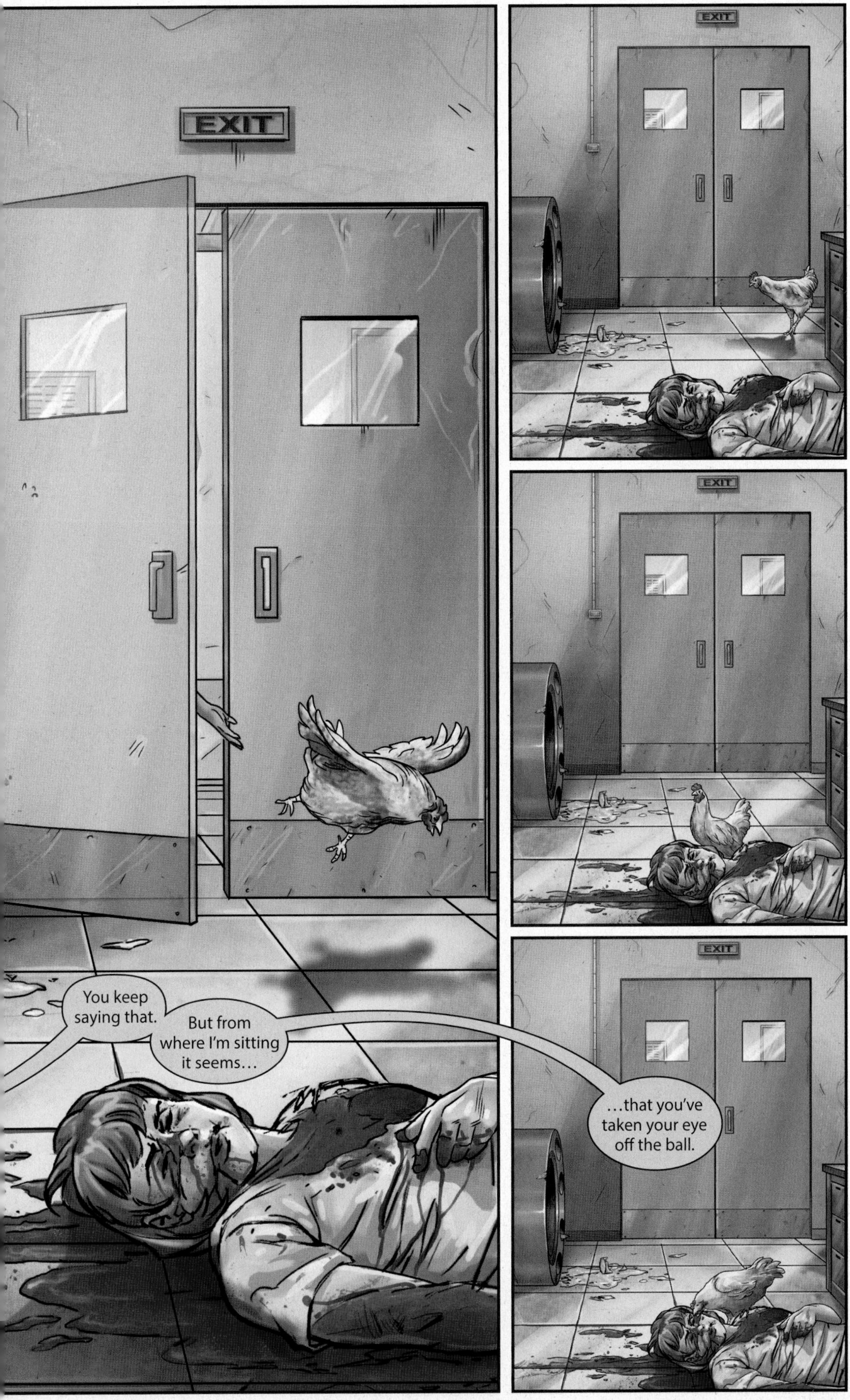
EXIT
EXIT
EXIT
EXIT
You keep saying that.
But from where I'm sitting it seems…
…that you've taken your eye off the ball.

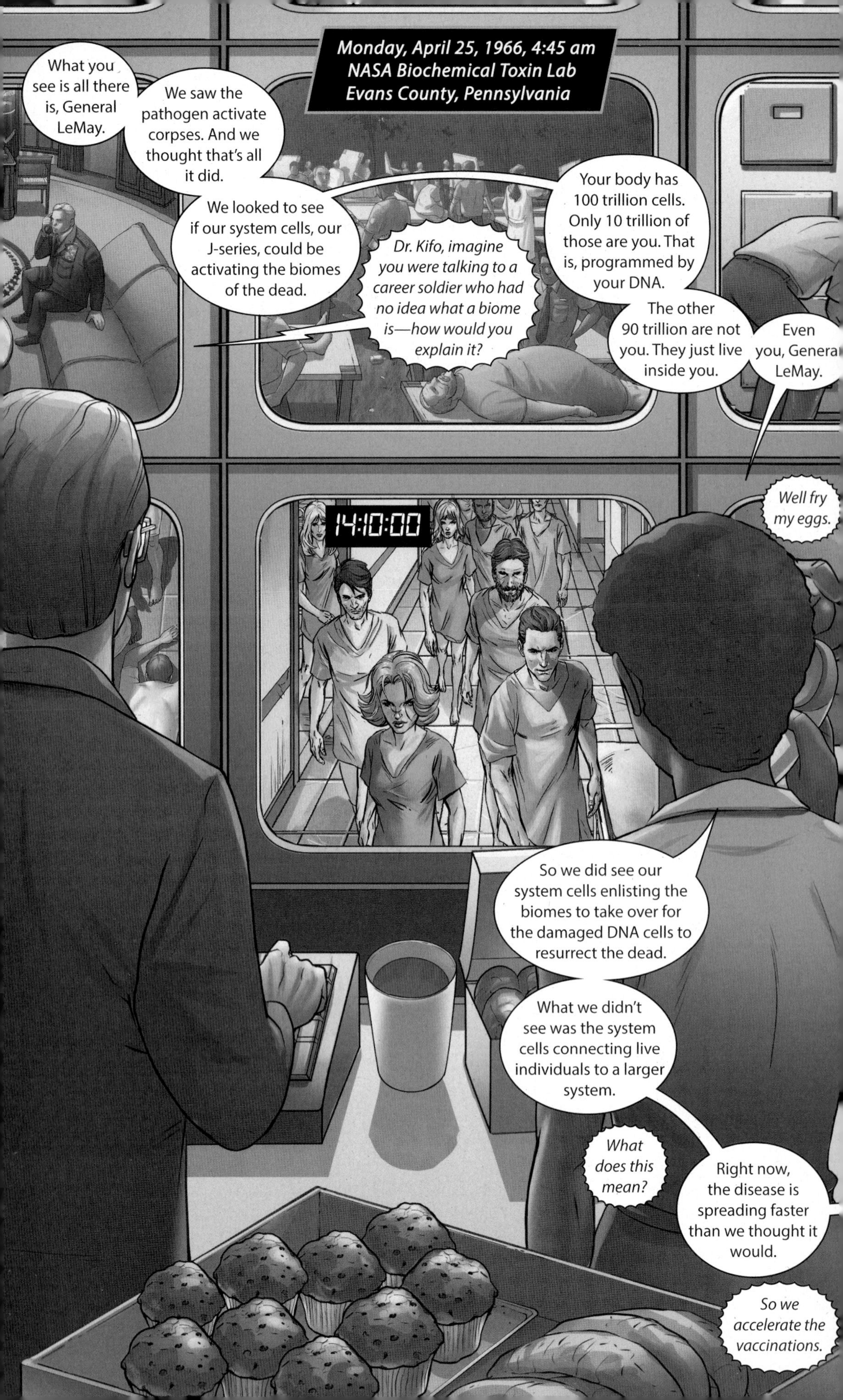
Monday, April 25, 1966, 4:45 am
NASA Biochemical Toxin Lab
Evans County, Pennsylvania
What you see is all there is, General LeMay.
We saw the pathogen activate corpses. And we thought that's all it did.
We looked to see if our system cells, our J-series, could be activating the biomes of the dead.
Dr. Kifo, imagine you were talking to a career soldier who had no idea what a biome is—how would you explain it?
Your body has 100 trillion cells. Only 10 trillion of those are you. That is, programmed by your DNA.
The other 90 trillion are not you. They just live inside you.
Even you, Genera LeMay.
Well fry my eggs.
14:10:00
So we did see our system cells enlisting the biomes to take over for the damaged DNA cells to resurrect the dead.
What we didn't see was the system cells connecting live individuals to a larger system.
What does this mean?
Right now, the disease is spreading faster than we thought it would.
So we accelerate the vaccinations.

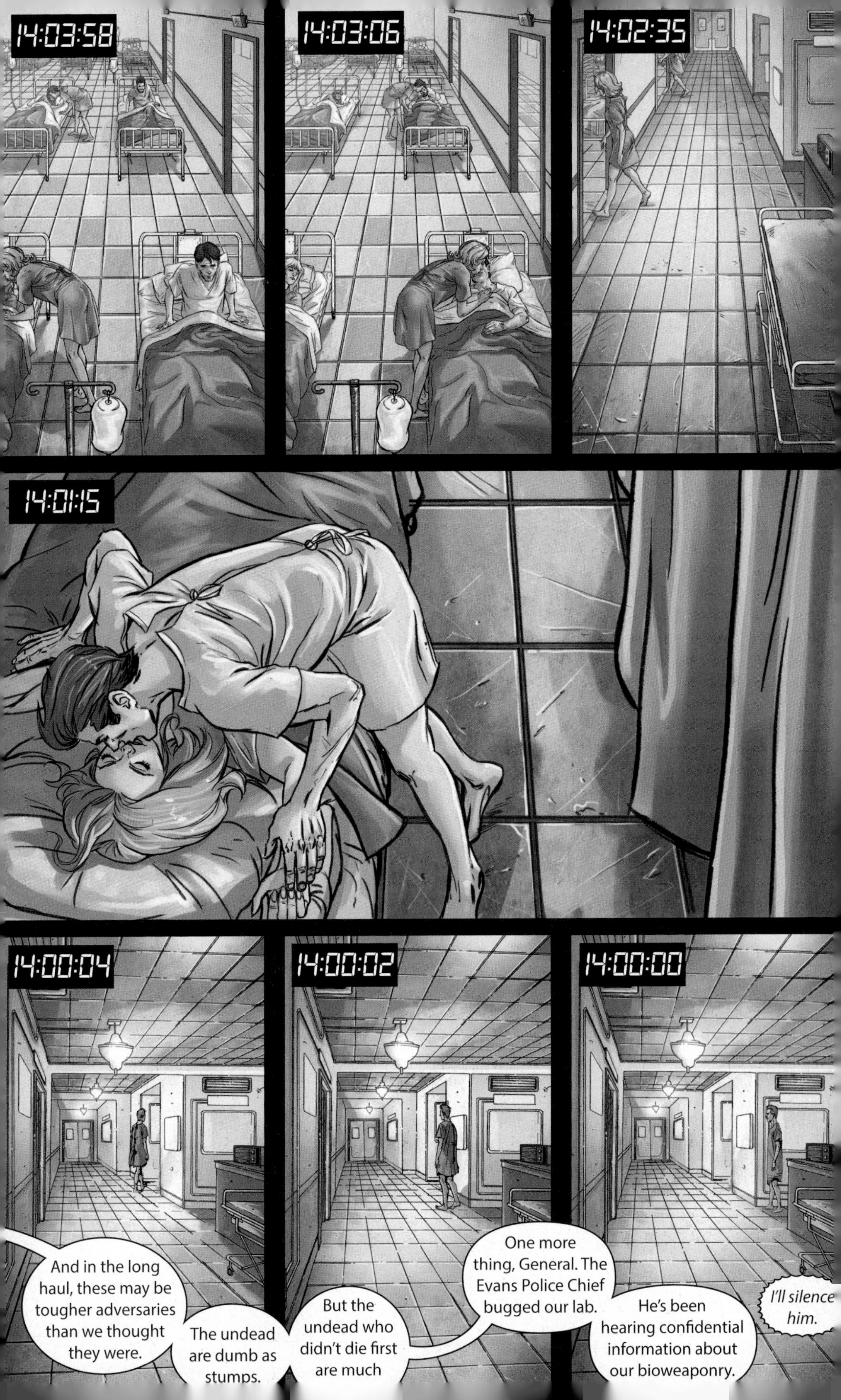

14:03:58
14:03:06
14:02:35
14:01:15
14:00:04
14:00:02
14:00:00
And in the long haul, these may be tougher adversaries than we thought they were.
The undead are dumb as stumps.
But the undead who didn't die first are much
One more thing, General. The Evans Police Chief bugged our lab.
He's been hearing confidential information about our bioweaponry.
I'll silence him.

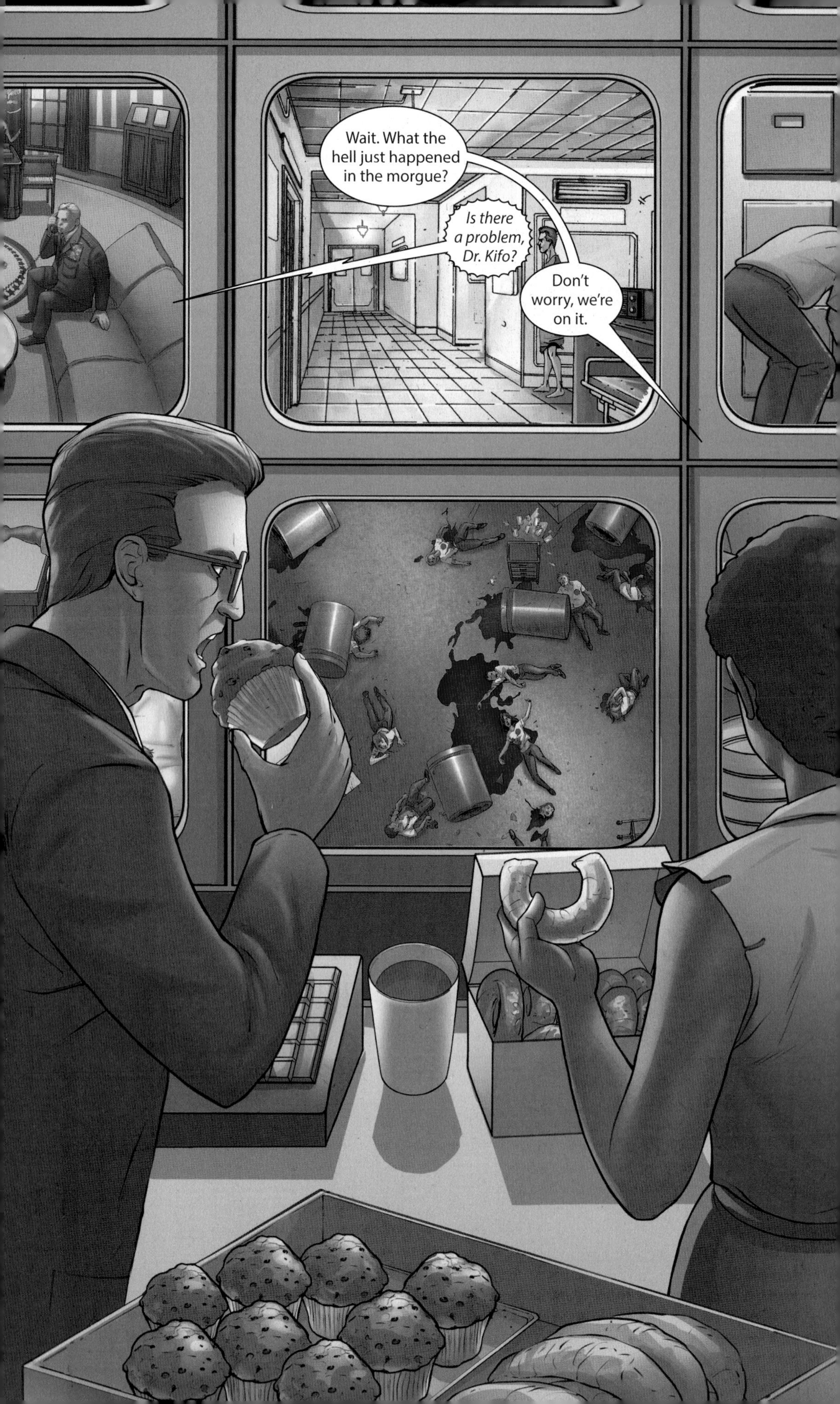
Wait. What the hell just happened in the morgue?
Is there a problem, Dr. Kifo?
Don't worry, we're on it.

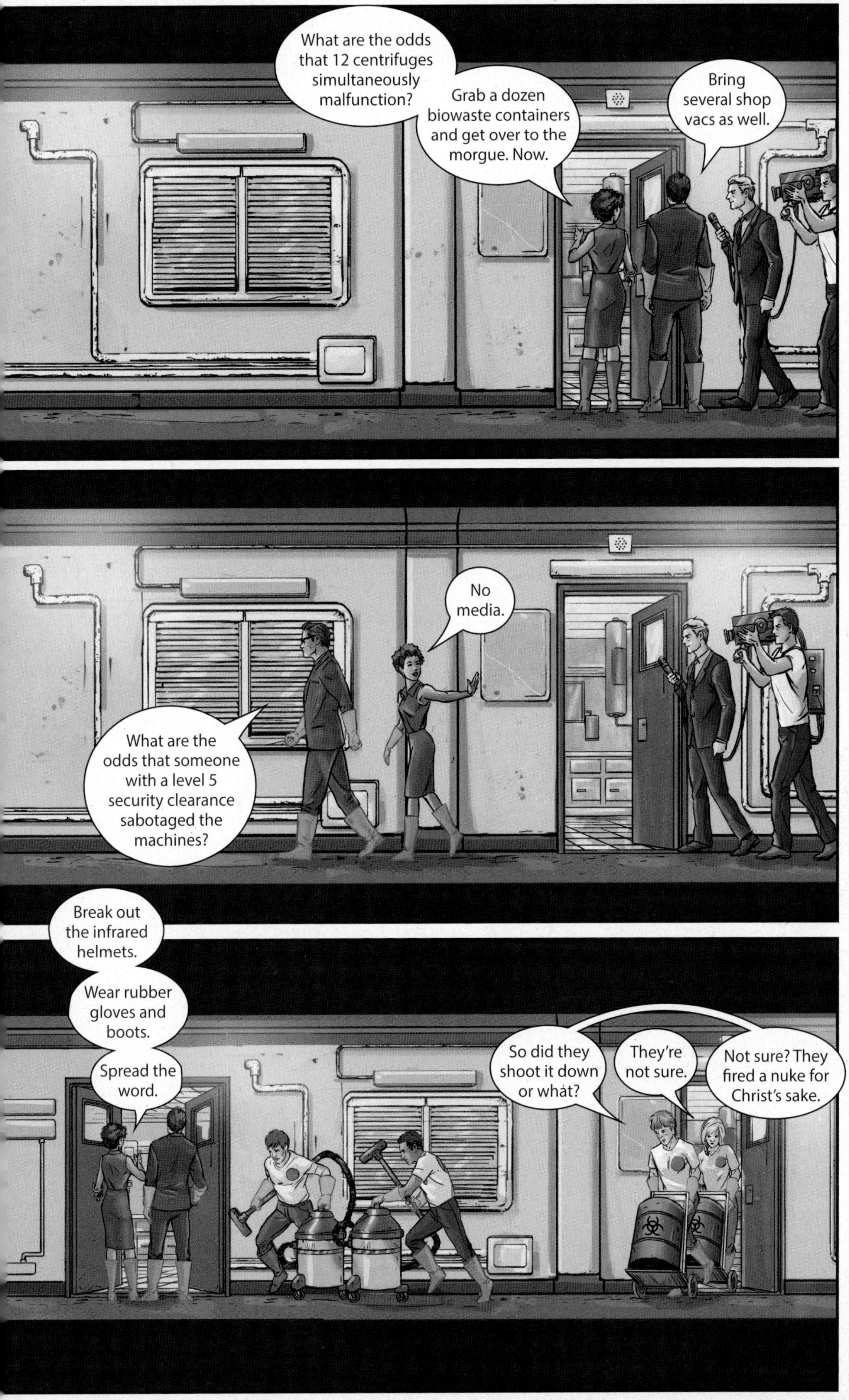
What are the odds that 12 centrifuges simultaneously malfunction?
Grab a dozen biowaste containers and get over to the morgue. Now.
Bring several shop vacs as well.
No media.
What are the odds that someone with a level 5 security clearance sabotaged the machines?
Break out the infrared helmets.
Wear rubber gloves and boots.
Spread the word.
So did they shoot it down or what?
They're not sure.
Not sure? They fired a nuke for Christ's sake.

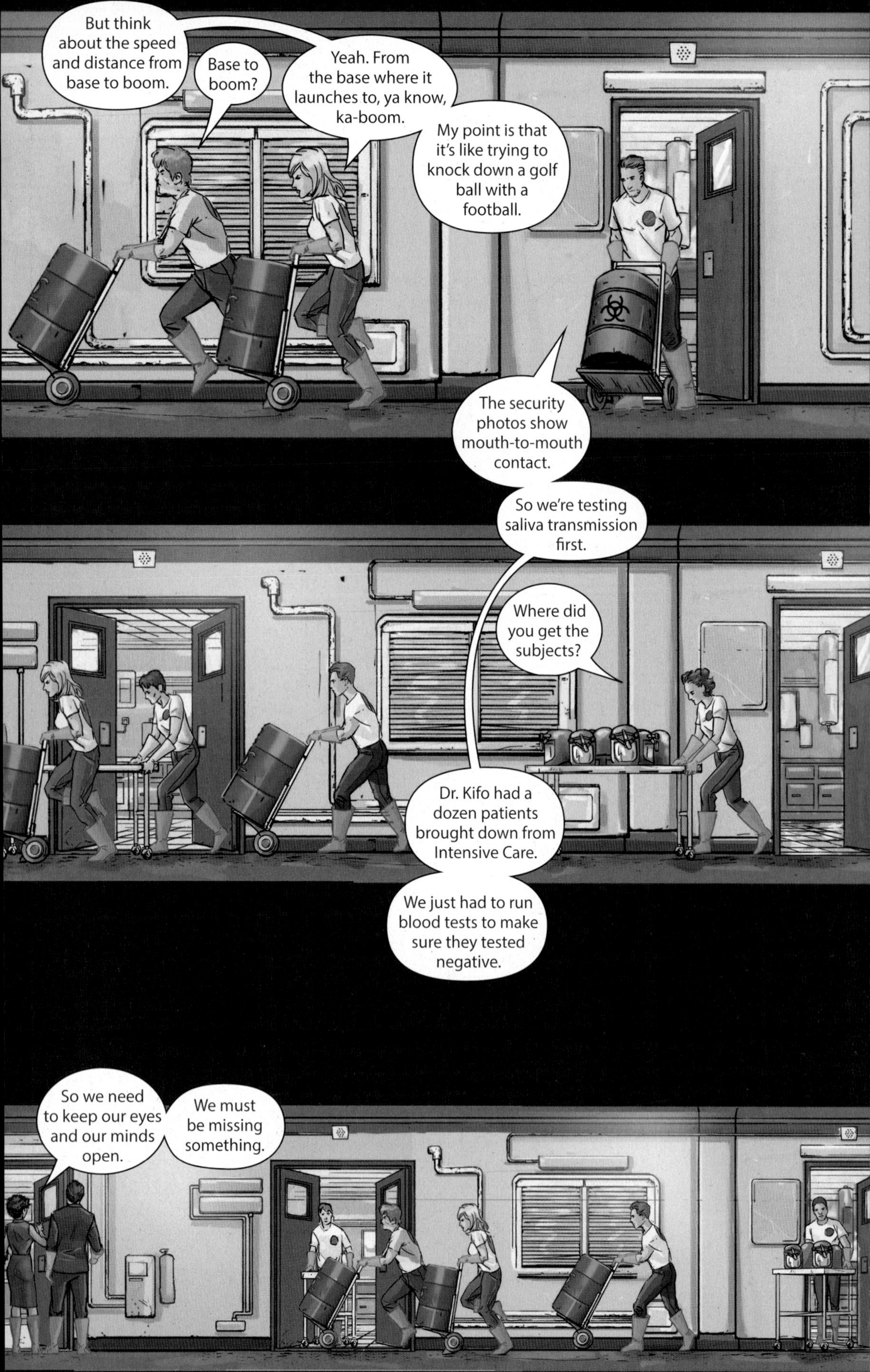
But think about the speed and distance from base to boom.
Base to boom?
Yeah. From the base where it launches to, ya know, ka-boom.
My point is that it's like trying to knock down a golf ball with a football.
The security photos show mouth-to-mouth contact.
So we're testing saliva transmission first.
Where did you get the subjects?
Dr. Kifo had a dozen patients brought down from Intensive Care.
We just had to run blood tests to make sure they tested negative.
So we need to keep our eyes and our minds open.
We must be missing something.

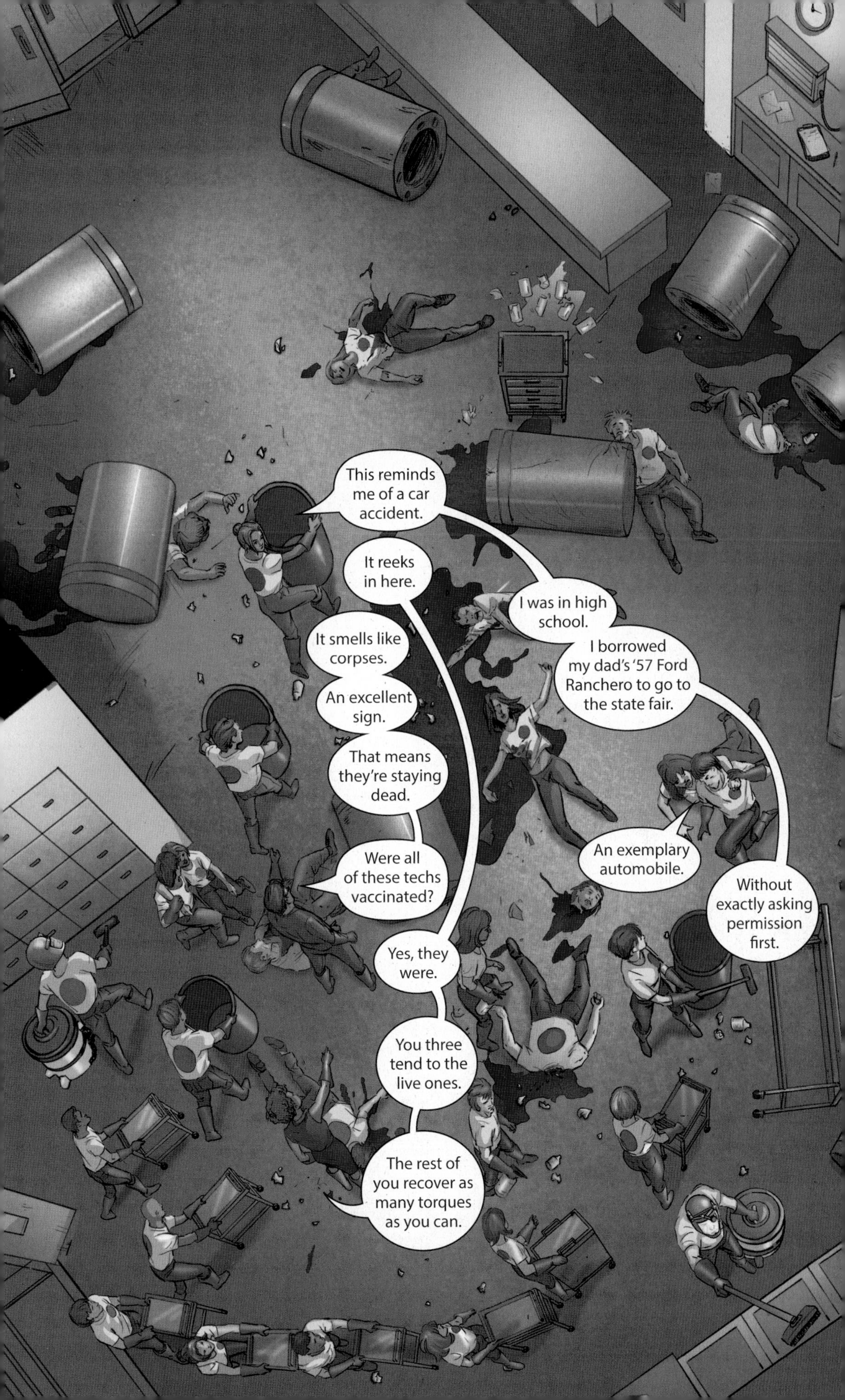
This reminds me of a car accident.
It reeks in here.
It smells like corpses.
An excellent sign.
That means they're staying dead.
I was in high school.
I borrowed my dad's '57 Ford Ranchero to go to the state fair.
An exemplary automobile.
Without exactly asking permission first.
Were all of these techs vaccinated?
Yes, they were.
You three tend to the live ones.
The rest of you recover as many torques as you can.

NATURE'S ZOMBIES

The modern zombie is usually a cadaver or living human infected with a virus that alters the host's behavior. Our zombie fiction may be closer to reality than imagined. From protozoans to wasps, these parasites manipulate their hosts' behaviors for their benefit (and to their hosts' detriment).

Credit: Flickr / Stig Nygaard

TOXOPLASMA GONDII: A mouse finds itself in the cat's territory; it should be wary from the scent of cat urine. But this mouse is not behaving normally: it is less averse, having been infected with a parasitic protozoan called *T. gondii*. The cat easily snatches up the infected prey. The parasite ends up exactly where it wants to be: in the cat's intestinal tract, which is the only place where it's known to reproduce, and it will spread through feline excrement. While *T. gondii* seems to primarily alter behavior in mice, the parasite can infect almost all warm-blooded animals. An estimated 30 to 50 percent of the global human population may be chronically infected with *T. gondii* after exposure. While infection in humans is mostly asymptomatic, some studies suggest that the parasite may be associated with a number of neurological disorders in humans (e.g., schizophrenia).

JEWEL WASP OR EMERALD COCKROACH WASP
AMPULEX COMPRESSA: Located in South Asia, Africa, and the Pacific Islands, the female jewel wasp uses a cockroach as its living nursery. First, she paralyzes the roach's front legs; then, she stings the roach's head with a venom disabling the roach's escape reflexes. Instead of running, the roach will groom extensively, and become sluggish. Next, the wasp leads the roach to its burrow by pulling on one of the roach's antennae (much like a leash). Over the next eight days, her larva consumes the roach's organs. The roach stays alive until the larva pupates.

Credit: Brett A. Goodman, Pieter T.J. Johnson

PARASITIC FLATWORM – RIBEIROIA ONDATRAE: The *R. ondatrae* is a microscopic flatworm that first attacks a snail's reproductive organs, turning it into a vehicle to release thousands of larvae that burrow into tadpoles' budding limbs. As infected tadpoles develop, cysts from the flatworm larvae cause deformities, such as extra limbs. These frogs are crippled and easy prey for waterbirds. Once consumed, the waterbirds carry the parasites in their stomach to another body of water.

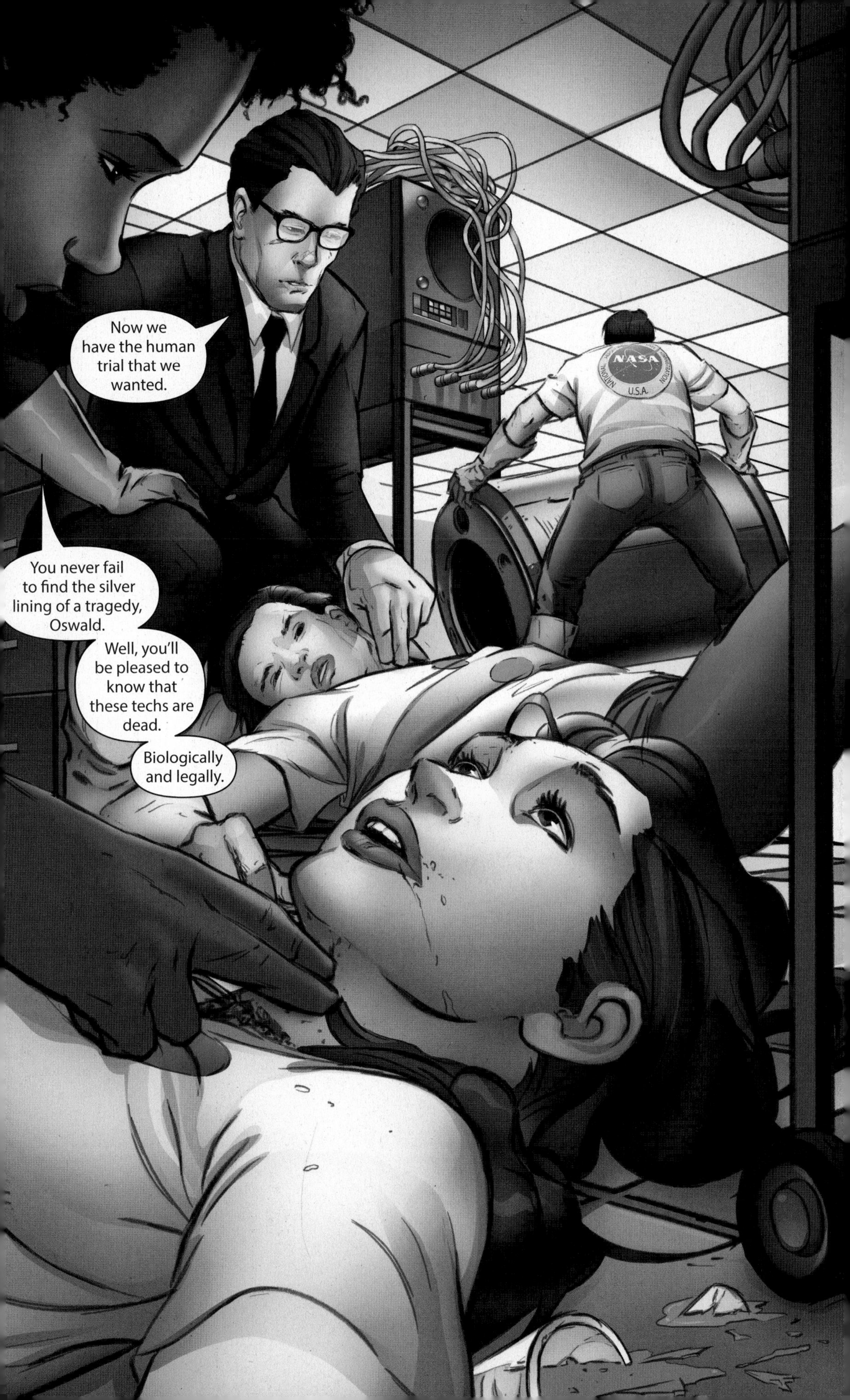
Now we have the human trial that we wanted.
You never fail to find the silver lining of a tragedy, Oswald.
Well, you'll be pleased to know that these techs are dead.
Biologically and legally.
NASA
U.S.A.

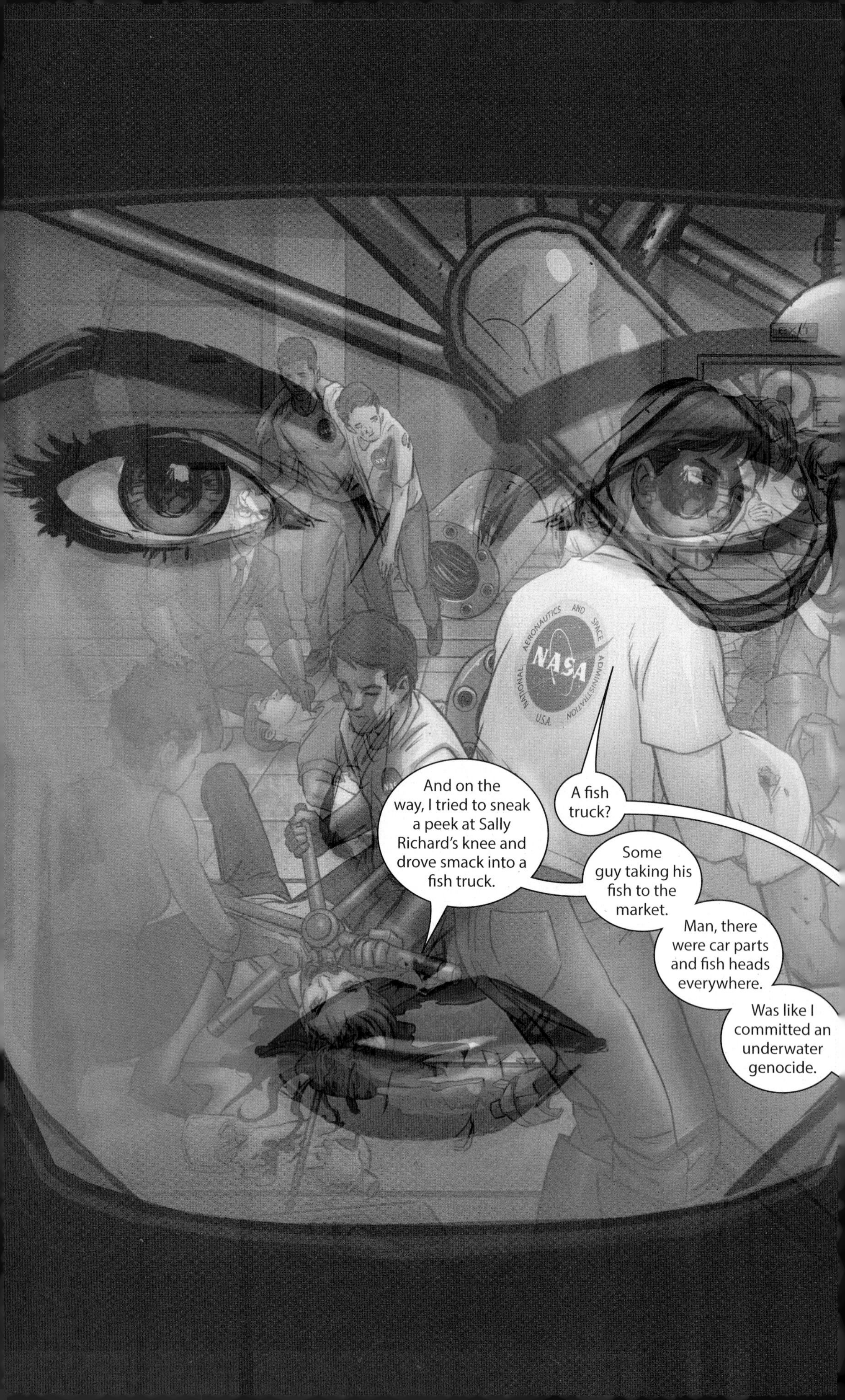

And on the way, I tried to sneak a peek at Sally Richard's knee and drove smack into a fish truck.
A fish truck?
Some guy taking his fish to the market.
Man, there were car parts and fish heads everywhere.
Was like I committed an underwater genocide.

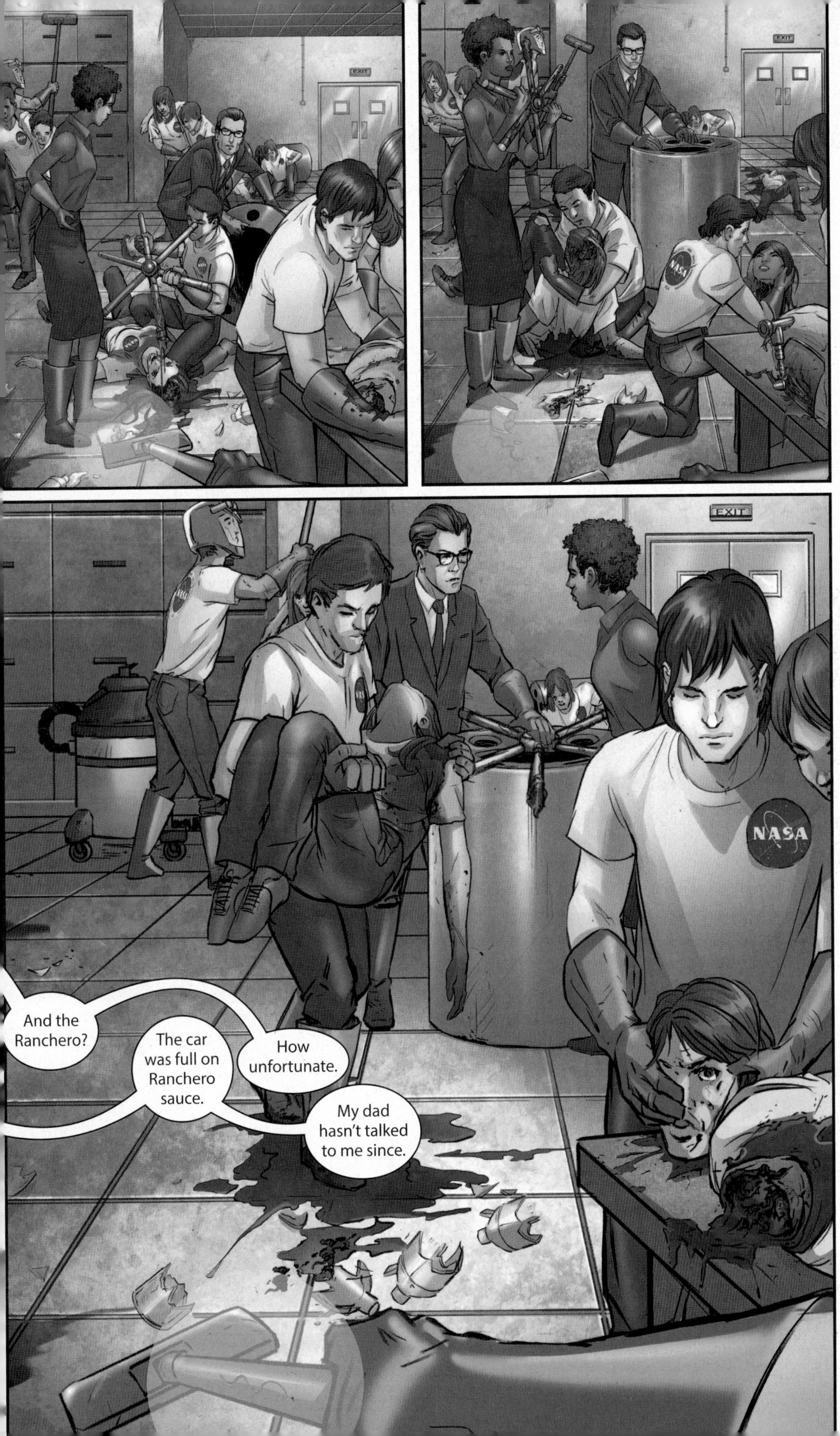

EXIT
And the Ranchero?
The car was full on Ranchero sauce.
How unfortunate.
My dad hasn't talked to me since.

THE NATIONAL AIR AND SPACE ADMINISTRATION

October 4, 1957 – The Soviet Union launched *Sputnik*, the world's first man-made satellite, into space.

November 3, 1957 – The Soviet Union followed with *Sputnik 2*, which carried Laika, a canine. Laika survived the trip into space but died when the oxygen supply ran out.

January 31, 1958 – The United States launched its first satellite, *Explorer 1*.

August 19, 1960 – The Soviet Union launched *Sputnik 5* with a grey rabbit, 42 mice, two rats, flies, several plants, fungi, and two canines, Belka and Strelka; all passengers survived the trip to and from space.

April 12, 1961 – Soviet cosmonaut Yuri Gagarin became the first human in space.

May 5, 1961 – Alan Shepard became the first American in space.

May 25, 1961 – President John F. Kennedy rallied Congress and the nation to support the first manned mission to the moon, which became the Apollo program.

February 3, 1966 – The Soviet Union landed the first spacecraft on the moon; the United States followed with *Surveyor I* on June 2.

July 2, 1969 – American astronauts Neil Armstrong and "Buzz" Aldrin became the first men on the moon.

September 1976 – American probe *Viking 2* discovered water frost on Mars.

August and September 1977 – *Voyagers 1* and *2* were launched; each would transmit images of the outer planets over the decades while on their (still ongoing) journeys.

April 12, 1981 – The United States launched the first space shuttle *Columbia*.

August 6, 2012 – NASA's *Curiosity* rover landed on Mars.

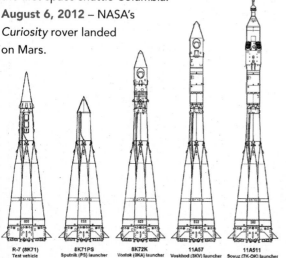

R-7 (8K71)
Test vehicle
1957

8K71PS
Sputnik (PS) launcher
1957

8K72K
Vostok (3KA) launcher
1960

11A57
Voskhod (3KV) launcher
1963

11A511
Soyuz (7K-OK) launcher
1966

SINCE *SPUTNIK'S* LAUNCH IN 1957

SATELLITES SENT INTO ORBIT	2,271
ACTIVE SATELLITES	1,381
UNITED STATES	568
RUSSIA	133
CHINA	177
ALL OTHER COUNTRIES	503
ACTIVE MILITARY SATELLITES	295
UNITED STATES	129
RUSSIA	75
CHINA	35
ALL OTHER COUNTRIES	56

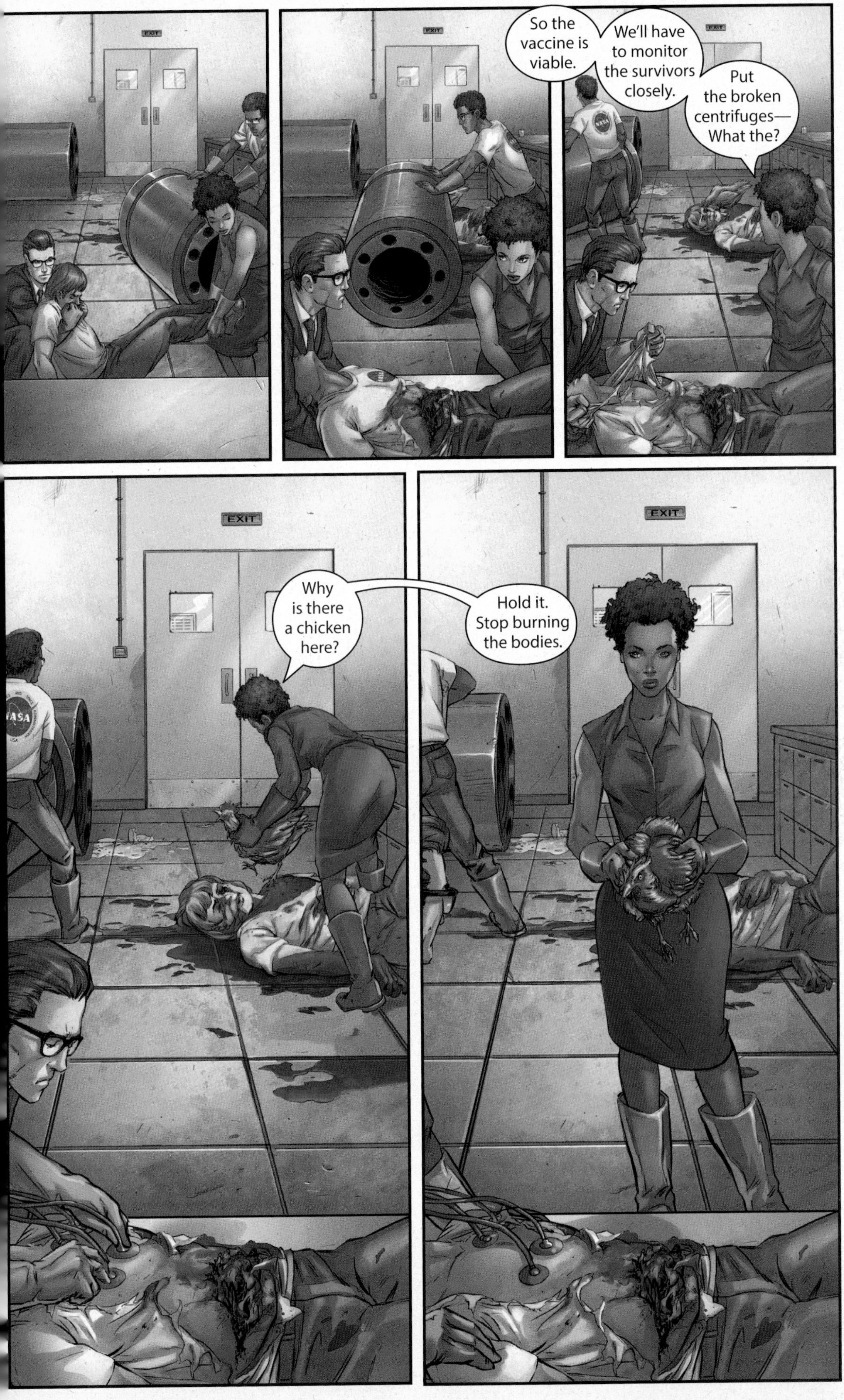
So the vaccine is viable.
We'll have to monitor the survivors closely.
Put the broken centrifuges— What the?
EXIT
Why is there a chicken here?
Hold it. Stop burning the bodies.

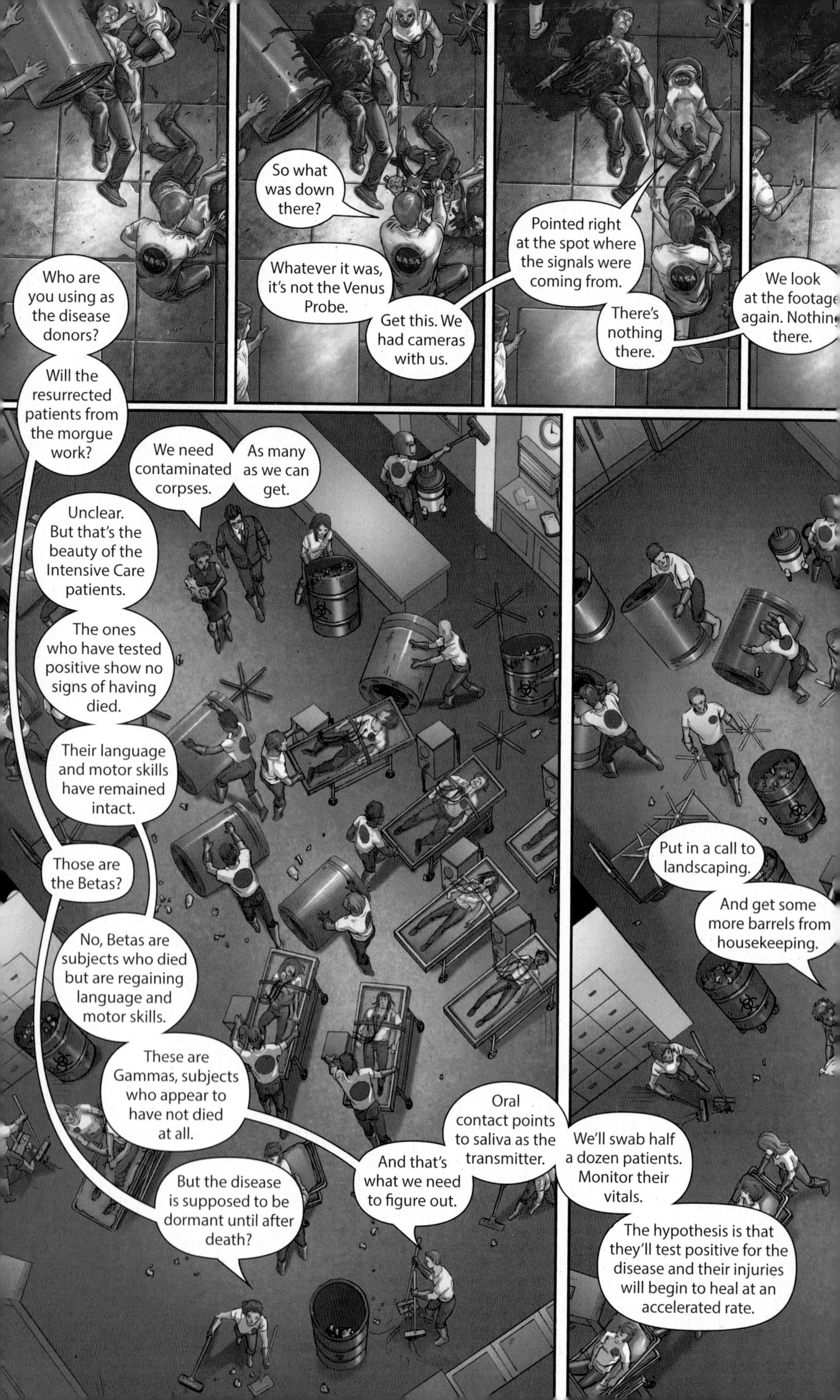
So what was down there?
Whatever it was, it's not the Venus Probe.
Get this. We had cameras with us.
Pointed right at the spot where the signals were coming from.
There's nothing there.
We look at the footage again. Nothing there.
Who are you using as the disease donors?
Will the resurrected patients from the morgue work?
We need contaminated corpses.
As many as we can get.
Unclear. But that's the beauty of the Intensive Care patients.
The ones who have tested positive show no signs of having died.
Their language and motor skills have remained intact.
Those are the Betas?
No, Betas are subjects who died but are regaining language and motor skills.
These are Gammas, subjects who appear to have not died at all.
But the disease is supposed to be dormant until after death?
And that's what we need to figure out.
Oral contact points to saliva as the transmitter.
We'll swab half a dozen patients. Monitor their vitals.
The hypothesis is that they'll test positive for the disease and their injuries will begin to heal at an accelerated rate.
Put in a call to landscaping.
And get some more barrels from housekeeping.

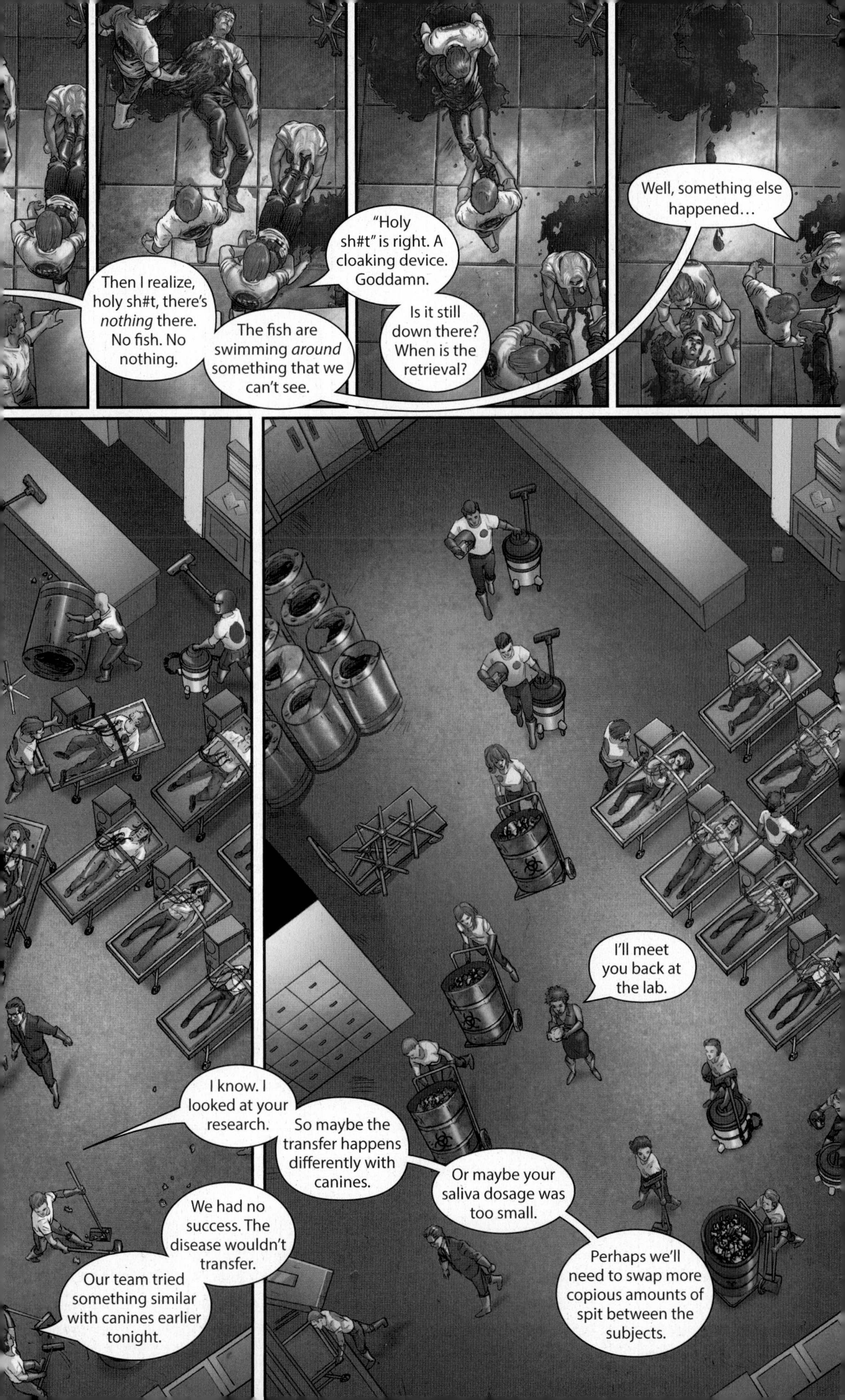
Then I realize, holy sh#t, there's *nothing* there. No fish. No nothing.
The fish are swimming *around* something that we can't see.
"Holy sh#t" is right. A cloaking device. Goddamn.
Is it still down there? When is the retrieval?
Well, something else happened…
Our team tried something similar with canines earlier tonight.
We had no success. The disease wouldn't transfer.
I know. I looked at your research.
So maybe the transfer happens differently with canines.
Or maybe your saliva dosage was too small.
Perhaps we'll need to swap more copious amounts of spit between the subjects.
I'll meet you back at the lab.

AN EXPERIMENTAL SUBSCRIPTION TO THE **2T BOOK-OF-THE-DECADE CLUB** WILL DEMONSTRATE HOW DEVOTE MEMBERSHIP IS THE BEST INSURANCE AGAINST MISSING OUT ON THE BEST BOOKS FROM BYGONE DECADES.

YOUR CHOICE OF ANY 3 FOR ONLY $1

TO KILL A
Mockingbird
A NOVEL BY
HARPER LEE

An idiot's guide.

Cat's Cradle
a novel by KURT VONNEGUT, JR.

Yes, humans can cause climate change.

The Godfather
A NOVEL
Mario Puzo

Guaranteed to include zero references to *The Godfather III.*

SLAUGHTERHOUSE-FIVE
OR
The Children's Crusade
A NEW NOVEL BY
KURT VONNEGUT, JR.

The most hilarious book about firebombing that you'll ever read.

An illustrated guide to conquering nature.

Tom Wolfe
The Electric Kool-Aid Acid Test

Makes for great reading on any trip.

THE
AGONY
AND THE
ECSTASY
the biographical novel of
MICHELANGELO
IRVING
STONE

50 shades of marble.

Please enroll me as a member. I am to receive for $1 the three books I've selected below. I will pay $300 for each book-of-the-decade I buy after. I agree to purchase at least 6 books-of-the-decade from 2T each year I am a member. I may cancel the subscription only if I pay 2T $1 million and give 2T the soul of my firstborn child.

SELECT THREE BOOKS ☐ ☐ ☐

NAME ____________________

Please do not actually

ADDRESS ____________________

fill this out and send it in.

CITY ________ POSTAL ZONE No. ________ STATE ________

Valley
of the
Dolls
A NOVEL BY
Jacqueline Susann

Downers are a girl's best friend.

Portnoy's
Complaint
Philip
Roth

Includes new liver recipe.

JAMES AND
THE GIANT PEACH
by ROALD DAHL

Story of the first GMO.

MAIL TO:

2T BOOK-OF-THE-DECADE CLUB
38 W. 39TH STREET 2ND FLOOR,
NEW YORK, NY 10018

Signing and mailing the coupon enrolls you into the 2T Book of the Decade Club ("2T Club") for life. You start with three books of your choice for $1 but thereafter are obligated to purchase at least six books-of-the-decade for $300 each within a twelve-month period after you enroll. You do not have the right to cancel your membership at any point until you have given us $1 million and the soul of your firstborn child, plus postage, handling, and any other expenses 2T feels like tacking onto your bill. We understand money can be tight so we accept payment plans. Any payment plans will be subject to a 15 percent interest to account for inflation and the ever depreciating value of your child's soul as your child ages. Please note, under no circumstances will 2T actually send you any books.

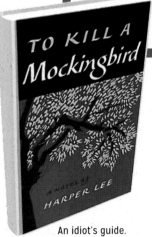

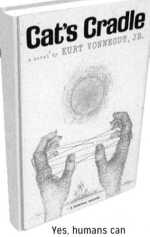

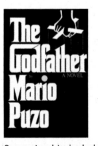

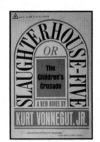

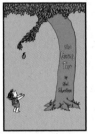

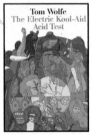

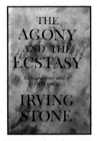

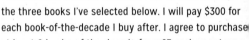

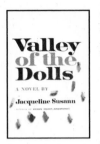

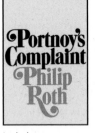

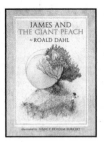

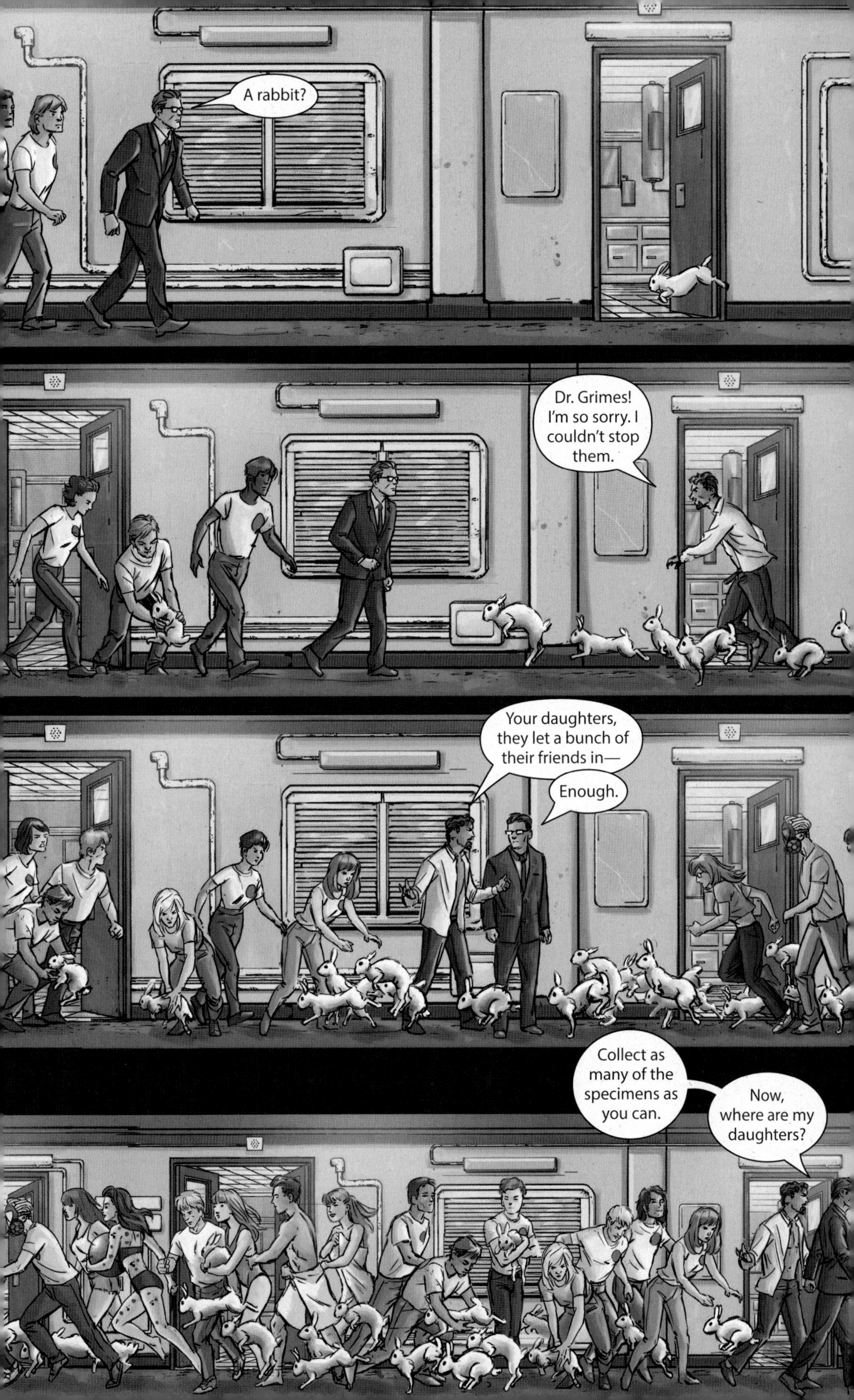
A rabbit?
Dr. Grimes! I'm so sorry. I couldn't stop them.
Your daughters, they let a bunch of their friends in—
Enough.
Collect as many of the specimens as you can.
Now, where are my daughters?

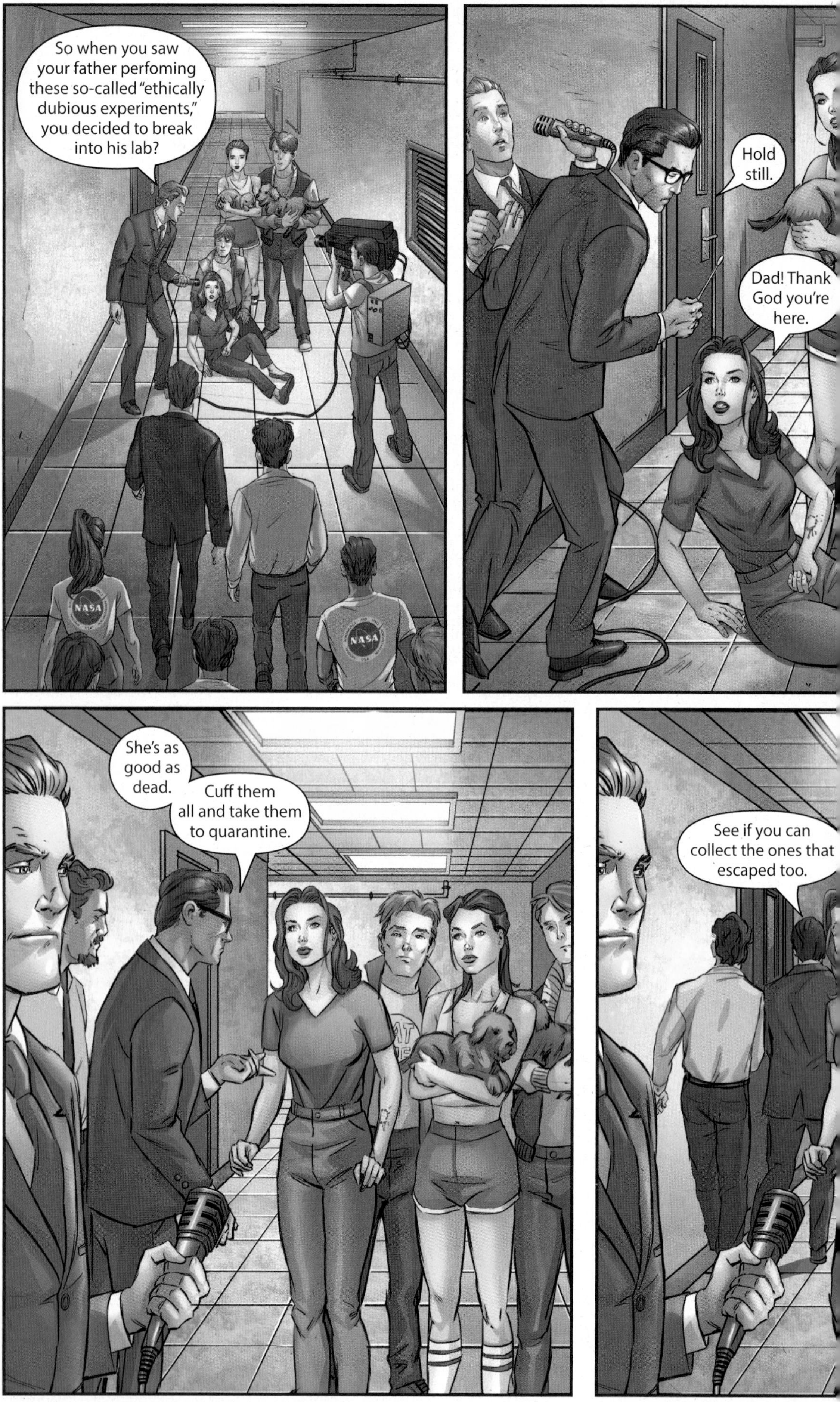
So when you saw your father perfoming these so-called "ethically dubious experiments," you decided to break into his lab?
Hold still.
Dad! Thank God you're here.
She's as good as dead.
Cuff them all and take them to quarantine.
See if you can collect the ones that escaped too.

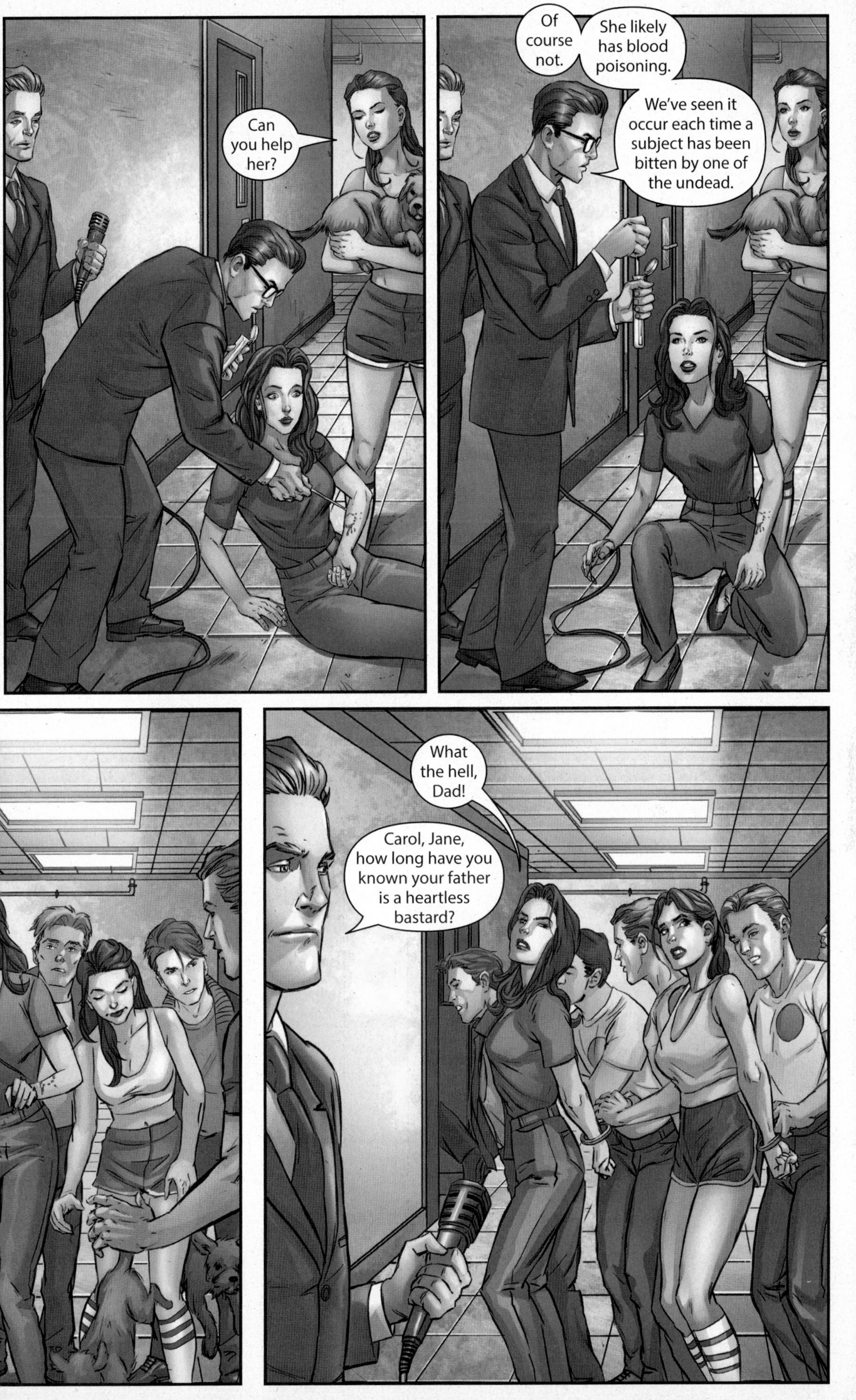
Can you help her?
Of course not.
She likely has blood poisoning.
We've seen it occur each time a subject has been bitten by one of the undead.
What the hell, Dad!
Carol, Jane, how long have you known your father is a heartless bastard?

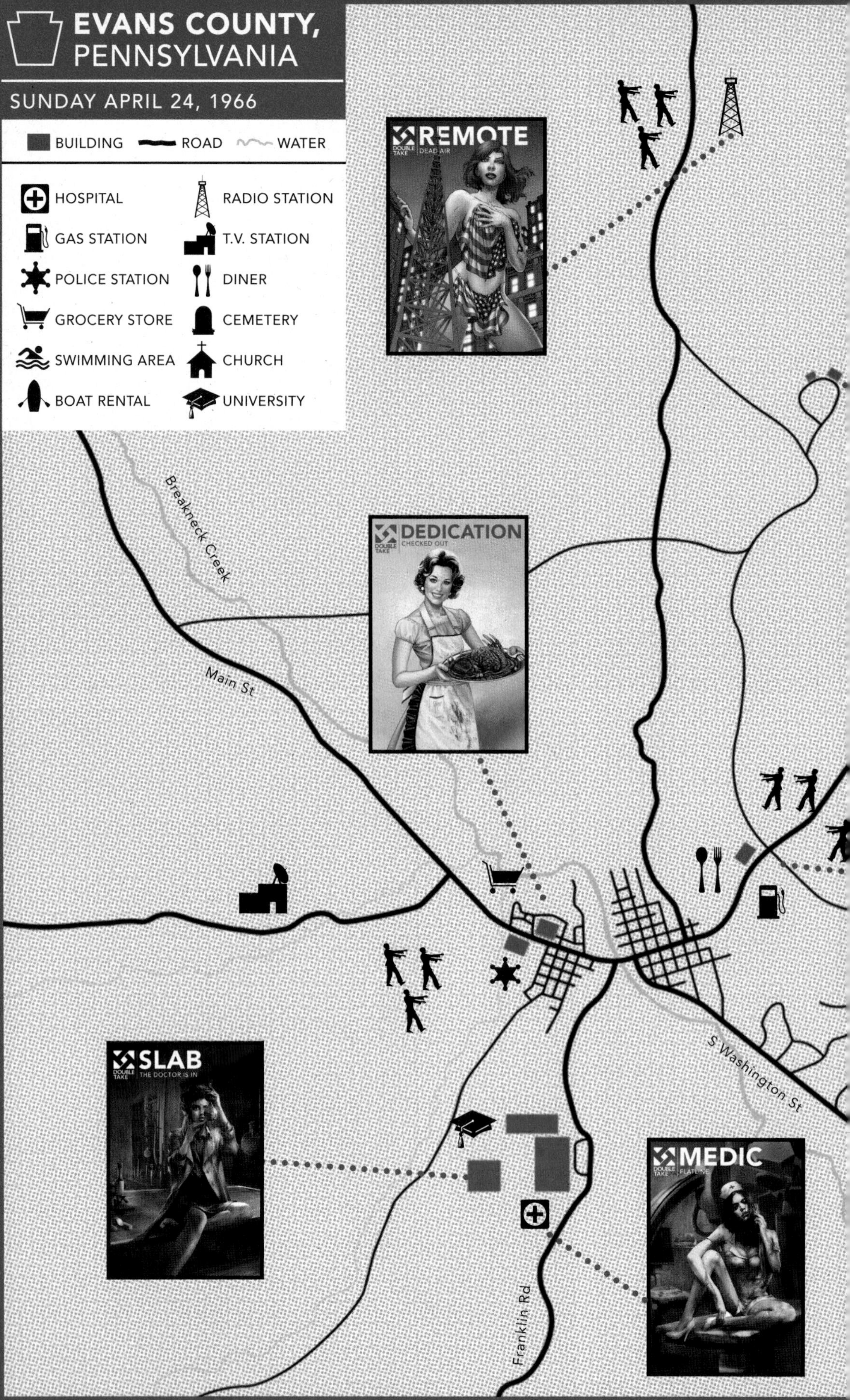
EVANS COUNTY, PENNSYLVANIA
SUNDAY APRIL 24, 1966
BUILDING
ROAD
WATER
HOSPITAL
RADIO STATION
GAS STATION
T.V. STATION
POLICE STATION
DINER
GROCERY STORE
CEMETERY
SWIMMING AREA
CHURCH
BOAT RENTAL
UNIVERSITY
DOUBLE TAKE REMOTE DEAD AIR
DOUBLE TAKE DEDICATION CHECKED OUT
DOUBLE TAKE SLAB THE DOCTOR IS IN
DOUBLE TAKE MEDIC FLATLINE
Breakneck Creek
Main St
S Washington St
Franklin Rd

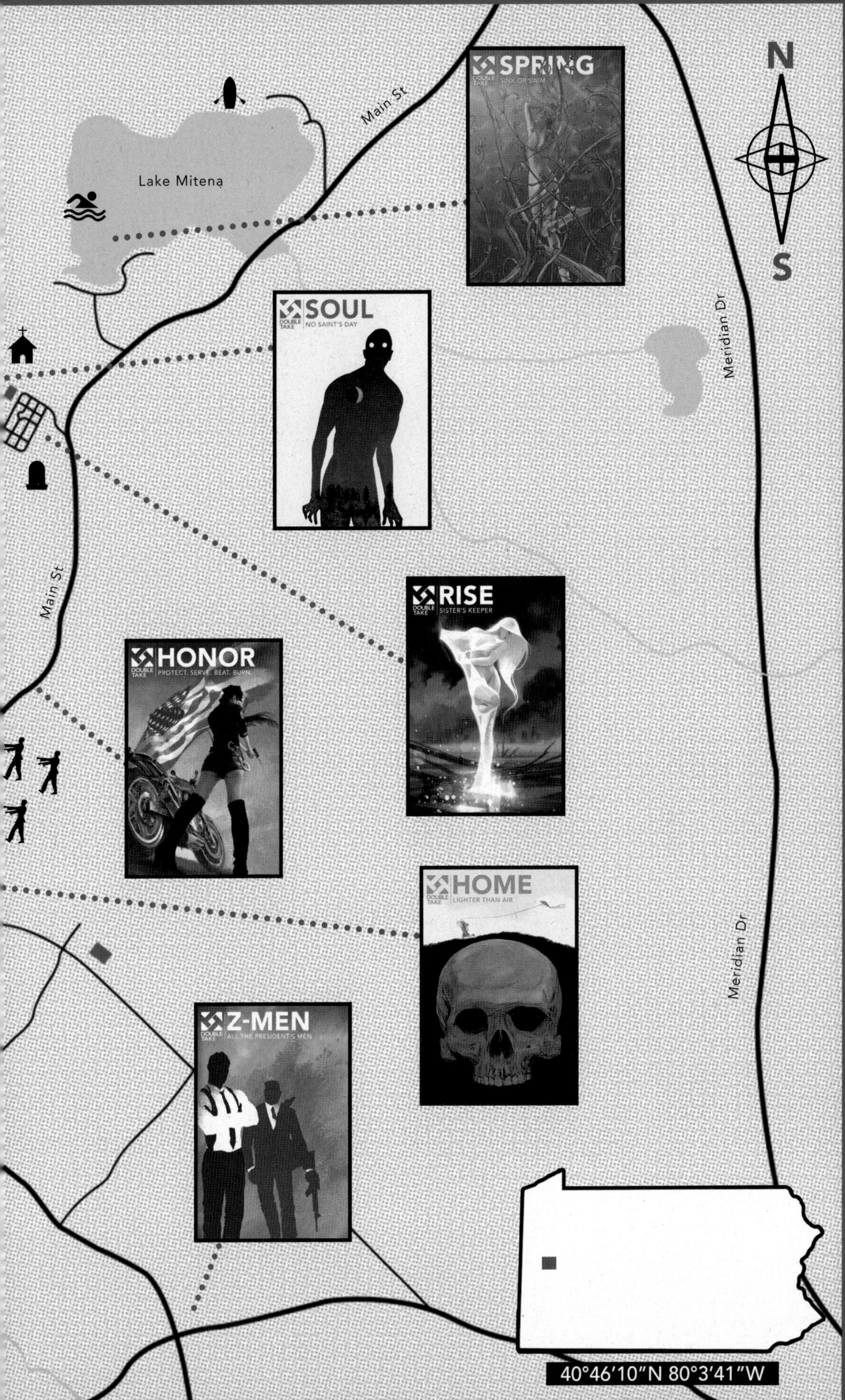

N
S
Main St
Lake Mitena
DOUBLE TAKE SPRING
SINK OR SWIM
DOUBLE TAKE SOUL
NO SAINT'S DAY
Meridian Dr
Main St
DOUBLE TAKE RISE
SISTER'S KEEPER
DOUBLE TAKE HONOR
PROTECT. SERVE. BEAT. BURN.
DOUBLE TAKE HOME
LIGHTER THAN AIR
Meridian Dr
DOUBLE TAKE Z-MEN
ALL THE PRESIDENT'S MEN
40°46′10″N 80°3′41″W

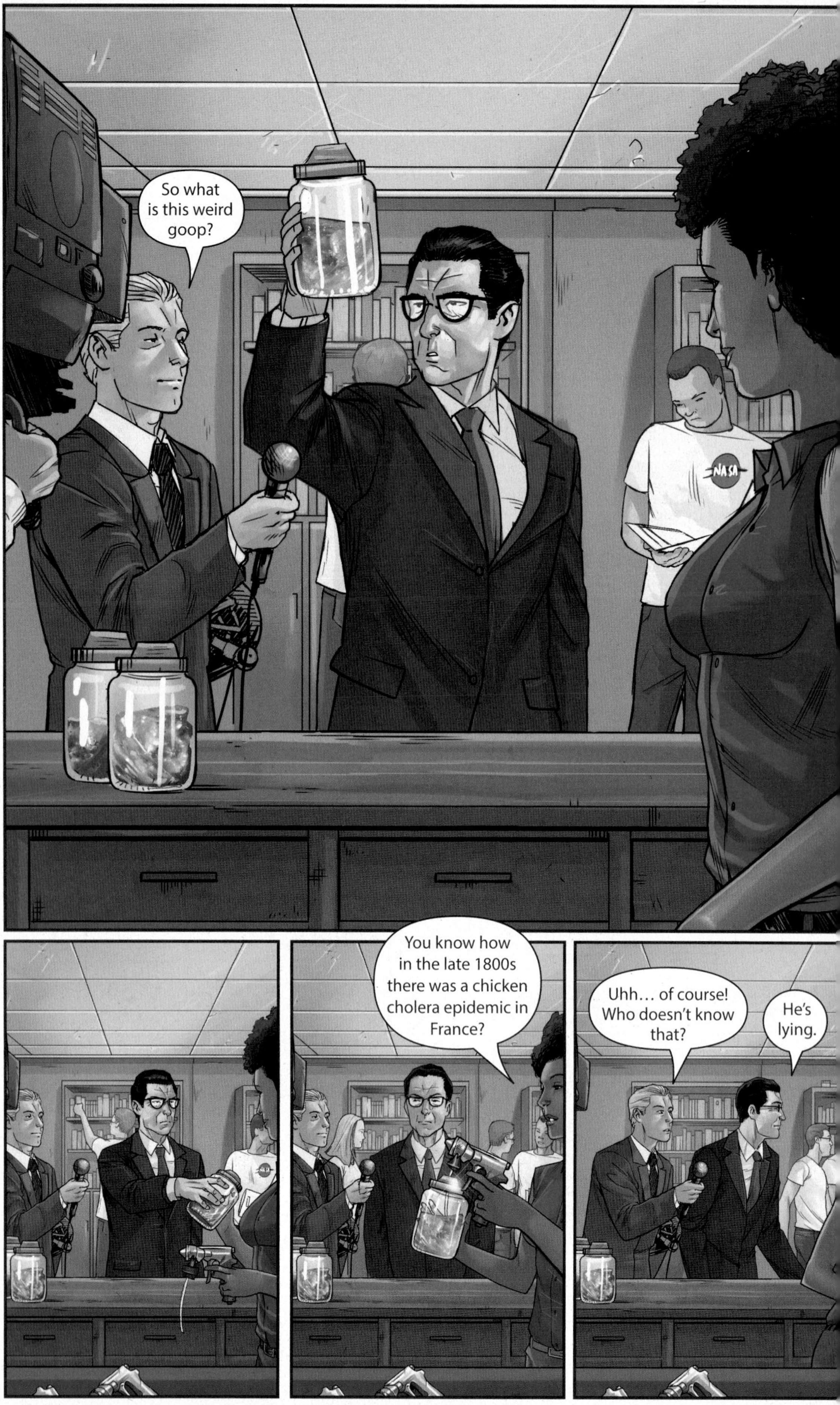
So what is this weird goop?
You know how in the late 1800s there was a chicken cholera epidemic in France?
Uhh… of course! Who doesn't know that?
He's lying.

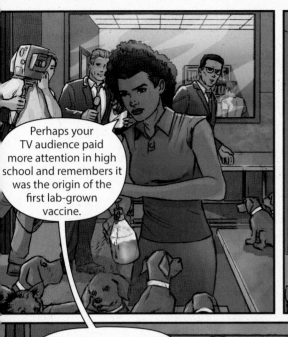

Perhaps your TV audience paid more attention in high school and remembers it was the origin of the first lab-grown vaccine.

Louis Pasteur had been injecting chickens with cholera to observe the disease, and he asked his assistant to perform some tests with fresh cholera before they took a vacation.

But the assistant forgot.

He took care of it when he got back, but that was a month later and the cholera culture was old.

The chickens lived.

So he tried again with a fresh batch of cholera.

The chickens lived through that too.

And from that, Pasteur extrapolated that giving a person a weakened version of the bacteria would help a person's body learn how to fight that disease.

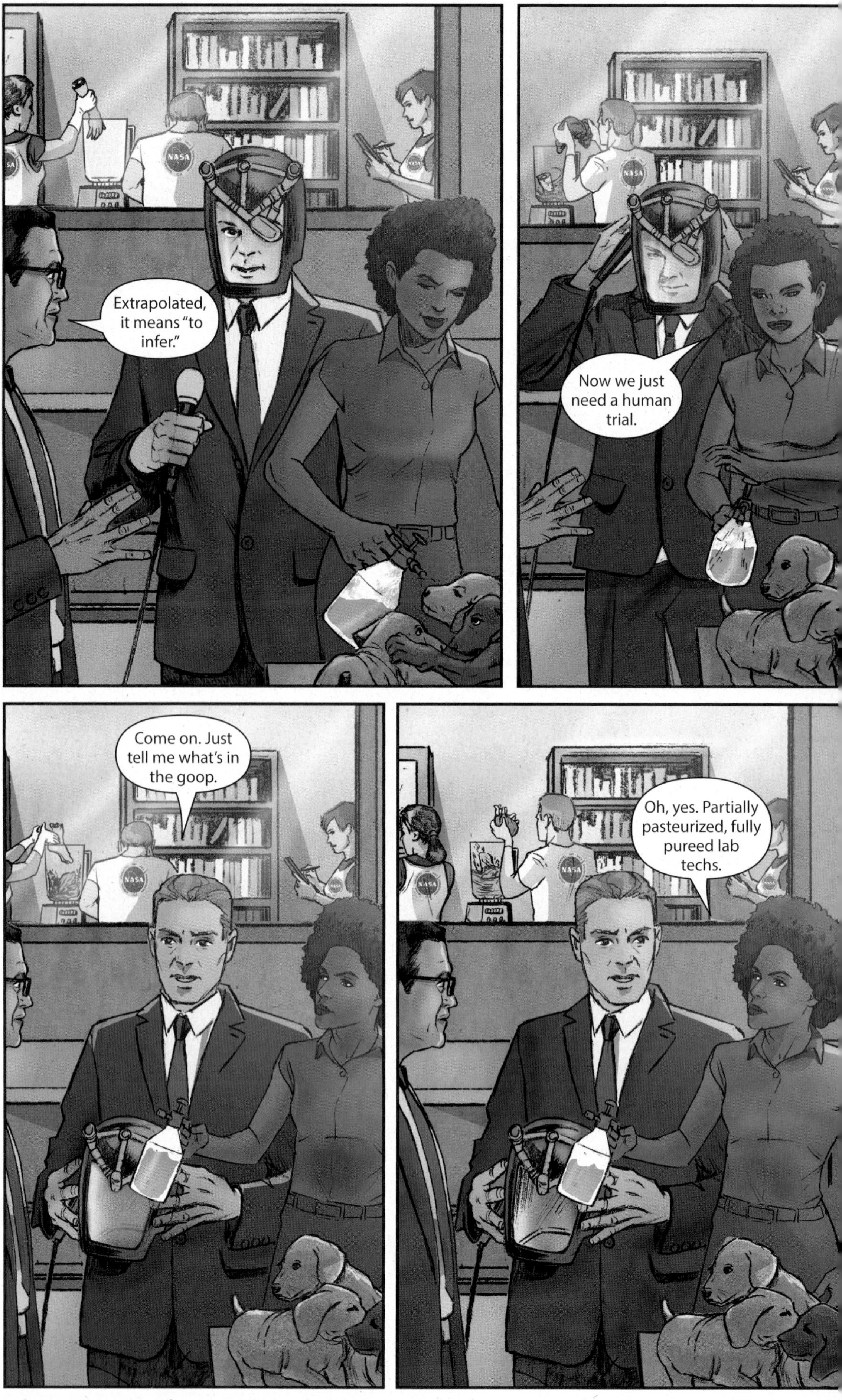
NASA
Extrapolated, it means "to infer."
Now we just need a human trial.
Come on. Just tell me what's in the goop.
Oh, yes. Partially pasteurized, fully pureed lab techs.

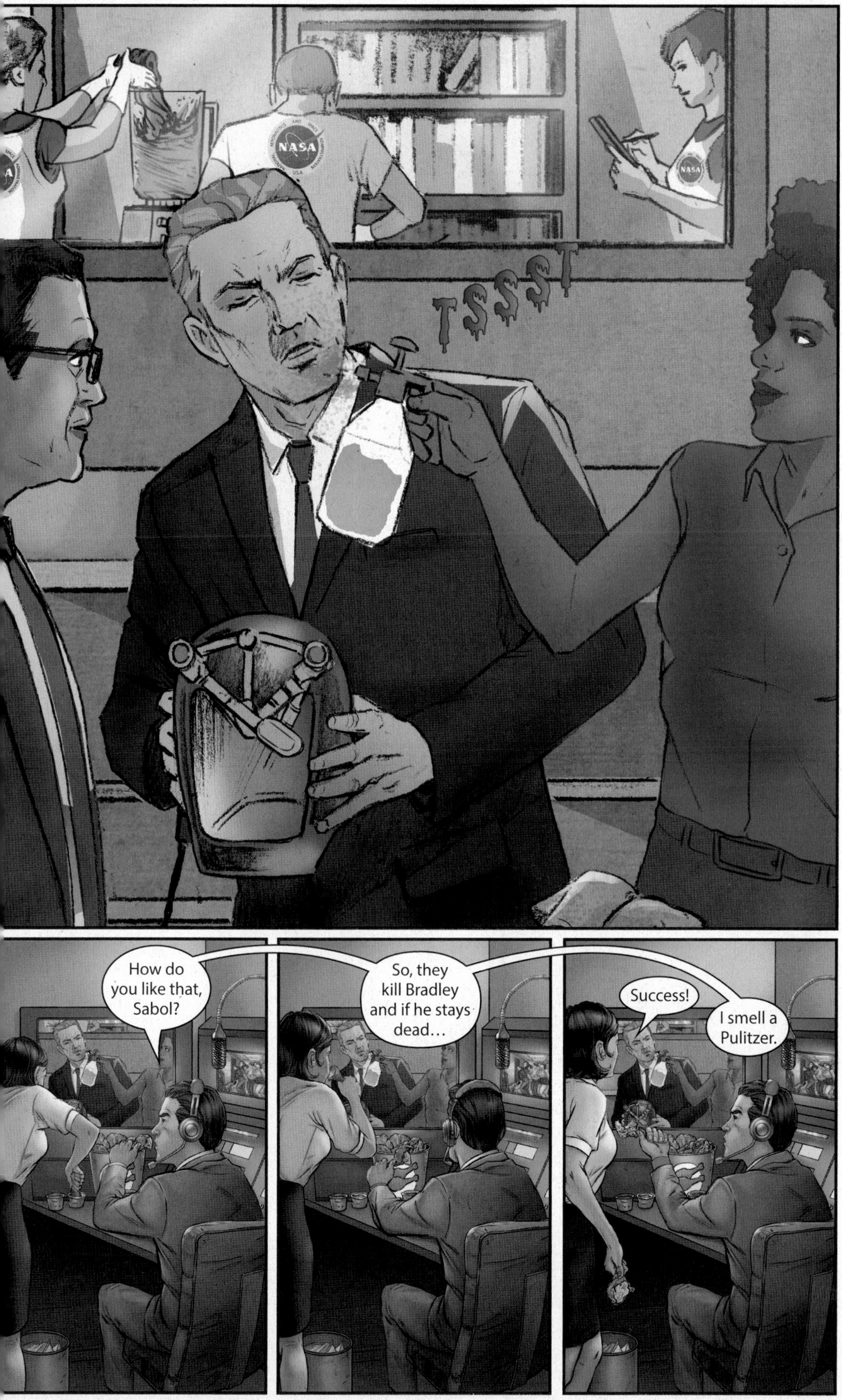
TSSST
How do you like that, Sabol?
So, they kill Bradley and if he stays dead…
Success!
I smell a Pulitzer.

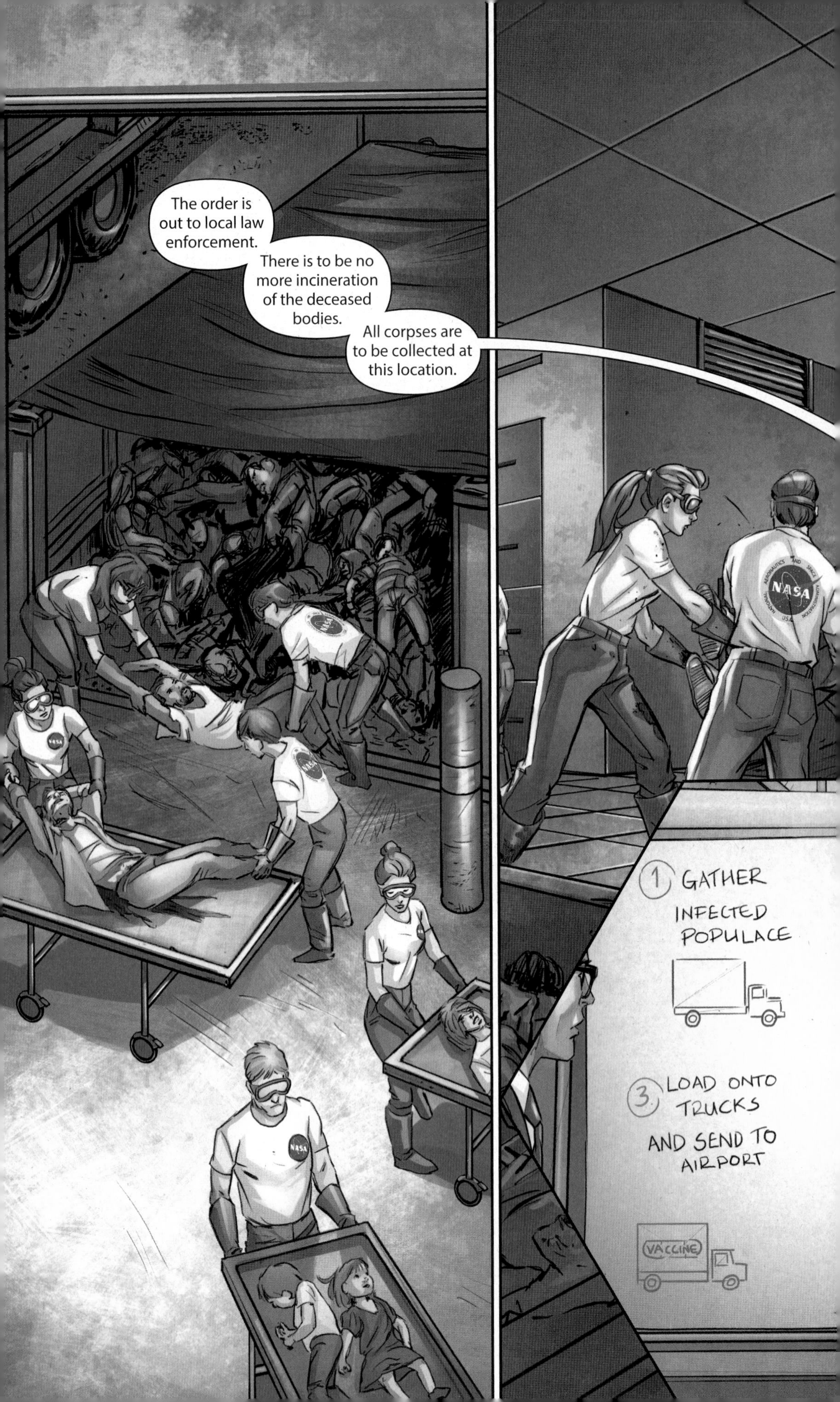

The order is out to local law enforcement.
There is to be no more incineration of the deceased bodies.
All corpses are to be collected at this location.
NASA
1 GATHER INFECTED POPULACE
3 LOAD ONTO TRUCKS AND SEND TO AIRPORT
VACCINE

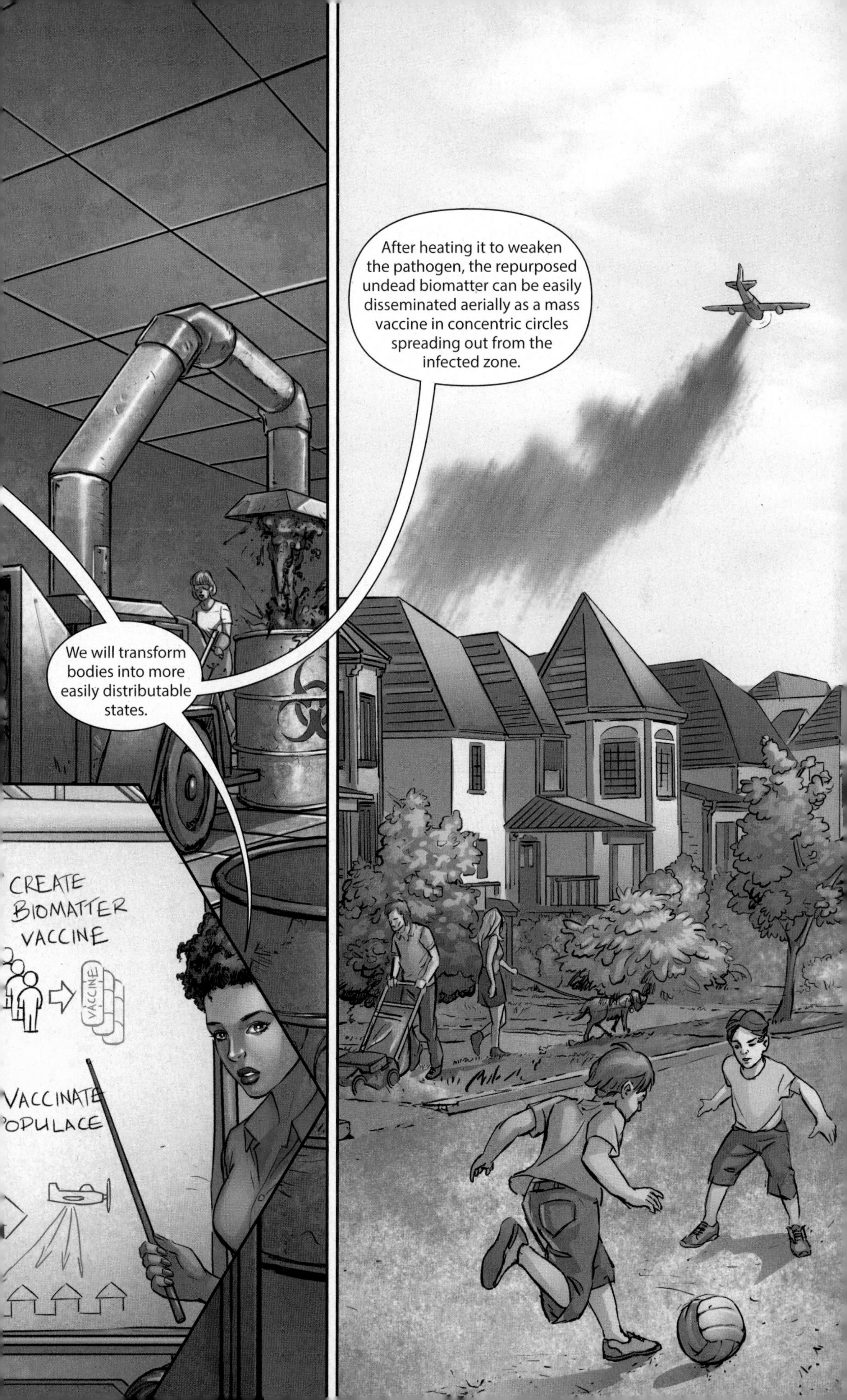
We will transform bodies into more easily distributable states.
CREATE BIOMATTER VACCINE
VACCINE
VACCINATE POPULACE
After heating it to weaken the pathogen, the repurposed undead biomatter can be easily disseminated aerially as a mass vaccine in concentric circles spreading out from the infected zone.

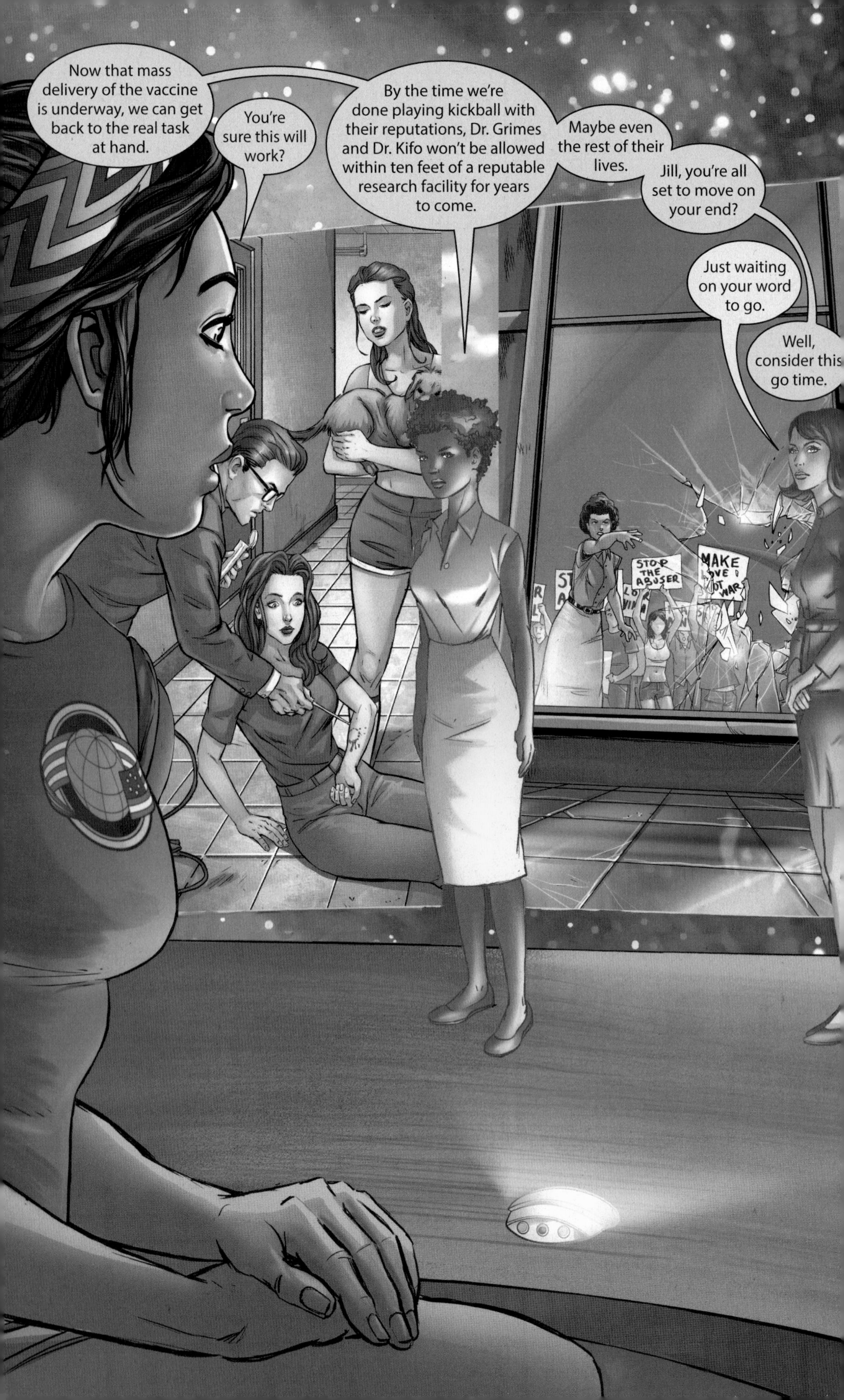
Now that mass delivery of the vaccine is underway, we can get back to the real task at hand.
You're sure this will work?
By the time we're done playing kickball with their reputations, Dr. Grimes and Dr. Kifo won't be allowed within ten feet of a reputable research facility for years to come.
Maybe even the rest of their lives.
Jill, you're all set to move on your end?
Just waiting on your word to go.
Well, consider this go time.
STOP THE ABUSER
MAKE

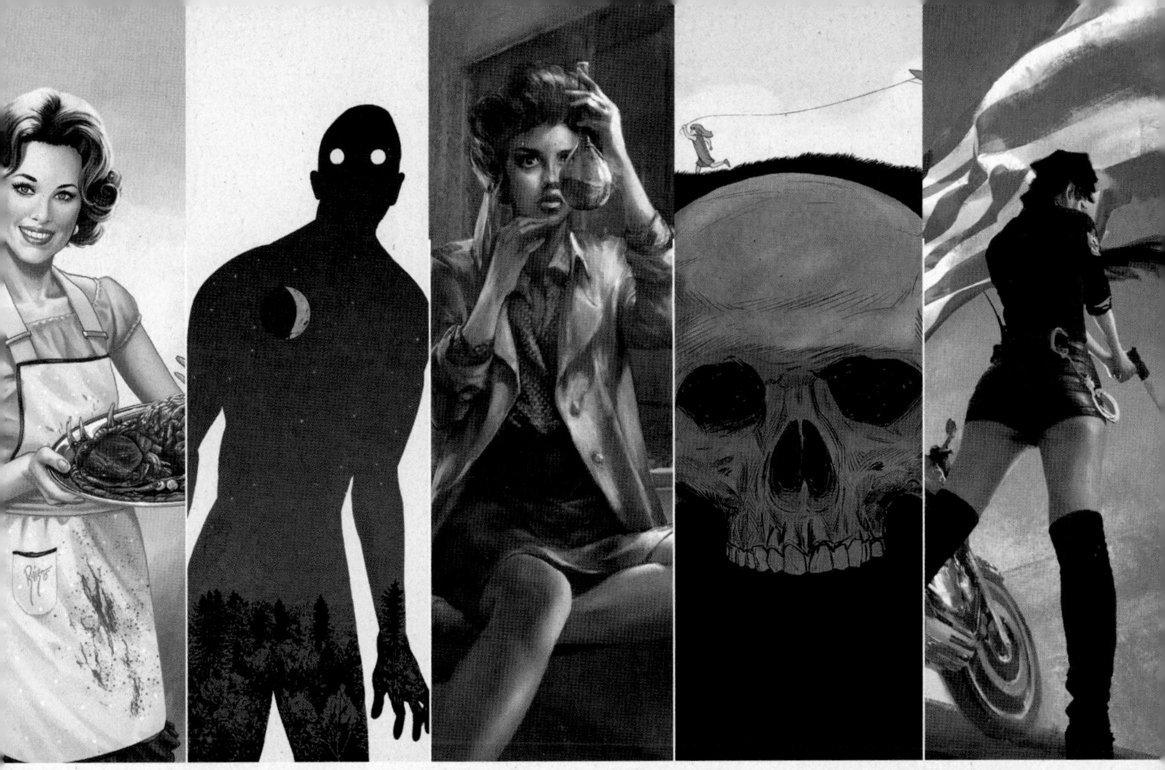

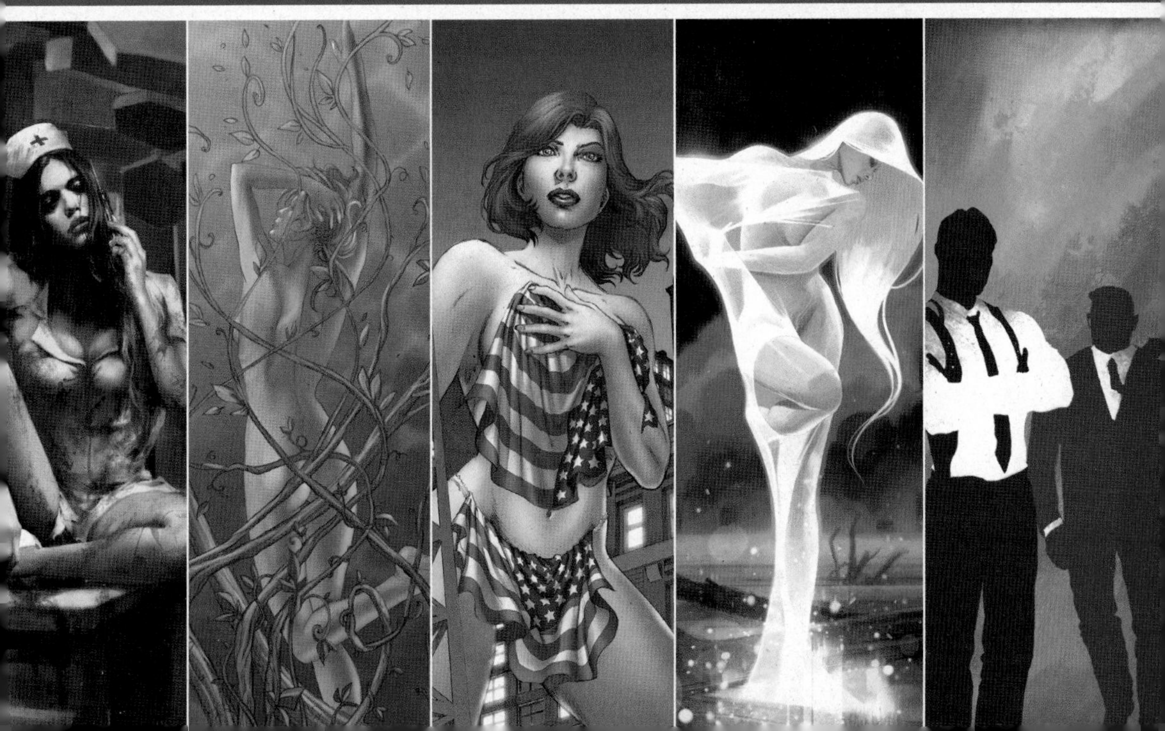

ULTIMATE Cocktail Party

Sidecar
¾ ounce triple sec
¾ ounce lemon juice
1 ½ ounces cognac

Martini
2 ½ ounces dry gin
½ ounce dry vermouth
Green olive for garnish

Classic Onion Dip

Ingredients
1 ½ cups chopped onion
½ cup mayonnaise
3 tablespoons butter
1 teaspoon black pepper
¼ teaspoon salt
2 cups sour cream
1 tsp garlic powder

Directions:
• Heat butter in a saucepan. Add black pepper, salt, garlic powder, and onions. Sauté for 10 minutes.
• Mix mayonnaise, sour cream, and sautéed onions in large bowl. Serve at room temperature or chilled, if desired.

Manhattan
2 ounces bourbon whiskey
½ ounce sweet vermouth
½ ounce dry vermouth
2 dashes Angostura bitters
Maraschino cherry

Cosmo
2 ounces vodka
½ ounce triple sec
¾ ounce cranberry juic
¼ ounce fresh lime juic
1 2-inch orange peel/tw

Swiss Fondue

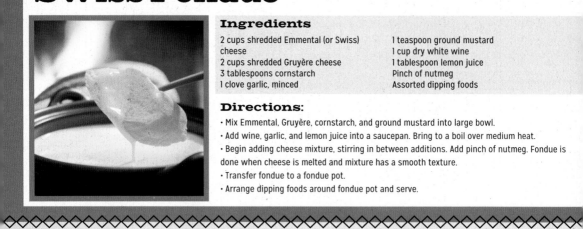

Ingredients
2 cups shredded Emmental (or Swiss) cheese
2 cups shredded Gruyère cheese
3 tablespoons cornstarch
1 clove garlic, minced

1 teaspoon ground mustard
1 cup dry white wine
1 tablespoon lemon juice
Pinch of nutmeg
Assorted dipping foods

Directions:
• Mix Emmental, Gruyère, cornstarch, and ground mustard into large bowl.
• Add wine, garlic, and lemon juice into a saucepan. Bring to a boil over medium heat.
• Begin adding cheese mixture, stirring in between additions. Add pinch of nutmeg. Fondue is done when cheese is melted and mixture has a smooth texture.
• Transfer fondue to a fondue pot.
• Arrange dipping foods around fondue pot and serve.

Deviled Eggs

Ingredients
6 eggs
2 tablespoons mayonnaise
1 teaspoon of yellow mustard

Salt and black pepper to taste
Paprika

Directions:
• Hard boil eggs and slice into halves.
• Separate yolks from egg whites and place yolks in a bowl.
• Mash yolks using a fork. Add mayonnaise, mustard, salt, and pepper and stir.
• Spoon mixture into egg whites using a teaspoon. Sprinkle paprika to garnish.
• Chill eggs for 1 hour and serve.